# Basic Systems Design

*Hutchinson Computer Studies Series*

# Basic Systems Design

## J. E. Downs

*Senior Lecturer in Computing, Manchester Polytechnic*

Hutchinson

London   Melbourne   Sydney   Auckland   Johannesburg

Hutchinson & Co. (Publishers) Ltd
An imprint of the Hutchinson Publishing Group
17–21 Conway Street, London W1P 6JD

Hutchinson Publishing Group (Australia) Pty Ltd
16–21 Church Street, Hawthorn, Melbourne, Victoria 3122

Hutchinson Group (NZ) Ltd
32–34 View Road, PO Box 40–086, Glenfield, Auckland 10

Hutchinson Group (SA) (Pty) Ltd
PO Box 337, Bergvlei 2012, South Africa

First published 1985

© J. E. Downs 1985

Set in VIP Plantin by Spire Print Services Ltd, Salisbury, Wilts

Printed and bound in Great Britain by
Anchor Brendon Ltd, Tiptree, Essex

**British Library Cataloguing in Publication Data**
Downs, J. E.
  Basic systems design – (Hutchinson computer
  studies series)
  1. Computer architecture
  I. Title
  001.64    QA76.9.A73

ISBN 0 09 159071 X

# Contents

# Editor's note

This book is one of a series of textbooks with a modular structure aimed at students of computer studies and designed for use on courses at most levels of academic and professional qualification. A coherent approach to the development of courses in computing has emerged over the last few years with the introduction of the BTEC National, Higher National and Post-Experience Awards in Computer Studies. The syllabus guidelines for these courses have provided the focus for this series of books and this ensures that the books are relevant to a wide range of courses at intermediate level.

Many existing books on computing cause frustration to teachers and students because, in trying to be all embracing, they usually include irrelevant material and fail to tackle relevant material in adequate depth. The books in this series are specific in their treatment of topics and practical in their orientation. They provide a firm foundation in all the key areas of computer studies, which are seen as: computer technology; programming the computer; analysing and designing computer-based systems; and applications of the computer.

There are ten books in the series.

*Computer Appreciation* is the introductory book. It is intended to put the computer into context both for the layman who wants to understand a little more about computers and their usage, and for the student as a background for further study. *Computing in a Small Business* is aimed specifically at the small businessman, or at the student who will be working in a small business, and sets out to provide a practical guide to implementing computer-based systems in a small business. It is a comprehensive treatment of most aspects of computing.

*Fundamentals of Computing* looks in considerably more depth than the previous two books at the basic concepts of the technology. Its major emphasis is on hardware, with an introduction to system software. *Computer Systems: Software and architecture* develops from this base and concentrates on software, especially operating systems, language processors and data base management systems; it concludes with a section on networks.

*An Introduction to Program Design* is about how to design computer programs based on the Michael Jackson method. Examples of program code are given in BASIC, Pascal and COBOL, but this is not a book about a programming language since there are plenty of these books already available. This title complements *Program Development: Tools and techniques*, which looks at the task of programming from all angles and is independent of program design methods, programming languages and machines.

*Data Processing Methods* provides a fairly detailed treatment of the methods which lie behind computer-based systems in terms of modes of processing, input and output of data, storage of data, and security of systems. Several applications are described. *Information Systems* follows it up by looking at the role of data processing in organizations. This book deals with organizations and their information systems as systems, and with how information systems contribute to and affect the functioning of an organization.

*Basic Systems Analysis* offers an introduction to the knowledge and skills required by a systems analyst with rather more emphasis on feasibility, investigation, implementation and review than on design. *Basic Systems Design*, the related volume, tackles design in considerable depth and looks at current methods of structured systems design.

The books in this series stand alone, but all are related to each other so that duplication is avoided.

*Barry S. Lee*
*Series editor*

# Preface

This book aims to give an understanding of how a data processing system can be designed, starting from first principles – the objectives of the enterprise. The intention is that a grounding in the fundamentals of design will lead to continual learning as the reader observes real systems and participates in design activities.

It should be a suitable text for students on computing courses, in higher education and elsewhere. It is also intended to be of use to those computing staff who wish to learn about systems design, either because they are about to embark upon their first design effort, or because they wish to put their experience into context and broaden their horizons beyond the familiar. Users of computer systems may wish to find out about design so as to take a more active part in achieving their own goals. This book aims to help such readers to extend their knowledge and skills, and will be most beneficial when read in conjunction with involvement in design activities.

A middle path is taken between a students' guide to standard data processing methods, and a state of the art design methodology for practitioners. The amount of material describing each stage of the design is related to how familiar the material is likely to be to the reader. This leads to an emphasis upon logical design, with the use of an extensive example, at the expense of some parts of detailed design. This is also in keeping with the emphasis on fundamentals rather than current technology.

The methodology of design described here, DM/1, can also be said to be a middle path between an intuitive experienced approach to design and a formal highly structured approach. The former tends to leave the learner wondering on what grounds a decision was made. With the latter the learner may lose sight of the decisions in an overwhelming mass of standards and document-ation. DM/1 is a segmented description of a struct-ured systems design process. It is particularly suitable for the design of transaction processing systems, and would need only slight modification to be appropriate for information retrieval types of system. It is based upon the flow of data and as such

would not be directly suitable for control-driven real-time systems. However, many of the concepts and the overall approach to organizing the design are appropriate to all design efforts.

The description is segmented to assist understanding, assimilation and use by the beginner, who needs only to concentrate upon one part of the design at a time. Each stage is described in a prescriptive manner and applied to a single example. The reader is encouraged to think about the stages and appreciate the concepts and functions which underly each stage. In this way an adaptable approach to design may be fostered. DM/1 has been used in the teaching of systems analysis and design to part-time students who have successfully applied it to projects at their place of work.

Part One provides a background to systems design, placing it in the context of systems development and describing alternative possible design strategies; DM/1 is introduced. The various tools used by a designer are described, including data dictionaries, charting techniques and the representation of procedure logic.

Part Two shows how a logical design of the new system can be developed, including both process and data modelling. The intention is to build the design from the objectives, making every decision explicit. Logical design is the specification of what an information system must do.

Part Three then considers how the logical system can be physically implemented. It describes outline and detail design, together with an overview of hardware selection for input and output and guidelines on program specification.

The questions at the end of each part are not just recall tests of material in the chapter. They are intended to promote the application of the ideas presented, discussion of them, and possibly further study.

Throughout the book attention is drawn to some of the basic principles by their identification as golden rules. Golden Rule 0 is the most important (see Chapter 11). Golden Rules 1 to 10 are ranked equal second in importance; these are the ten 'Selsdon Commandments'.

*Golden Rule 1*
Thou shalt use microelectronics in as broad a way as possible, and it will greatly benefit you, your home, your animals, your work and your money, and protect you against theft, fire and flood. But you will benefit more if you live in the North rather than in the South.

*Alexander King*

*Golden Rule 2*
Thou shalt use microelectronics to make life easier, more enjoyable and more democratic, but experimentation is required to learn how to do this and governments should encourage social experiments.

*G. W. Rathenau*

*Golden Rule 3*
Thou shalt trust your government to look after you and know your best interests, and you shall have the choice of selecting the solution so carefully prepared for you by the government.

*M. Jacques Condoux*

*Golden Rule 4*
Thou shalt care for the marginal, the misfits, the underprivileged and the women. Do not subject the computer illiterates to technical fixes and remember we are all potential misfits.

*Helga Nowotny*

*Golden Rule 5*
Thou shalt view technology as beautiful, produced by beautiful men and operated by beautiful women, and thou shall trust the technologist.

*John Fairclough*

*Golden Rule 6*
Thou shalt protect yourself against technology which is dangerous; designed for idiots by hard, leathery, exploiting men who use technology to increase their power.

*Michael Cooley*

*Golden Rule 7*
Thou shalt base information technology policy on the principles of:

Democracy (involving the user in the design)
Wholism (consider people, organizations, and society when designing technology)
Supportiveness (the role of technology is to support the user).

*Olof Johansson*

*Golden Rule 8*
Thou shalt ensure that information technology helps the sick, the old and the less intelligent as well as the average and regular case especially when organizing social services.

*Jürgen Reese*

*Golden Rule 9*
Thou shalt be an expert in human-centred design and forget machine-centred design that defines human skills as obsolete and imperfect.

*Howard Rosenbrock*

*Golden Rule 10*
Thou shalt go out into the future and spread the word of microelectronics. Thou shalt act with confidence but also with caution and awareness, especially of competition from Japan. Thou shalt have a clear strategy of joining them rather than fighting them.

*G. Lanzavecchia*

These ten golden rules are reprinted, with permission, from the proceedings of a European conference, and published as *Information Society, for Richer, for Poorer*, edited by Bjørn-Andersen *et al*. (1982). In order to fully appreciate these golden rules (or even to assess suspicions of sarcasm in them), the reader is referred to the full papers.

# Acknowledgements

The author gratefully acknowledges the permission granted by the National Computing Centre Ltd, Oxford Road, Manchester M1 7ED to use various forms and standards from their *Data Processing Documentation Standards Manual*, and by R. Howell to use the cartoon on page 185.

# Part One

# Background to design

# 1 Introduction to systems design

All design work is undertaken in order to achieve some objectives, and this chapter begins by placing the systems development project in the context of an organization's policies and plans. The role of users in design and the relationship with systems analysis are then discussed; thus some of the boundaries of design within a development project are described.

There are some common objectives and constraints applied to design work, such as performance, flexibility and project funding, the implications of which are described. This leads to a comparison of approaches to systems design and an overview of the design methodology used in this book. The word 'methodology' is used, not in the purist sense of a study of methods, but rather with its popular meaning as an integrated collection of tools and methods.

## The systems development project

The type of feedback model shown in Figure 1 is widely used to aid the understanding of systems and is found in psychology and sociology as well as in engineering and biology. The basic idea is that a system involves processes which are performed on inputs to produce outputs. The processes of the organization are controlled by sampling the outputs, comparing them with a set of rules and then, if the rules and outputs do not agree, effecting some change to either or both of them.

The rules against which performance is compared should be derived from a higher level of planning, that is the policy or strategy of the organization. This policy may or may not be explicit, but defines where the organization

intends to go in the long term and incorporates the overall objectives of the organization. For commercial companies the objectives may be 'to make a profit', 'to pay good dividends', or 'not to lose too much money so as to stay in business'; a government institution may be offering a service or administering a law. Whatever the overall objectives (there will usually be several interrelated but possibly conflicting objectives) the whole organization is supposed to be working together to achieve them. The policy document interprets the objectives over a relatively long period, e.g. five or ten years. From this is derived a more specific interpretation which ranges over one or two years and may be for use within a limited area of the organization's activities; thus

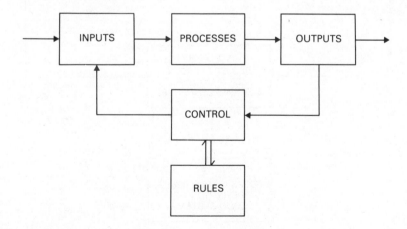

Figure 1   *Feedback model*

the plan is frequently much more concrete and quantitative than the policy. A hierarchy of objectives, policies and plans can be envisaged, with the highest level referring to the long term and global and the lowest level being comparatively short term and local. It is within this framework that computer projects should be initiated and controlled.

The project may be considered as a process which takes as its input the existing system and any new requirements, and works on these to produce a new system as output, all the time being monitored to ensure that the project contributes to the organization's objectives. The control function will act if the project deviates from the plan, e.g. by consuming more time or money than was anticipated. Such a situation demands a change to the project, e.g. replacement of staff, or to the rules, such as increase budget, or to both.

Within the project itself the rules by which it will be assessed and controlled may be considered as being divided into two areas. First, the terms of reference constitute the specific set of the organization's objectives which the project is

required to meet and may consist of such statements as:

1   Look at the stock control area and reduce order despatch time to three days.
2   Any new system must be operational by the beginning of the year, not require any new hardware and occupy no more than twelve programmer man-months.

This defines an area within which the project is bound (stock control), and states the overall objective (three-day despatch time) together with other objectives or constraints. These objectives may conflict with each other and the project leader is responsible for determining the viability of the project. If, either at the beginning or at any later time these objectives are not seen as feasible, this must be reported on, and either the terms of reference or the overall data processing plan amended. It is in fact the responsibility of all members of project to constantly review the objectives and the performance so as to be aware of problems and draw them to the attention of those exercising control. An example of this would arise if following on from the above terms

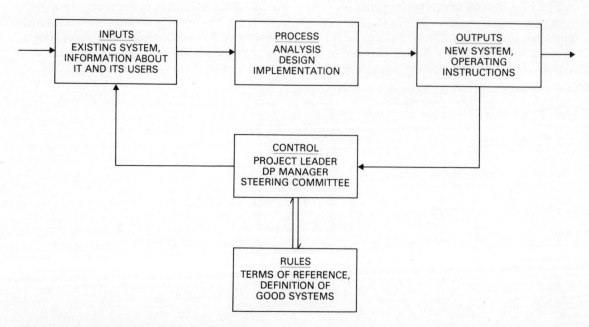

Figure 2   *Systems development: feedback model*

of reference a study revealed that the problem was one not of stock control but of order processing. It would hardly be professional or in the interests of the overall organization for the project to continue.

The second set of objectives is derived from the information processing staff themselves and is based upon what they see as constituting a desirable system. If the designers consider a system which uses the minimum of computer time and storage to be ideal, then the final system will be different from that designed by people who hold easy man/machine interface to be of prime importance. For example, the former would be unlikely to have much in the way of graphic output, which users might find very convenient but which adds to processing time. These objectives may be made explicit by means of a formal methodology for systems analysis and design, which is adopted by the organization. In the absence of such a methodology the objectives are simply embodied in the individual project members, and what they believe are the hallmarks of a 'good' system. The impact of this on the outcome of the project is significant, and readers are urged to give consideration to their own views on the matter. What do you believe constitutes good-quality systems design? More will be said on this when considering design methods.

Using the feedback model to describe the systems development project can result in Figure 2. In this way the model produces a neat, clean analysis of the project with distinct categories of information and activity. This is misleading. In the vast majority of projects, users do not just provide inputs of information but also, and quite rightly, get involved with analysing that information and in designing a new system. Similarly the process does not consist of distinct activities performed by different people at different times. The new system is not output from the process like a bicycle from a production line. The model does present a view of the development project which may be sufficient for those requiring a simple view but is not adequate for the present purposes. There is nothing intrinsically 'wrong' with the feedback model, but Figure 2 does little to help understand the development project itself. This leads directly to

*Golden Rule 11*
You cannot use tools without thinking.

This applies to the feedback model and to all other tools and techniques described in this book (including the golden rules themselves). It is essential to consider the objective which is to be attained and then assess the tool in terms of how effectively it helps to get to the objective.

Here the roles of the user, analyst, and designer will be considered further, but for a description of all the stages involved in a 'typical' project see another book in this series, *Basic Systems Analysis* (Lee, 1984).

## User participation

The role of the user in the systems development project has been growing ever since the beginning of commercial computers. Originally computer staff were high priests or technocrats to whom the user had to bow down in the absence of adequate knowledge and in the face of a special language. This image has been steadily eroding, and the widespread availability of the microcomputer has done much to dispense with it. The user is no longer a passive customer but actively participates in the project. Weinberg (1980) sees the system analyst as a partner of the user in an attempt to obtain a system which meets the user requirements. Semprevivo (1976) saw analysts in the role of helping users to understand their problems and appreciate possible methods for overcoming them.

The extent to which users will be involved in systems design work will vary with the organization, its management style, the role taken by any trade unions, and the interests of the users themselves. Apart from the moral aspects of user involvement, which are part of the law in some Scandinavian countries, there are benefits for the system itself. If a system is not acceptable to its users it will in all probability fail to meet any of its targets, even if it is technically sound. Alternatively, a technically poor system can become an effective working system. This choice, to make or break a system, may never be explicitly made and will follow from attitudes to the system. If a system is to be successful, it must therefore be seen in its broader social context, and effort must be spent in making it acceptable to the users and creating a positive attitude towards it.

The development of a positive attitude towards change in general, and involvement in making such change for the better, is a general responsibility of the organization's management. In the area of systems design there are several possible methods of obtaining involvement. At one extreme there is the one-way communication of the newsletter and briefing sessions, whereas at the other extreme users design their own systems, possibly using an organization's information centre as a source of technical expertise. A common compromise is the idea of user representatives who either work with the designers or sit on a steering committee. One significant problem with user representatives is that they may well become divorced from their former colleagues as they become more involved with the design of the system. However, where attention has been paid to this problem, and time set aside for the participation, this method has proved very successful. An alternative method of involving users in design is to specify certain areas which will be user designed. This is usually done

at the detailed design level and in particular covers input, output, and job organization. If left to this late stage, technical decisions may preclude some options. Mumford (1979) suggests that these areas are designed in parallel, whereas Damodaran *et al.* (1980) suggest designing the user aspects first. Once either the user or the technical system is fixed the number of options in the other area is reduced, but in many cases computer efficiency is the least significant factor. Where a more traditional approach is taken to the demarcation of work roles, Farrow's *Computerization Guidelines* (1979) can help avoid pitfalls by increasing understanding of the design process and the responsibilities of the participants.

This section has briefly outlined some of the issues related to user participation in design, which to a large extent will be determined by the project managers rather than by the individual designers. The designer will have to be able to adopt a variety of roles in relating to system users, work democratically at times, and consider far more than merely technical factors when making decisions. These are not new to many good designers. In this book the term 'designer' will range in application from the individual, computer specialist, designer to a whole committee of people from a variety of backgrounds who are designing a system. The specific human aspects of systems design will be included where relevant, but for a fuller treatment of this important topic the reader is directed towards the referenced texts.

## Systems development

On way to describe the activities which often come within the scope of 'systems development' is to define a sequence of stages which, when performed correctly, lead to the implementation of a working system. These stages may be called:

Feasibility study
Systems analysis
System design
System testing

Implementation
Review.

The description of these stages is often accompanied by a statement referring to the iterative nature of development. This is sometimes referred to as the project 'life cycle' and may be useful for developing project control systems and dividing the work into separate manageable tasks. It also provides a useful framework for teaching newcomers to the topic.

However, many practitioners would find difficulty in identifying these stages in their own work and would be likely to lay more emphasis on the iteration than the sequencing of distinct tasks. This is not due to any deficiency on the part of the practitioners, but rather due to a failure in the description of systems development. One reason for this failure is that the time-scale for development combined with the availability of resources may mean that design work is done before analysis is complete. A further reason is that it is often difficult to specify what the system requirements are without at the same time specifying part of the design. A more general reason for the iteration is that the development process is largely a learning process. As time goes on the developers learn more about the application area, about the users and about designing feasible systems. It is only to be expected that this learning will lead to a change in previously held ideas. Indeed, where this is not the case suspicions should be aroused, particularly about the appropriateness of the 'solution' to the 'problem'.

Most descriptions of development do adopt the divide and describe approach; that is the method used in this text and by many consultancies who employ their own formal methods for systems development. It is a useful organization for learning, and follows in part from the nature of printed material. The example of design used in this book went through many iterations prior to appearing in its present form.

The interface between the areas of systems analysis and systems design is often seen as being a document which specifies precisely what the new system is required to do. This document has such names as 'User system specification' or 'Definition study report'. Even where the stages of analysis and design are clearly separate, the interface is usually much more complex than a single report, the detailed specification of system requirements frequently taking place in parallel with design work.

Ideally a specification of requirements would be complete, consistent, unambiguous, free of design assumptions and correct. Following on from such a sound basis, design could proceed with a good idea of the potential benefits and within an accurate plan. The design could be checked against these requirements throughout the design process. Moreover, a clear specification of requirements relatively early in a project would help avoid the inbuilt assumptions and errors which otherwise may only be discovered when the system goes live. The earlier mistakes are built into a system, the more costly their impact, e.g. a decision to provide an unnecessary enquiry facility has more extensive impact than a bug located in a single program. The specification of requirements is therefore a very important part of the analysis/design interface. Together with it there must also be a large amount of detail which describes the application area. However, this detail is often collected when required without too great a consequence.

System requirements are derived from users, but very often the users are unsure of what they require, or what problems are facing them. The objectives of different groups of users may conflict with each other. Frequently requirements are stated very ambiguously and it is difficult to determine what would satisfy the requirement. One systems development methodology, ISAC (described by Lundeberg, 1981), has progressively increased the emphasis it lays upon defining the requirements, and suggests that only when the objectives are well defined is it worth building an information system.

One way of organizing a statement of requirements is to associate each objective with the users whom it is supposed to assist, thus emphasizing the organizational context of any change. Each requirement would then be accompanied by

1 An identification of the user group(s) who support the objective;
2 A statement of the organizational objectives of the user group(s);
3 A statement of the problems which face the users in trying to achieve these objectives.

The requirement could then be derived by comparison of two and three. Where possible this can be accompanied by further statements defining the criteria which will be used to judge the fulfilment or otherwise of the requirement, and a statement of the value of achieving this requirement. Given all this information, design becomes relatively straightforward. In all but the most simple and structured situations this information will not be available, or will be subject to constant revision. Much of the skill of good systems design lies in leaving as many options open as long as possible so that there is the maximum chance of learning (by both designer and user) before making decisions.

As yet the problems of the analysis/design interface are largely unresolved (unresolvable?), although attempts to define high-level languages for this task continue. In practice many designers will need to continue to rely upon voluminous written and spoken communications from analysts and users. Systems will need to be checked by those responsible for the requirements wherever possible, such that omissions and errors can be identified and corrected as soon as possible.

Over recent years the possibility of developing a prototype of a new system has become ever more real and frequent. Prototypes are generally developed with the aid of high-level languages, such as APL, or software generator packages. Typically they will perform the necessary functions of a system, but inefficiently in terms of computer resource. The reduced cost of hardware and increased software costs have led to some of these prototypes being accepted as live systems.

A prototype system can be used with users to help define their requirements. There is an inherent danger here, that users' requirements will be tailored to suit that which can be shown in the prototype. This can be very much a bottom-up method of specifying requirements, with the danger of getting bogged down in the detail at the expense of the overall objectives.

The use of prototyping has been welcomed as a means for eliminating the so-called project life cycle and its emphasis on explicit user requirements. Prototyping allows the system and the requirements to be developed in unison until they are defined in sufficient detail to satisfy the users. Its use does, however, need to be carefully controlled so that it is integrated into a coherent project strategy, rather than the technique itself being allowed to determine the development methods.

One methodology described by Jenkins for developing systems with the aid of prototypes states that the first step is to define the users' basic information needs, prior to refining both them and the design. This presumes that an information system will meet the needs of the user and that users will take an active part in systems development. The prototype system can be regarded as a model for the final operational system, but a model that is closely linked to available technology. In some situations this will be a viable design strategy, particularly if the users have some computing experience. Jenkins (1983) adds further criteria of appropriateness, suggesting that prototyping is particularly useful when

Project development time is limited;
The project is of reasonable scope, e.g. one user or five programs;
The users need to learn about their requirements and conduct experiments;
The system is mainly concerned with reporting and management support;

but not useful when

The organization's software and data is not well defined and organized;
The prototyping tools are not well understood;
Users and systems staff are not jointly involved with systems development.

Prototyping is a very powerful technique. It may not replace the traditional methods for designing systems which have many users or have large volumes of transactions. However, even if only used as part of a development method it will assist user involvement and the design of those systems which interact with people to a large extent.

# Design objectives and constraints

Prior to the consideration of methods by which systems can be designed, it is necessary to look at the general objective of design and some of the more common constraints. Many of these are concerned with the product of design, the operational system. Three are concerned with the process, the project: project funding, project life, competence. These are not independent of each other; for example, in order to achieve a very secure system, project funding may need to be increased and performance levels lowered.

The overriding objective of any information system must be to contribute to some activity of the organization. The place of the development project within the organizational plans, and the difficulties of defining exactly what is required to make this contribution, have already been described. Despite these difficulties the final system should effectively support the organization, and this objective needs to be kept in mind throughout the project. It should be used at all decision points in evaluating the merit of a particular option or of the project as a whole. Information systems have little value in their own right and exist to serve other areas of human activity; thus service is the primary objective.

## Performance

Performance used to be regarded as of major importance, and was assessed in terms of run time for batch jobs and response time for real-time work. Systems designed for performance tend to be built around specific hardware and system software, exploiting its capabilities. Further, these systems tend to have large and complex data structures manipulated by equally large and complex programs, with the data and programs closely related for fast processing. Typically some parts of a system are optimized for performance at the expense of less critical areas. These factors lead to fast systems which are difficult to change because a modification to either the data, the processes, the system software or the hardware involves ramifications throughout the tightly interwoven system. The advent of relatively cheap processing power has led to the reduced importance of performance as a major design objective for most application systems.

## Storage requirements

Storage requirements also used to be minimized as part of the design effort and complex packing and unpacking routines developed, together with the use of highly compressed codes. These techniques save storage space but require processor time. Again, the relative cheapness of hardware has led to a change in the order of magnitude of the problem, and many commercial designers can afford to disregard it altogether. Designers of on-line information retrieval systems and text processors may well consider how to store gigabytes of information and more importantly how to access it quickly, but even here the use of data base machines and content addressable storage systems will reduce the importance of optimizing on storage. Similarly, few users of micros would be able to financially justify designing a system around storage when the question would be better put as a choice between upgrading the processor and using a packing routine or buying another disk drive.

## Flexibility

Flexibility in the design is currently believed by many to be of prime importance. This follows from the very high maintenance costs incurred by installations which for one reason or another have disregarded flexibility in the past. The major part of the budgets of many installations is devoted to maintenance work. It is impossible to stop the need for changes to a system because the requirements placed upon it change. The goal here is to design a system where the impact of change is minimal. The result of optimizing for flexibility is a system composed of relatively small modules each of which performs a single task with as little dependence upon other modules as possible. In this way, a change in one part of the real world is contained in that part of the computer system which relates directly to it, and there is no secondary effect. An example would be the separation of sales order header information from the detailed order lines; then if a change was made to the contents of an order line any tasks which only needed to use the order header information could remain unchanged. The total effect of the change is less than it would have been if the two types of information had been held in one record.

## Portability

Portability, such that a system can run on different types of hardware and software, is a specific type of flexibility. This goal may be important to a software house developing a package, an organization with a mixture of hardware at different sites, or a company which thinks it may change its hardware or software in the foreseeable future. It is virtually impossible to develop a truly portable system, but it is possible to concentrate the hardware- and software-dependent routines in one module. If all calls to backing store are calls to a common module then the change of medium need only involve a change to this one module, which acts as the interface between the physical storage and the processing tasks. Portability can also be enhanced by confining the design to standard features which are likely to be found in other hardware or software; for example, by only using the standard parts of a programming language and not a particular manufacturer's extensions to it.

If the design is optimized in terms of flexibility then there will be a price to pay in terms of performance and possibly storage requirements. It is because of the changes in the relative cost of hardware and staff that there is now much more emphasis on flexibility. Not only is the hardware cheap enough for flexible systems to be afforded, but also the cost of maintenance is such that flexible systems are essential for anyone adopting a long-term view.

## Security

Security of the system, including the privacy and confidentiality of the data, may be of major importance, and this will lead to extra processing requirements and data storage to control access to programs and data. The system could be divided up into clearance levels, which can mean a reduction in performance and flexibility.

## Reliability

Reliability of the system in terms of hardware reliability and data integrity has parallels with security. There are accepted methods by which reliability can be improved, again at a price in terms of performance and flexibility.

In the cases of both security and reliability, the costs incurred need to be balanced against the benefits gained. There are not many sites which can justify the use of four mainframes, all doing the same job and cross-checking their results in order to ensure accuracy. However, there are not many sites controlling manned flights to the moon!

## Project life

Project life is a factor which can be varied and will have an impact on the design. If a major objective is a system which is working in a very short period there are several possible consequences, which include the development of a system which is familiar to the designer rather than the optimum solution to the problem. The system may require continual modification to incorporate hitherto unconsidered aspects of the system. An example would be the use of a package about which staff already had experience, although it does not meet the requirements. The use of software generators is an alternative which reduces project life at the expense of performance.

## Project funding

Project funding may be considered as a separate factor from project life, although there are obvious interactions. Given that the date a system must be implemented by is not fixed, then the time spent on the project can be varied in inverse relation to the number of staff/consultants employed for any given budget. In practice this relationship is often very complex and difficult to manage accurately.

Funding will also affect the type of hardware and software which can be used both during development and by the final system. The funds available should be directly related to the potential benefits which the project could bring, and which should have been quantified during the feasibility study. In some cases application development tools may be costed against increased productivity over several projects, but this is really a matter of accounting and management. In practice financial limitations are usually expressed as a restriction that the system will require no significant hardware or software purchases. This limitation is so common that it is rarely stated, with what counts as a 'significant purchase' being a matter of common knowledge in a given installation. Only a minority of projects are of sufficient size for the terms of reference to allow for hardware and software changes.

Most organizations upgrade following a review of performance covering all systems using the equipment, albeit allowing for future plans. If the hardware and software to be used is defined, this does not mean that the designer's work is almost complete, or that the equipment can be blamed for a poor system. A large number of potential systems could be built, and the designer has many decisions to make even when these restrictions apply.

### Integration

Integration with existing and planned systems is often high on the list of objectives. This may well mean that the designer is limited in the hardware and software which can be used. For example, if current systems all use a CODASYL data base, then even though the best design for a particular system might incorporate a relational data base it would be implemented in CODASYL.

Integration of data may lead to the possibility of new information, e.g. combining training data with staff workload data leading to skill availability information. Similarly, a designer may need to conform to documentation, design, message or other standards for the sake of integration, although they may not be ideal in a particular instance. In this situation the individual project is suffering for the greater good of the whole organization, this greater good possibly being the use of a common data base management system for all data or standardized documentation.

### Competence

Competence at designing systems is a constraint which applies in many projects and may be the consequence of either a lack of ability or experience or both. It is unlikely that a system will be developed which is a complete failure and for which responsibility can be fully allocated. More likely is a system which works, just about, but is known to be difficult to use and maintain. This situation is not uncommon, and follows in part from the rapid changes in the information technology field which necessitate regular and costly retraining. The designer facing a novel situation may resort to installing a familiar system which does not take advantage of opportunities offered by the present situation. Alternatively, an attempt to design in new features can lead to success if learning can also take place, that is if the time and facilities to learn are available.

*Golden Rule 12* Be aware of when you need help, and ask for it.

It is dangerous to pretend to have a level of competence beyond that which one actually has because, apart from the fact that this is lying, it can also lead to a great deal of unnecessary work on the part of the designer and colleagues. Somewhat more dangerous is the incompetent who is unaware of the situation, for whom there is little hope, and who should be avoided.

## Approaches to design

There is no one right way by which systems can be designed. This is not wholly explained by the fact that there is no such thing as the perfect system, and the best that can be hoped for is a system in which the compromises between objectives have been carefully chosen. To use a colloquial expression, there is more than one way to skin a cat, which translates into general systems terminology as the principle of equifinality. Design methods, strategies and methodologies are tools for the designer, and Golden Rule 11 applies to them. Systems cannot be designed without thought, because the tools need selecting and applying carefully. It follows that a good designer may employ a design standard but will constantly be reviewing its effectiveness and looking for improvements. In order to do this effectively the designer needs to be aware of some of the common methods and emphases in systems design. The three *methods* in design are top down, bottom up and critical first.

## Design methods

### Top-down design

Top-down design is based around the idea that there are various levels of decision which need to be made, varying from those concerning the goals of the project and the overall system boundary down to the detailed level of allocating data to disks and the layout of printed reports. An example is a management information system where the goals and boundaries of the management are defined prior to specifying the elements of data to be used. Progressively analysing higher-level functions into more detail is referred to as 'functional decomposition'; 'stepwise refinement' refers to gradually increasing the precision of a statement. These may both be considered as specific varieties of top-down development methods. Top-down design involves answering the higher questions before the detailed ones and at all times trying not to limit the range of choices which are left for consideration at a more detailed level. Iteration here is the process of stepping back to a higher level to review the impact there of lower-level decisions, and it may be necessary to change previous decisions in the light of lower-level information. This method leads to well-structured systems, with the various components being well defined, having simple interfaces and working together towards the overall goal. A common criticism of this method is that its success depends upon the experience of the project staff and their ability to make implicit assumptions about what is practical at a detailed level. It is also true to say that few systems possess a clearly defined hierarchy of decision points and that the true overall objectives of most projects are never clearly defined. It follows from these criticisms that a purely top-down method of design is unlikely to be sufficient for most projects and other methods may need to be employed.

### Bottom-up design

Bottom-up design starts with basic units of the system, and from these the design builds up to higher levels. A system created in this way could start with the design of input documents and output layouts, eventually arriving at the point where a management information system has been built. This method has a longer history than the others and some authors claim it has a better success rate than top-down design. In the example here at least the managers would get reports which are of use to them even though it is almost certain that the overall system will not form a coherent whole. The notion of suboptimization refers to the situation where elements of a system are optimized individually with the effect that the whole system does not function at its best. For optimum functioning of the whole it may be necessary for elements to be compromised; e.g. in designing a mini car, optimizing each component on its own is likely to lead to a design for a Rolls Royce! Bottom-up design also tends to produce systems with complex interfaces between modules because the modules were not designed to be interfaced in the first place. An area where bottom-up methods are particularly useful is that of program and system testing.

These two methods do not necessarily emphasize the needs of the system users. It is possible to have as the top objective of a project the need to integrate an existing system with recent developments, any possible user benefits being given low priority. A bottom-up design could begin with the acquisition of some graphics software followed by a search for an application. Because these situations frequently exist the term 'outside-in' has been coined to emphasize that the end users of the system, on the outside, should come before the internal aspects of the system.

### Critical-first design

Critical first design is a method of system design which emphasizes the identification of the most critical component in the system. If potential problem areas can be identified at an early stage it is possible to try to solve these before going on to further design work. This can apply to technical problems, such as whether it is possible to connect a particular micro to a given network; a negative answer here could lead to the end of a project without needing to define all higher levels of project objectives. Similarly, the functional boundaries of two departments in an organization may need defining before any work on a joint system could prove fruitful. It is very difficult to know for certain at the beginning of a project what constitutes the biggest potential problem, but tackling the most critical component first is a very practical way of commencing system design. This method could be used to design a whole system by ranking all parts of design in terms of difficulty and working down the list, although this is not frequently done.

The design methods described so far suggest a sequence by which decisions should or could be made. However, as proponents of these methods state, design is not simply a sequence of steps through which one moves, going only in one direction. It is always necessary to go back and review the impact on previous decisions of the current decisions. This iteration tends to lead to a loss of distinctness of the methods in practice, and to the design oscillating between hardware-dependent features on the one hand and management policy on the other. This is right and proper and if labels are required, may be termed the hybrid method. Top-down design may be used to obtain the overall integration, and critical-first and bottom-up design to contribute to the detail. In fact any combination of the methods may be used which the designer can justify as being the most appropriate in a given situation.

## Design emphases
Independent of the sequence of decisions, the design may concentrate upon either the processes or the data; these are the two *emphases* in system design, and each has its own proponents. If the emphasis is upon the operations which need to be performed, e.g. processing goods received by a

factory, then there will be less choice available when it comes to defining data storage because how it is to be used will already have been defined. Conversely, if data design is the focal point of attention then the stored data and input/output messages may be defined without regard to how one will be generated from the other. Emphasizing the processes is the more traditional design method and is advocated as leading to efficient systems with good performance characteristics.

### Process-driven design
Process-driven design looks at a system as a series of functions, e.g.

1 Obtain orders
2 Validate orders
3 Output error details
4 Update customer file
5 Update stock file
6 Acknowledge order.

These are jobs which need to be done, and consideration of exactly what constitutes an order or an error detail is of secondary concern.

### Data-driven design
Data-driven design has been advocated for some time in program design and more recently has gained popularity with systems design. The arguments here are that if good structuring of stored data can be achieved, a very flexible system can be developed and processes built around this. It is also argued that the end users are interested in the data messages, not the processes that handled them, and that it is with these that design should begin. For the preceding example, concern would be placed upon (1) the definition of orders, error details and order acknowledgement, and (2) the definition of the data stored about customers and stock in such a way that it could support this and other applications.

If emphasis is placed upon a definition of the messages which are conveyed the design method can be referred to as data flow. Conversely, if the emphasis is upon the organization of the stored data the method is data structure driven. Data flow design argues that both processes and structures are subordinate to the messages which are the purpose of the system. Data structure design advocates point to the need for a stable organization of the stored data which will support new applications and changes to existing ones at a relatively low cost.

Once again, each method has arguments both in its favour and against it. As already pointed out, a system needs all three components – processes, messages and stored data – and they need to be integrated. At any one point in the design it may be wise to concentrate upon one aspect rather than the others, but eventually the design must be considered from each point of view in an iterative manner.

## Classification of design approaches

The various approaches have been grouped together under six headings (Wood-Harper and Fitzgerald, 1982), and these are worth consideration to remind the designer of the wide range of possible problems and methods which may be encountered.

### General systems theory

General systems theory emphasizes the place of a specific system in a larger system and tries not to limit the range of possible solutions. The generality and the attempt to optimize at a very high level tend to mean that practical results are currently impossible. Solutions to high-level questions tend to involve very far-reaching changes and are beyond the scope of most project controllers, e.g. solving payroll tax deduction by introducing a state-controlled economy.

### Human activity systems

Human activity design, as developed by Checkland (1983), addresses itself to soft problems. These are problems which are difficult to define because they are complex, unstructured and typically human. The aim is to look at the problem in its environment, considering the organization and attitudes as well as procedures. The purpose is to create a situation in which the problem can be solved and changes introduced. It

is these soft problems and their lack of resolution prior to computer systems design which has led to many systems being developed which do not tackle the real problem, i.e. there is no 'top' from which to design down.

### Participative approach

Participative design is associated with Mumford (1979) or the NCC, and emphasizes the need for users to be actively involved in the design activity itself. The motivation here is partly to ensure user involvement and acceptance of a design, without which the 'best' solution will be a failure. It is also true to argue that the users know their application area and are in a good position to state their requirements of a new system. This method does not attempt to tackle the whole problem range, but concentrates on the immediate users.

### Traditional approaches

Traditional approaches to analysis and design are very widespread and emphasize the analysis of an application area in terms of first its processes and second its data. Design has concentrated upon replacing existing systems with new equipment which performs the job more efficiently. This approach assumes that the existing system for processing information is basically sound and mainly needs modernizing – a dangerous assumption.

### Data analysis

Data analysis, derived from data base design methods, seeks to establish a neutral base from which problems may be solved. It attempts to make the data structuring as independent of the organization and its spectific managers as possible. The objective is a structuring of the data based upon the real world which will outlast the present applications. For example, the fact that an organization's customers each have one order outstanding at a time does not mean that the system can build upon this fact, because in the future a customer may place two or more orders with the organization and this should be allowed for. It is worth nothing that some of the sophisticated application design aids ask the designer to specify the data stores and input/output, and then generate automatically the code to process these.

*Structured systems analysis*
Structured systems analysis and design provide a variety of 'new' documentation techniques, but also bring to the project an emphasis upon logical design prior to physical implementation considerations. This follows on from the freedom from hardware restraints, which means that

designers can now decide what is wanted prior to looking at how this will be achieved.

These six classifications overlap to some extent, and the perfect designer would need to be able to solve problems at all of the levels described. An alternative approach, and one that is much more realistic, would be to look at these six approaches as each offering something towards the design of a system.

# Design methodology 1 (DM/1)

This name has been given to the approach to designing computer systems expounded in this book. It is a hybrid, using techniques of data analysis, structured analysis, top-down design, critical-first design and others. DM/1 attempts to face the general problems of designing a system. It therefore follows that its use will not provide a solution to a specific problem on its own. These methods, along with all others, need to be treated critically, modified where necessary, and applied with thought. You are expected to invent or develop DM/2 yourself. Further increments of the design methodology will need to be made for each new design effort and following each design experience.

The model which underlies this methodology considers a system as consisting of data stores, data flows and processes as well as users. Figure 3 shows the relationships. All these components need to be attended to by the design. The stored data is treated as the property of the whole organization rather than as a single application area. This follows the increasingly held view that the stored data is a shared resource which must be managed by criteria different from those relevant to specific applications. For example, a project may require information to be made available about people and their homes, at short notice, following an enquiry giving a person's name. This could be achieved by storing home information with person information using the person's name as a key. If this course was taken the information stored would be of little use to the person wanting a quick answer to the

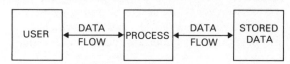

Figure 3  *Design methodology system*

question 'who lives in home X?' There can be a conflict of interest which needs to be resolved by reference to an organizational policy on data storage. The difference is between an organization's view of its data and the view of a single application area.

DM/1 addresses itself to definable problems typical of operation-level data processing systems. Where variable or not predefined output is required, as in a management information system, the necessary flexibility may well be best provided by the use of query language. This could derive data from the data model built for other objectives. The extent to which the data model is able to accurately and simply reflect the interests of the organization will determine the extent to which it will be able to support demands made on it.

There is also a distinction to be made between logical and physical design. Logical design is the development of a model of what is required of the new system, irrespective of how this can be implemented. This model may exist on paper and possibly in a prototype system. In this model, consideration of how a job will be done (e.g. by a person or a machine), should not relevant; the logical design concentrates upon a definition of the job to be done.

The physical design has two aspects,. The first is the outline design of the system, which involves the selection of processing methods and media based upon such considerations as response times and the project budget. In moving from the logical to the outline compromises and tradeoffs need to be made, and it is proposed that these are done on the basis that the most critical components are designed first. This implies that during the original specification of the requirements by the users and management the objectives were ranked into order of importance either in terms of the financial benefits involved or for other reasons. This prioritization can then be carried over to the design by giving priority in resource allocation to tasks and data which support the most important requirements. Many iterations will usually be needed at this stage in order to balance all the variables in something like an optimum manner. Detailed physical design is the second stage, and involves the design of files, reports, dialogues, processes and the like.

In theory, it is possible to develop and implement the stored data model independently of any application considerations. This may be done by taking the logical data model developed, and mapping it on to any data management software in as acurate a manner as possible. Some installations operating data base systems adopt this approach because of the importance of a stable organization of the stored data. Many sites consider that the outline physical design of the application and the data should be done together. The objective is to achieve the optimum result

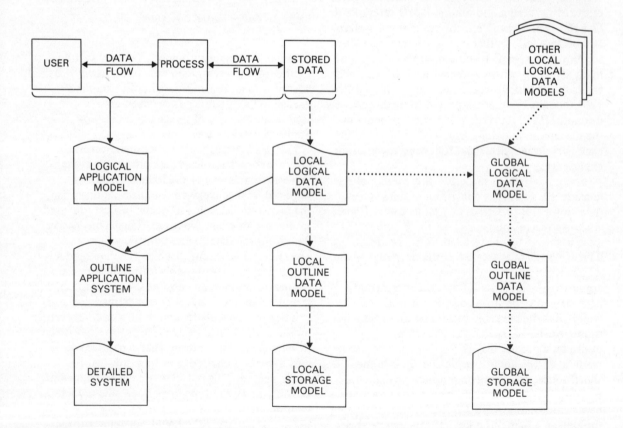

Figure 4   *Overview of DM/1 (continuous lines). Possible relationships with (a) an organization-wide data model design (dotted lines) (b) the development of the data model for the application area (dashed lines)*

allowing for compromises in both areas of design. Similarly, detailed design decisions about either the application or the data could have an effect on the other component, and revisions may need to be made.

Where an organization wishes to maintain an overall data model distinct from that of a specific application, then the logical data model will contribute to that overview; the overall model eventually incorporates and supports the local view. DM/1 as described here does not assume an overall data model, and implements the logical data model as part of the application system (see Figure 4).

The design therefore proceeds from the logical through outline to the physical, and constitutes a top-down approach in general terms. This does not imply that a single clearly defined 'top' is a prerequisite; rather, it accepts that most designers have an idea of the direction in which the goal lies and will be refining the definition of the goal throughout the project. This is consistent with

*Golden Rule 13*
Constantly question the purpose of the project and your actions.

The good designer, like the realistic person, will accept the inevitability of change and misunderstanding. By maintaining an open, positive and critical attitude the designer will be able to keep on course for the project goals, identifying and correcting errors as early as possible.

# 2 Design aids

## Standard documentation

Standardized documentation is widely advocated as being a good, professional and worthwhile part of the job of systems design. It is also frequently the cause of complaints, moans and sighs emanating from those who have the responsibility for producing it. It is therefore worth spending some time on the topic in general, prior to describing particular techniques.

### Documentation
This is the recording of all the information which is pertinent to a system for subsequent use. It is usually kept together in one place, be that a manual, a file or a set of filing cabinets.

*What information?*
The short answer to this question is 'everything'; however, one possible structuring of this information is into inputs and outputs of the design effort.

The *inputs* to the design are the raw data collected from previous documentation, users, those requesting the project etc. All the data which will be used to design the new system (including that gained from informal conversations) should be written down and stored. It is important that each item has the date/time and source of that information added to it. As well as inputs from outside the design team there are the ideas, suggestions, and plans generated by the designer and colleagues. Again, these need to be written down and stored, together with a note identifying the date/time, source and whether or not the idea is an interpretation of facts, a question to be answered, a problem identified or a solution discussed, i.e. how far was the idea followed up.

The *outputs* from the design are copies of every report, memo or conversation that relates to the system; these contribute to the documentation. The date/time and destination of these outputs should be recorded. This information usually involves a summarization of the design effort and may prove sufficient in its own right to meet the demands made on the documentation without referring back to the source data on which the output was based. (For a list of the typical documentation outputs, see Figure 12 in Lee, 1984.)

If all the inputs and outputs are stored, then the documentation will be the sum total of the information on the project, which if kept up to date would all but eliminate the stage of fact-finding when maintenance or redesign are required in the future.

*Why document?*
The primary reason for documenting a system is to avoid the loss of information which will later prove to be useful. It is because it is impossible to predict all the changes the future may hold that everything is kept – just in case. If at some time in the future (either within the project or after its completion) a problem needs to be solved which has been tackled before, a duplication of effort can be avoided by the study of the previous solution.

Recording ideas on paper forces the designer to formalize these ideas, which leads to clarification of them. This would be done eventually if the ideas are incorporated into the working system, but the sooner fuzzy thinking is cleared up the less time will be lost following up dead ends. It is certainly no loss to store the unused ideas, because as there are changes in the environment within which the system works it may be that these rejected possibilities will become valid, and new solutions can be built on them. Similarly, recording all assumptions and reasons which go into making a design decision enables the impact of changes in these variables to be assessed and the design revised, in a much more intelligent and economic way than would be possible without an understanding of how the decision had been arrived at. A further advantage of this storage of ideas is that overall quality of the design work can be improved by learning from one's own and one's colleagues successes and mistakes. This leads to the allocation of responsibility for both the good and poor ideas, and if all inputs to the design process have identifiable sources, then responsibility for misleading information can be apportioned. This is important, particularly when a legal contract exists between the design team and the user, and problems arise when the designer is given false information which leads to the design of a system which either does not work or does not meet the objectives.

Finally, once the information on a system is safely written down, an organization is no longer in the vulnerable position of depending upon the memories of individuals. There is the morality of this situation – it is possible for the individuals to effectively blackmail the organization. The more likely occurrence is that the designer will be relied upon to provide answers when questions arise in the short and long term, with the danger of indispensibility leading to stagnation.

## Standardization

### Why standardize?

For many people involved in the work of designing systems or the study of the design process, effective communication is seen as a major factor in producing success. The designer is responsible for communicating with

The systems analyst(s)
User management and staff
Programmers
Computer operators
Project managers.

In some organizations, the systems analyst and designer will be the same person, or will share work between themselves in a project team, perhaps with the analyst specializing in 'business analysis'. With this possible exception, all the other people involved often come from different backgrounds, with their own goals, problems and most importantly their own technical language. It is also true that a project does not occur at a single point in time and may extend over months and years. In the light of this a communication problem may exist within the project. This could

happen when people change jobs or forget what they knew, because of either breaks from the job, or the pressure of other work, or simply the passage of time. The potential problem increases when one considers the subsequent maintenance of the system by staff who may never have met the original designers.

Kit Grindley (1975) describes the problems as

1   To produce a statement of requirements, which is complete, unambiguous, short, and free from programming strategy;
2   To obtain the users' agreement and, better, his understanding of what he has agreed;
3   To communicate these requirements to programmers and to minimize their chief time-waster, the systems query;
4   To maintain an up-to-date description of what the company's computer system does.

Standards are first and foremost an attempt to establish a language which will be useful in communicating information to all the parties concerned with the project. However, attempts to produce a language which is at a level high enough to meet everyone's needs have generally found little support in the industry – partly because the effort involved in learning the language is prohibitive. There are times when it is necessary to provide different versions of the same information to meet the languages of different people, but the use of an appropriate set of standards helps to keep this to a minimum.

Over and above these benefits, there are several other reasons for standardizing the documentation:

1   The time and money spent on training staff who transfer into the project team is reduced because the new member knows where to find information and can learn about the current state of the design with relatively little assistance.
2   Standards by definition apply to the general case and not all sections will be useful in a given situation. However, by having an extensive checklist the designer is reminded of the information which might be needed. This

means that omissions are more likely to be intentional than accidental.

3  In developing a set of standards the experience of many systems designers is used, and so, by following the standards, designers are forced to obtain and use information that has in the past improved the quality of the design.

4  Standard documentation can lead to standardization in other areas, particularly in the use of transapplication software aids, e.g. module libraries, test generators and harnesses, preprocessors, menu processors and the like.

As a final comment on the use of standards in system design, it is worth noting the acceptance that programming standards have found in both the program design and coding areas; the problems of programmers are similar to those of designers.

*Which standards?*
The standards adopted need to match the job being asked of them. Thus it would be unlikely that standards developed for use with mainframe batch systems design work would be ideal for the designer working with on-line distributed minis. However, many sets of standards do attempt to cover a wide range of hardware and processing modes, and these may usefully be employed as they will have the benefit of not being abandoned when, for example, the type of equipment is changed. This flexibility is important because the world is bound to change, and the users and systems staff are going to have to learn a completely new set of standards for recording information if the old standards are not able to cope with the new types of system. An indication of the failing of standards is increasing incorporation of explanations and appendices into the documentation. If this situation is found to be occurring, then the data processing management need to look into the possibility of enhancing the standards and helping them to evolve, as a matter of urgency.

It would be unusually fortuitous if a single set of ready-made standards met all an organization's needs. A common practice is to use a set of general standards as a basis from which the organization builds its own standards to suit its own specific needs.

In short, the best standards are those with which everyone is familiar and which are applicable to the problem in hand. If no standards are currently in use, general purpose standards, e.g. those developed by the NCC, should be adopted.

**Problems with standardized documentation**
A common complaint about standard documentation is that the time spent producing it is unproductive. In response to this one only has to ask the person who later has to maintain the system, or even the designer who has forgotten the good idea of only a couple of days ago, to realize the benefits of standardized documentation. If the only measure of efficiency is the solving of problems and not their prevention in the first place, then documentation may be regarded as inefficient. This short-term view is not recommended.

A more realistic assessment of the complaints would often reveal that the true cause is the repetitive clerical nature of the tasks involved, which are for much of the time very boring. The glimmer of hope in this area is the use of software to help produce the documentation, although this cannot remove the necessity for producing and entering the detail into the computer in the first place.

A significant problem in much documentation is the duplication and consequent redundancy of information. Apart from increasing the tedious part of form filling, this situation is also dangerous in that as soon as a piece of information is held in two separate places the possibility of inconsistency arises. As an example of this, consider the situation in which copies of record layouts are kept as part of the documentation for each procedure which uses them. If a decision is made to alter a field length then all these copies need to be found and altered. If an end-of-year procedure is not kept up to date, then it may be programmed and tested with the wrong field length; this may lead to costly later modifications.

Some documentation systems, particularly those based around data dictionaries, try to avoid this problem; others should have some explicit method of cross-referencing to try to reduce the likelihood of inconsistency.

Another substantial problem is that no system of documentation can possibly meet all the needs of all the people wishing to use it. Programmers would like to see documentation organized around the programs, each program specification including details of all files it uses. The designer may wish to have all the information on files in one place to help with disk allocation, and a user may wish to see the outputs of the system grouped together in chronological order. These and many other requirements conflict, and need to be resolved by either (1) training everyone to find their own way around a complete set of documentation, or (2) producing subsets of information for each person – with the consequent cost and dangers which follow this duplication.

This problem is true of all information retrieval systems, and again some comfort may be found in the use of software-based documentation which will allow people to see the information as though it were organized from their point of view while still retaining the advantages of a single master copy.

## Data dictionaries

In its most basic form a data dictionary is simply a documentation aid which holds data about data. As with other dictionaries it offers a standard name and a definition of the basic elements. It may also hold information on the possible values, the picture, any alternative names used and the elements' relationship to other elements also found in the dictionary. Thus all the information relating to a particular data item is held in one place.

The advantages of using a data dictionary for documentation purposes include:

1  A reduction in the work involved in producing and maintaining documentation by reducing redundancy and duplication.
2  Easier identification of synonyms (more than one name for one thing) and homonyms (one name for more than one thing).

The dictionary may be held manually, e.g. on cards in alphabetic sequence, or on a computer. Many data dictionary packages are available which offer a great number of ways of using the data dictionary information, e.g. the production of data division source code in COBOL, the production of test data, listings of synonyms and incomplete elements as well as printing subsets of the dictionary for users or programmers. Figure 5 is a possible data element layout for a data dictionary.

| Name | System(s) |
|---|---|
| Aliases | |
| Description (including origin/maintenance/deletion) | |
| Values (min) (max) (avg) | Security |
| Format/picture | |
| Other elements related to (including functional dependencies) | |
| Relationships with structures/stores/processes/flows | |
| Function/purpose | |
| References(s) | |

Figure 5   *Data element layout*

The basic idea of a data dictionary has been extended until it includes within it virtually all the documentation on the whole system and becomes not only a way of structuring the documentation but a way of organizing the design process. Thus as well as data elements the following may also be found in some data dictionaries.

## Structures

Structures are information about the way in which elements are grouped together. Typically these are records but may also be structures used for input, e.g. a VDU screen of input or output, a report layout. The structure may not even correspond to a single physical record and may be a part of one physical record or consist of two or more physical records. However a structure is defined, the important thing is that it describes a group of elements which will be treated in a similar manner by programs and hardware. The contents of a typical structure entry in a dictionary are given in Figure 6. Note that the composition allows reference to be made to the data elements in the dictionary. To allow two-way cross-referencing the elements would have to hold information saying what structures they were part of.

A useful notation to briefly describe a data structure, and which shall be used here, is illustrated by the following examples:

STUDENT-DATA (STDT-NO, STDT-NAME, [ADDRESS/HOME-ADRS], COURSE* (UNIT-NO, UNIT-NAME, [RESULT]))

The name of the group of data is STUDENT-DATA and the parentheses () describe the items which compose a group. STDT-NO is chosen as the unique key and underlined, although the fact that STDT-NAME could have been a key is denoted by the dashed line under it. Items are separated by commas. Where separators are absent the existence of the item is qualified by the statements from which it is not separated. The brackets [] enclose optional fields. The slash / corresponds to a logical OR and a plus + corresponds to a logical AND. In this example either ADDRESS or HOME-ADRS must be present. [ADDRESS], [HOME-ADRS] would mean that one, both or neither addresses could be present, while ,[ADDRESS]/ [HOME-ADRS], would mean that one or neither might occur. The asterisk * denotes repetition which may involve numbers of occurrences ≥ zero. In this example a whole group of items is repeating. The item COURSE is defined in more detail by the items within the brackets which follow COURSE. Note that no comma separates COURSE and its detailed definition. The symbols for 'and' and 'or' can be combined in several ways to specify alternative groupings of data.

| Name | System(s) |
|---|---|
| Aliases | |
| Description | |
| Elements/composition | |
| Physical information | |
| Moved by | |
| Stored by | |
| Function/purpose | |
| Reference(s) | |

Figure 6 *Structure layout*

## Flows

Some dictionaries have a special type of entry to

describe the channels along which data moves, defining the source and destinations of the flows. Apart from reference to the data elements or structures which are moved, other details which can be held are an identification of the search argument (key) used to define the flow, the frequency and/or volume of the data moved, the timing constraints such as response times or deadlines, a specification of the necessary freshness of the data, and the definition of the physical medium of transfer, e.g. Figure 7.

### Stores

These may also be defined separately, and describe what data is stored in the system, how it is stored, which data flows put data into the store and which take data out from the store.

Even systems which make extensive use of data base management software have a large amount of data held in temporary non-data-base files or manual files. These, as well as the whole data base, could be specified as data stores. Figure 8 is a possible layout.

### *Processes*

These are the other essential part of any system and may also be described in a data dictionary. The flows in and out would need to be identified, as well as physical information on how the process was to be carried out, its frequency of execution and its probable duration, together with a brief summary of the process logic.

| Name | System(s) |
|---|---|
| Aliases | |
| Composition (including search argument) | |
| Source | |
| Destination | |
| Volumes/timing/freshness | |
| Physical medium | |
| Function/purpose | |
| Reference(s) | |

Figure 7   *Flows layout*

| Name | System(s) |
|---|---|
| Aliases | |
| Composition (including unique identifiers) | |
| Flows in | |
| Flows out | |
| Organization and access methods (including direct access fields) | |
| Function/purpose | |
| Reference(s) | |

Figure 8   *Stores layout*

| Name | System(s) |
|------|-----------|
| Aliases | |
| Logic summary | |
| Flows in | |
| Flows out | |
| Method | |
| Timing | |
| Function/purpose | |
| Reference(s) | |

Figure 9   *Processes layout*

Note that not all processes physically alter data; a validation program may use a transaction file to which no physical changes are made but which become the valid transaction file and the end of the run. Figure 9 shows a possible layout.

In an extended data dictionary, as described here, the true strength is in the cross-referencing capability, which means that data about the system is recorded once only and at all other times it is only referred to. This leads to a saving in putting information into the dictionary (and maintaining it), but more work when information is wanted out from the dictionary as all the references need to be followed up. Here computer packages help as they can produce reports containing all and only the relevant information, for example if it is required to know what the impact of changing an element would be. Using text handling capabilities packages could produce all the necessary information for a programmer or a user. Similarly, a graphics facility would allow the production of system flow charts and the like.

One problem remains with most dictionary systems: they only describe a system at one point in time and do not allow for incorporating alternative proposed systems, the old and the new systems, and logical/outline/detail system designs. One way around this is to include a system reference for each entry in the dictionary, which gives the name and version of the system of which this entry is a part. All output requests would then need to specify which system they were referring to. In this way the dictionary could hold information which may not be important at the time but probably would be as soon as it was discarded.

It is worth noting that there are very-high-level languages in which systems can be specified, the most famous of which is probably PSL. Originally intentions were to specify the requirements of the system, which would then be processed by software to generate the final system. PSL, as commercially available, assists the designer in building an extended data dictionary and deriving information from it, and is independent of the systems optimization and design algorithm (SODA) which was part of the original project.

## Software aids

The ever-increasing gap between the cost of hardware and manpower has led to the greater use of application development software. In the past report writer and enquiry facilities have existed separately from the screen generator or file definition software used by programmers. Packages exist which integrate these and many other functions to provide a very powerful tool.

Systems may be programmed in days or weeks rather than months or years; this programming may be done with user-friendly question and answer sessions between 'programmer' and the development package. The area which will be most influenced by the widespread use of such packages is traditional programming, these development aids having been designed specifically to reduce the time taken to program systems. Apart from the cost of buying or leasing the package itself there is the further cost in terms of programs which can be less efficient in their use of processor time or storage space than the COBOL programs they are replacing. In terms of overall costs and benefits, many organizations are making this move to what are, in effect, higher-level languages.

One impact of this for the designer is in the area of detailed design. If 'programming' with these aids is so simple, then it may well be quicker to program a system than to specify it in detail. This can cover such areas as program, input, output, communications and data store specification together with the implicit specification of codes and security. Prior to sitting at a screen and specifying this detail the designer will need to have made all the major design decisions. The use of the development software is then equivalent to the use of a word processor upon which to write the specifications which can then be handed to traditional programmers. This may appear to have relatively little impact for the designer until one considers that most designers spend a large proportion of their time answering 'systems queries' from programmers. Another time-consuming activity is system testing, and although the use of development aids cannot eliminate system errors they should reduce program errors, particularly if programs can be developed which are provably correct. A further impact of this change in the detailed design area is that users themselves can become more involved with the design. If agreement has been reached regarding the outline design of the system, the detailed layout of the input and output can best be done by the users themselves, further reducing the possibility of misunderstanding between people.

In the past there have been several attempts to produce software which will automate the systems design process. No such software has gained widespread use, possibly because of the heuristic and fuzzy nature of many of the problems which are addressed. In the future it may be possible for such problems to be tackled by computers, but currently machines are limited to assisting the designer with specific, algorithmic tasks. Soon many major design methodologies will be supported by extensive and integrated software aids.

Data dictionaries, as stated earlier, may be computerized. They may be linked to graphics facilities which can produce and possibly read system charts such as flow charts or data flow diagrams. If hard copy of documentation is required it can be generated to whatever standards are written into the software. The design of the data model can also be automated as long as the system is aware of the relationships between elements, which can be extracted from the data dictionary. In this case the software would be able to perform many of the quasi-mathematical checks for undesirable dependencies between elements which few designers have either the skill or the time to perform. System performance estimating is another area which can usefully be programmed, and the outline design processed against hardware parameters. It would be possible for the software to try several alternative implementations of the system to see which was the most effective in optimizing the project's performance goals. This is often an algorithmic task which is rarely done well because of the time involved. Some consultancies use computers to match available products with clients' requirements, and one manufacturer is currently developing an expert system to do performance estimating.

In the future it is quite possible that designers will spend more of their time designing systems and less of it on clerical specification, answering queries and repetitive tasks, thereby increasing the productivity of each designer. This can be extended to the idea of designers working in information centres as advisers to users who are designing their own systems; the advice given will cover such topics as how to use development aids, select hardware, likely pitfalls and the resolution of technical problems. In this context an organization may also require designers to work on such general issues as documentation standards, design standards and data base administration.

## Team working

Very little work is done in isolation from other people, and team working is often unavoidable. Even where it is avoidable a better result almost inevitably follows the use of several people's ideas rather than one person's. There is a game/scenario where people are asked to decide which items, out of a list of about ten, would be of greatest use in surviving in a desert. The idea is that few people 'know' the answer, but general knowledge and logic can be used. The items are ranked by individuals, and then by groups. The interesting part of the game is that, when the results are compared with those of 'experts' in desert survival, the group scores are always higher than the individual ones – much to the initial surprise and dismay of many. In system design, team work is effective.

This can be assisted by good team management, the allocation of responsibilities, progress reporting and the like. Certain attitudes and practices need to be encouraged. A non-possessive, co-operative attitude is of paramount importance. Work done is the property of the team rather than the individual; members should be encouraged to pursue the interests of the team rather than vie with each other.

The use of walkthroughs can be of great benefit. Here one member of the team methodically describes a situation, leading the team through it. Other members make comments as appropriate. Walkthroughs can be used for intragroup communciation, to check for mistakes prior to progressing with the design, or as a means of tackling a particularly difficult problem. Remember Golden Rule 12 on page 21.

# 3 Representing procedure logic

Several techniques have been developed which assist the designer in describing procedures. The objective of these techniques is the clear and unambiguous representation of the logic involved. The more common techniques will be described, together with information on how to produce and use them. A comparison will then be presented.

## Narrative

This is the most widely used, and many would say over used, technique for representing logic. It appears to be the easiest way of presenting one's ideas to others, but there are many pitfalls. Even though the person writing the narrative may be perfectly clear in his or her own mind about what is intended, the reader is very likely to misunderstand. A common cause of this is the fact that at the time of writing one is likely to be completely immersed in the design of a procedure, and therefore may not make explicit certain pieces of information which are essential if the reader is to fully understand what was intended.

Further, the production of good technical literature, which is both readable and precise, requires considerable skill in itself. The author, and doubtless the reader, of this book is only too well aware of the limitations of the average person in this area.

Narrative does have the full power of a natural language to call upon and can therefore be particularly useful for describing fuzzy, imprecise and human situations, e.g. to record the attitudes of staff to a change in work practices. However, this is not usually the problem being tackled with procedure logic.

If narrative is employed, it should be structured into sections and use cross-references where possible in order to reduce the total amount of narrative. The aim is to produce a 'scientific' report incorporating precise statements, not necessarily complete sentences. If the narrative can also be a work of art, so much the better, but this is of secondary importance in this situation.

The following is an example of logic representation using narrative.

**Example using narrative: calculating renewals**

*Initial processing*
Load the RENEWAL FORMS (ref. xyz) into the printer and then open the POLICY FILE (ref. xyz). Print the TEST PATTERN until the operator signifies stationery is aligned.

*Main processing*
As long as there are records on the file read one and calculate the PREMIUM (ref. xyz) as follows:
If the GROUP (ref. xyz) is less than 4 the PREMIUM will be $50+ (10 \times GROUP)$.
If the GROUP is 4 or 5 the PREMIUM will be $60+ (8 \times GROUP)$, and if GROUP is 6, then the PREMIUM is 120.
To this figure must be added surcharges which are calculated as follows:
If there has been a claim in the last year, add 100 to the PREMIUM for drivers over 25, and 200 to the PREMIUM for those 25 or under.
For those who have not had a claim in the last year, add 10 to the PREMIUM for over 25s, and add 20 to the PREMIUM for those 25 or less.
Print the NAME and ADDRESS (ref. xyz) on the RENEWAL FORM and then print the PREMIUM.

*Final processing*
Close the POLICY FILE.

## Structured English

Structured English is the designer's equivalent of structured programming in that it reduces all logic to imperative, decision, and repetition statements. There are many standards for producing structured English, but in general they contain most of the following:

1  Verbs should be specific, and words like 'do', 'handle', 'process', and 'control' should be avoided.
2  The object of the action should be made explicit.
3  All nouns should be documented elsewhere, often in a data dictionary.
4  Adjectives and adverbs should only be used when they are self-explanatory or are documented elsewhere, e.g. what is meant by a 'high-value order' should be given as a figure.
5  Indentation should be used to highlight the levels of control operating within the procedure and improve the readability.
6  If more than two levels of nesting are required, consideration should be given to putting part of the procedure into a separate module.
7  Capital letters should be used for nouns and key words, all other words being in lower case.
8  IF and ELSE statements should be connected by dotted lines.
9  ELSE statements should be followed by a statement of the condition(s) under which the actions will be taken. This to be written within brackets.
10  Use positive logic wherever possible.
11  Use END- statements to delimit blocks and connect these to the beginning statements with dotted lines.

Typical keywords in a structured English (sub) language are:

IF . . . ELSE . . . END-IF
DO-WHILE . . . END-DO-WHILE
(The condition is tested before any processing is done.)

REPEAT-UNTIL . . . END-REPEAT-UNTIL
(The condition is tested after the processing is done.)

CASE. . . IF . . . ELSE-IF . . . ELSE-IF . . . END-CASE
(For discrete selections from a list of alternatives as implemented in COBOL by GOTO DEPENDING ON. Strictly speaking this is pseudocode, not structured English.)

The following is the same insurance premium renewal example, but this time using structured English.

**Example using structured English: calculating renewals**

Load RENEWAL-FORMS into printer

REPEAT-UNTIL stationery aligned

   Print TEST PATTERN

END-REPEAT-UNTIL

Open POLICY-FILE

Read POLICY-FILE

DO-WHILE records on file

   CASE
      IF GROUP < 4
         PREMIUM = 50 + (10 × GROUP)

      ELSE-IF GROUP 4 OR 5
         PREMIUM = 60 + (8 × GROUP)

      ELSE-IF GROUP 6 PREMIUM = 120
   END-CASE
   IF a claim in last year

      IF over 25

         add 100 to PREMIUM

```
    ELSE (≤ 25)

        add 200 to PREMIUM

    END-IF

ELSE (no claim in last year)

    IF over 25

        add 10 to PREMIUM

    ELSE (≤ 25)

        add 25 to PREMIUM

    END-IF

END-IF

    Print NAME and ADDRESS

    Print PREMIUM

    Read POLICY-FILE

END-DO-WHILE

Close POLICY-FILE
```

As can be seen from the example, structured English lies somewhere between a high-level programming language and natural English. It is therefore useful not only when communicating with programmers but also when dealing with users who have some familiarity with program statements. Some standards exclude the END-keywords as they are not found in natural English, and others include AND, THEN, and SO as keywords to make it more readable, although this may obscure the logic.

## Structure charts

The purpose of these charts is to depict how various elements within a system interrelate. They are therefore concerned more with the logic of how the elements fit together than with the detail of what goes within the components, each of which can be regarded as a 'black boxes' for this purpose. Structure charts can be drawn at a variety of levels from total information systems of an organization, through application systems, application subsystems and systems as seen by specific subgroups (e.g. users or operators), to programs and modules within them.

At their simplest, structure charts are a graphic way of representing a hierarchy, and within the hierarchy all elements at a particular level are controlled by an element at a higher level. A typical set of guidelines for the production of structure charts might include the following:

1 All components will be drawn within rectangular boxes.
2 Each component will be named, and this name serves as a reference to further information on the component, e.g. an entry in a data dictionary or another structure chart.
3 Connecting symbols may be used to extend the chart beyond one sheet.
4 Where a level of components cannot be drawn

as a row, a linked column may be used.

5   Lines from one component to another show the passing of control, as in a COBOL PERFORM statement. The general assumption is that control will pass back to the higher-level component upon completion of the task.

6   The lines of control connecting one level with another will be drawn parallel to the edges of the paper.

In order to accommodate more realistic structures (networks) where one component may be used by several other components, possibly at different levels, a further guideline is often included:

7   A component which occurs more than once in a set of structure charts will have an asterisk in the top right-hand corner.

It is important to understand that these charts do not attempt to show the time dimension. Thus while charts are frequently read left to right and top to bottom, this should not be taken to imply the sequence in which control will be passed.

Further additions to structure charts were suggested by Weinberg. The first was the use of symbols to denote whether control was exercised on the basis of a decision ($\Diamond$) or repetition ($\circlearrowleft$). This could be included into the above guidelines by placing the appropriate symbol on the line going down to the component. The second was the indication of the data which was passed between components by means of arrows ($\circ\rightarrow$) alongside the control lines. Each arrow would have written alongside it a name which could be referenced to obtain more detail on the data flow. The inclusion of a symbol to describe the basis for passing control to a lower-level component has gained acceptance, and the idea has been incorporated into many sets of guidelines. The inclusion of information on data flows into the structure charts has not come into general use. Apart from the problems of keeping the chart clear and easy to follow, there are also objections

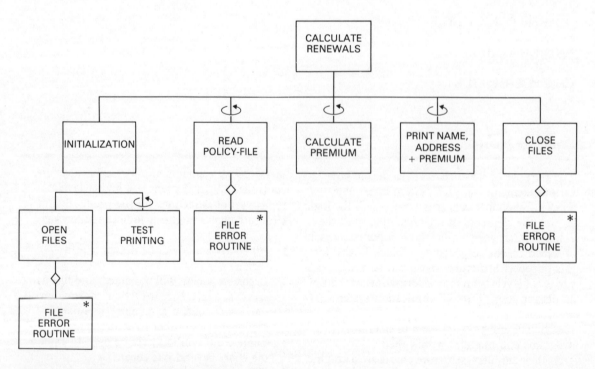

Figure 10   *Structure chart for renewals calculation*

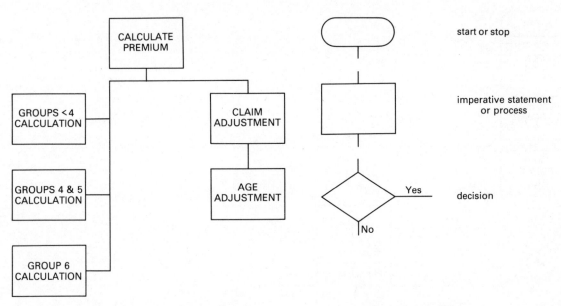

Figure 11   *Structure chart for premium calculation*          Figure 12   *Flow chart symbols*

to putting information about data into a diagram which is designed to show the organization of control. The point is that data and control are two different things which may or may not go together; for example, when selecting a program from a menu on a VDU, the menu controller need not pass any data to the program but may just pass control to it by executing it.

Figure 10 shows a structure chart for the example of renewal calculation. If, in this chart, the calculation of the premium was sufficiently complex, its organization could be described using a further structure chart, e.g. Figure 11.

## Flow charts

It is not the intention of this section to describe the techniques of flow charting in detail. It is assumed that most readers will be familiar with their use, and for those who are not in this position many introductory books on programming or data processing cover this area. As with the other techniques, flow charts are useful at a variety of levels of detail, but it is important to ensure that the level of detail given in any one flow chart is reasonably consistent.

In general, most flow charting standards are extensions from the three symbols in Figure 12. All procedure logic can ultimately be represented by these symbols. The lines entering and leaving each box, within which a brief description is given, correspond to the sequence of events in time. The charts are drawn top to bottom and left to right. Only when the sequence of execution of these steps does not follows this rule are arrows normally included on the lines. Consider the renewals calculation flow chart in Figure 13.

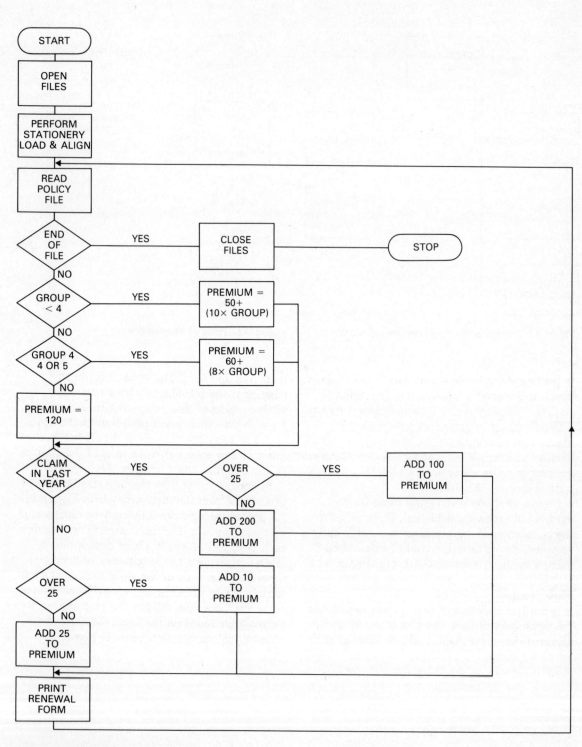

Figure 13   *Flow chart for renewals calculation*

# Decision trees

These are graphic techniques which are used to show how a series of decisions relate to each other, e.g. Figure 14. In writing decision trees, the following guidelines are generally adhered to:

1   The sequence of decisions is from left to right.
2   The questions are placed at the nodes of the tree, with possible results being branches going from the decision.
3   Each branch should have a label to denote exactly what outcome of the decision it represents.
4   Nodes should line up vertically so that the levels of the tree can clearly be seen.
5   The most discriminating tests are best placed on the left.

In the simple decision tree of Figure 14, each node has exactly two branches which represent 'yes' and 'no'. It is easy to check that all possible combinations have been covered. In general, if $M$ is the number of branches which go from each and every node and $L$ is the number of levels of nodes, i.e. the number of columns which contain decisions, there will be $M^L$ leaves or terminators on a given tree. The situation becomes more complex when all nodes do not have the same number of branches, and it is then difficult to check for completeness.

It is unusual for a series of decisions to follow one another without any intermediate processing, and decision trees may be extended to include this by putting processes at the nodes as well as the decisions, e.g. Figure 15.

Normally the processes are written vertically at a node so that the sequence of the actions is clear and ends with the next decision. The processes may be simple statements, performs or gotos, and as the decision tree will be given a name it is possible to loop back to the beginning of the decision tree or start on a new decision tree. It should be noted that it is only possible to start a decision tree with the single decision at the beginning, its root.

Decision trees are easy to create and to read if they are simple. However, this advantage can soon be lost if an attempt is made to put too much

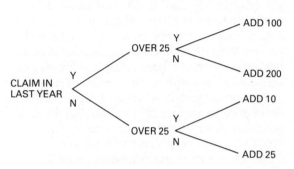

Figure 14   *Simple decision tree*

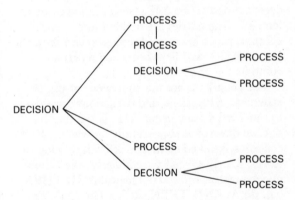

Figure 15   *Complex decision tree, including processes, variable number of branches at the node, and all leaves not being at the same level*

information into a single tree. The criterion used in this case is whether or not the tree is clear and easy to follow, as it is primarily a graphic technique. Complex decision trees involve a great deal of repetition on the part of the person creating them and, apart from the boredom this causes, there is an increased likelihood of inconsistencies. Note that no attempt is made here to put the whole of the renewals calculation example into a decision tree.

# Decision tables

Attitudes to decision tables vary from 'the best aid the designer ever had' to 'an old-fashioned, confusing waste of effort'. Much of the criticism comes from people who do not feel confident in the use of decision tables, either because they do not fully understand them, or because very few of the other people with whom they are trying to communicate understand them. In some cases decision tables are seen as beneficial, but the time necessary to create and condense them is not available and designers resort to quicker (although less rigorous) techniques, such as narrative.

The decision table is divided into four parts (Figure 16) which show (1) conditions as distinct from actions, and (2) explanations (of the decisions and actions) as a 'stub', followed by the 'entries'. The entries are divided into vertical columns which are termed the rules, and show the actions which will be taken when a certain combination of conditions exists.

The conditions are the equivalent of the IF statement in decisions, and the actions correspond to the THEN statements. This is not usually written down, but may usefully be read in. Each condition is linked to the one below it by a logical AND, e.g. IF $C_1$ and $C_2$. Similarly, the actions may be seen as linked by a logical AND THEN, e.g. do $A_1$ AND THEN do $A_2$. The rules are related by means of a logical OR, only one of the rules being chosen for a given performance of the table.

The simplest form of decision table is the limited entry decision table, where the condition entries must be

| | |
|---|---|
| Y | condition is met |
| N | condition is not met |

and the action entries must be

| | |
|---|---|
| X | do whatever is said in the action stub |
| Blank or – | do not do the action |

Some standards insist that the hyphen be used to indicate that a possible action has been considered

Figure 16   *Decision table*

| RULE | 1 | 2 | 3 | 4 |
|---|---|---|---|---|
| CLAIM IN LAST YEAR | Y | Y | N | N |
| OVER 25 | Y | N | Y | N |
| ADD 200 TO PREMIUM | – | X | – | – |
| ADD 100 TO PREMIUM | X | – | – | – |
| ADD 25 TO PREMIUM | – | – | – | X |
| ADD 10 TO PREMIUM | – | – | X | – |

Figure 17   *Limited entry decision table: adjustments calculation*

and decided against, rather than just forgotten, e.g. Figure 17.

The action stubs can include such verbs as GOTO or PERFORM which may be followed by the name of another procedure which could itself be represented by a decision table. It therefore becomes possible to describe a complex process by means of a group of decision tables which could be organized as a hierarchy or nested together. In this case a structure chart could be used to show how the tables related to each other.

The steps in constructing a decision table are:

1 Decide on the decisions which are to be included and write the condition stubs.
2 Calculate the number of rules which will be needed. This is $2^c$, where $c$ is the number of conditions.
3 Fill in the condition entries to include all possible combinations of conditions.
4 Identify all possible separate actions and write the action stubs.

5 Associate the actions to be taken with the rules and complete the action entries.

It is possible at this point to revise the table with the following objectives:

6 The conditions should be written in order of priority so that the most important decisions appear at the top of the list of conditions.
7 The actions *must* be written in the sequence in which they are to be executed. This may mean that it is necessary for an action stub to occur more than once.
8 The sequence of the rules may be changed so that the combination of answers which is most likely to occur is written nearest to the stubs and the rules to the right of this become progressively less likely to occur.
9 It is also important to identify any logically possible, but practically impossible, rules which may exist, e.g. 'age less than ten' AND 'more than three children' as these should produce an error message of some form.
10 Rules where two or more sets of conditions lead to the same set of actions should be identified and a note to this effect made.

An extension of the limited entry decision table is to allow the use of a hyphen in the condition entry to signify that the outcome of a particular decision is not relevant to a rule. Using this facility it is often possible to combine rules which lead to identical actions as referred to in 10 in the list. It can also be used in the situation described in nine, where following the decision that someone is 'less than ten' years old, the question of how many children they have is considered immaterial. It should be noted that, if the hyphen is used, checking for completeness becomes more difficult. The maximum number of rules is still $2^c$ but, in adding up the number of rules, each rule with a hyphen in its' condition entry counts as $2^H$ rules, where $H$ is the number of hyphens in the condition entry for that rule.

A further extension which is often used to reduce the number of rules in a decision table is the *else rule*. This is written on the extreme right-hand side of the table and, in effect says: 'If

| GROUP IS | <4 | <6 | 6 | E L S E |
|---|---|---|---|---|
| BASIC PREMIUM IS | 50 | 60 | 120 | — |
| ADD (GROUP X —) | 10 | 8 | — | — |
| GOTO CALCULATE ADJUSTMENTS | X | X | X | — |
| GOTO ERROR ROUTINE | — | — | — | X |

Figure 18  *Else rule: initial premium calculation*

none of the other possible combinations of conditions have covered the situation, do this.' The else rule has no condition entries. This is frequently used to trap impossible combinations which mean that an error has occurred. One effect is that, no matter what the input, the table knows what to do. However, this does not mean that the designer can relax; rather, prior to using the else rule, a full table should be constructed and then the else rule introduced. It would replace two or more rules which had identical actions, e.g. the only action entry for the else rule could cause a report to be generated detailing the data which caused the else rule to be used (Figure 18).

Moving further away from the simple decision table, we have the extended entry table, where the possible entries are no longer limited to Y, N, X, — . The entries may be anything which is meaningful when read in conjunction with the stub. In some cases a legend or key is given at the bottom of the table to explain the meaning of symbols found in the entries section of the table.

In extended entry tables it is possible to calculate the total number of rules using the following formula:

$$\text{total number of rules} = N_1 \times N_2 \ldots \times N_C$$

where $N_C$ is the number of significant values condition C may have. In Figure 18 there is only one condition which may have one of four significant values, namely < 4, 4 or 5, 6, > 6.

It is worth noting that software preprocessors are available which use as input a decision table drawn up to appropriate standards, and output source code in a high-level language on to a printer and a storage medium for subsequent inclusion into a program.

## Grid charts

Again, controversey exists as to the usefulness of grid charts, but they are included here, although not strictly intended to represent procedure logic, to remind the designer that a simple tabular arrangement of information may improve communications and save a great number of words (Figure 19).

| FILES \ PROGRAMS | CLIENT-MAINT | QUOTE MOTOR | QUOTE OTHER | INS-CO-UPDATE | CLIENT-ENQS | CLAIM-PROC |
|---|---|---|---|---|---|---|
| CLIENT | U | | | | R | U |
| MOTOR-INS | | R | | U | | |
| HOUSE-INS | | | R | U | | |
| CONT-INS | | | R | U | | |
| COMM-INS | | | R | U | | |
| POLICIES | U | | | | R | U |
| CLAIMS | | | | | R | U |
| DEBTS-DUE | U | | | | R | |
| PAYMENTS | U | | | | R | |

U = FILE MAY BE UPDATED
R = FILE IS READ ONLY

Figure 19   *Grid chart: use of files by programs*

## Comparison of procedural logic techniques

Figure 20 provides a comparison of some of the more common techniques used to represent procedural logic. As with any other technique or tool, the selection should be made bearing in mind why the job is being done and what will achieve the objectives in the most efficient way.

| Type | | Use with | Unam-biguous | Concise | Check comple-tion easily | Amend easily |
|---|---|---|---|---|---|---|
| Narrative | Needs to be structured and cross-referenced. Easily understood and very flexible. Ambiguity almost inevitable. | Over used! | N | N | N | Y |
| Structured English | Need some program familiarity to understand. Easily coded from. | DP staff and some users | Y | Y | — | — |
| Structure charts | Represent segmentation of a procedure and flow of control between tasks | Mostly DP | — | Y | N | Y |
| Flow charts | Flow of all logic in time. Widely used by those who understand the symbols. | DP | Y | Y | — | N |
| Decision trees | Graphic representation of logic. Simple to understand but complex trees lose this advantage. | Users | Y | Y | Y, if balanced | N |
| Decision tables | Need training to use. May use preprocessor to generate source code. | DP | Y | Y | Y | Y |
| Grid charts | Table of interactions of any two (possibly three) variables. Widely applicable. | DP and users | Y | Y | N | Y |

Figure 20  *Comparison of procedural logic techniques*

# 4 System charting techniques

Grouped together here are several techniques which attempt to show the flow of data (and, in some, the flow of control) throughout a whole system. These techniques are frequently associated with the design of new systems, but serve equally well to document existing systems. The emphasis is upon data flow diagrams developed in the mid 1970s, and how they can be constructed. The more traditional charting techniques are described in much less detail.

## Data flow diagrams

These diagrams represent a system using four basic elements, the symbols for which are not intended to imply any physical media (Figure 21).

As with other graphic techniques there is a limit to the amount of detail which can be shown while retaining the essential clarity of the diagram. It is therefore necessary that every symbol is given a name which can then be looked up in the documentation to obtain more details. The simple situation is where data flow diagrams and data dictionaries are used together with corresponding entries in the dictionary for each process, store or flow. However, data dictionaries are not essential and data flow diagrams can cross-reference to any type of documentation.

There are several methods by which data flow diagrams can be constructed, each corresponding to a systems design method. One large multinational uses a bottom-up approach, starting with a flow to or from a user (external entity) and progressing through the whole system at this detailed level. Gane and Sarson's (1979) book did much to popularize data flow diagrams; they emphasize the use of a top-down approach, starting with the most global/high-level functions and the major data flows in and out of these. A diagram with a small number of boxes is constructed to represent the top level. This is then expanded to produce a more detailed diagram, and so on. A halt is called when each process box corresponds to a single task or module which can be clearly and simply defined. Gane and Sarson recommend that errors and their processing are only included once the design has reached quite a detailed level. One institution advocates the use of data flow diagrams for documenting the existing system, designing the logical system and then for

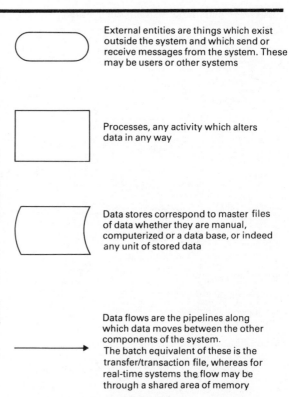

External entities are things which exist outside the system and which send or receive messages from the system. These may be users or other systems

Processes, any activity which alters data in any way

Data stores correspond to master files of data whether they are manual, computerized or a data base, or indeed any unit of stored data

Data flows are the pipelines along which data moves between the other components of the system.
The batch equivalent of these is the transfer/transaction file, whereas for real-time systems the flow may be through a shared area of memory

Figure 21   *Elements used in data flow diagrams*

designing the new physical system. They are a very useful and flexible charting technique.

The following example illustrates a combination of top-down and critical-first methods. In Figure 22 there are only three boxes; these show that the basic function of the SALES LEDGER SYSTEM is to process the INVOICES and PAYMENTS.

The second version (Figure 23) describes the

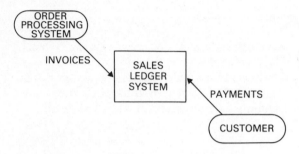

Figure 22   *Sales ledger system: basic function*

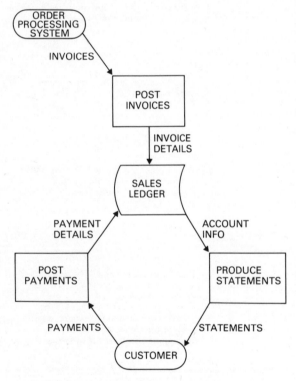

Figure 23   *Sales ledger system: additional functions*

SALES LEDGER SYSTEM in more detail, showing that apart from accounting for INVOICES and PAYMENTS a very important function is sending STATEMENTS to CUSTOMERS. The system itself is seen as consisting primarily of three processes and one data store.

In the third diagram (Figure 24) no more detail has been shown about the functions present on the second chart. There is, however, an additional process to perform maintenance of the ledger by inserting, amending or deleting accounts. The inclusion of this function on this diagram and not on the preceding one indicates that a less critical level of importance is attached to it. The system *must* POST INVOICES, POST PAYMENTS and PRODUCE STATEMENTS, but in the event of a serious lack of processing power, e.g. due to frequent equipment failure, LEDGER MAINTENANCE need not be run. Thus a fall-back position is identified at an early stage which a designer could subsequently build into the system.

The next diagram (Figure 25) is more complex than its predecessors but does not in fact show any more detail about the processes and flows already described. It does add processes which produce a LEDGER SUMMARY for the AUDITOR, allow ACCOUNT ENQUIRIES to be made, and perform an INVOICE/CREDIT ANALYSIS. These processes may be considered even less critical than the preceding ones and constitute an early fall-back position, or they may never be built into the system if resources are constrained.

The three levels of importance of requirements may be termed essential, necessary, and desirable, and form a crude way of prioritizing the system requirements. The relationship between Figures 22, 23, 24 and 25 is shown in Figure 26.

Graphically, the level of detail shown can be increased for the whole system and included on a larger diagram, or alternatively each of the major functions can be broken down into more detail with its own data flow diagram. In Figure 27 the function of posting payments on to the SALES LEDGER is shown in more detail. This diagram shows that prior to posting the payments they are recorded in a CASH BOOK as being received. They are then validated using reference information from a PARAMETERS store. Errors are assessed for severity and may be held as PENDING PAYMENTS until a suitable explanation for the payment is received from the CUSTOMER, upon which the ASSESS SEVERITY process releases them to be posted as

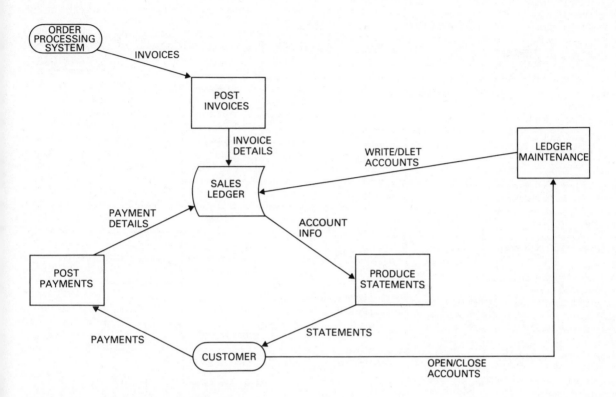

Figure 24  *Sales ledger system: further functions*

ACCEPTABLE PAYMENTS. All transactions which update the ledger are recorded on an AUDIT TRAIL. An analysis of the payments received is produced for the ACCOUNTANT, who together with the SALES LEDGER and the CUSTOMER can be considered external entities.

In moving to a more detailed level no attempt has been made to produce three separate data flow diagrams showing essential/necessary/desirable classes of requirements. These are present in the one diagram and would need to be specified explicitly in the supporting documentation. Effectively the relationship between Figures 25 and 27 is shown in Figure 28.

In general data flow diagrams are used to describe what the system will do independently of how this will be achieved. For example, the process ASSESS SEVERITY could well be done by a person but could be mechanized; similarly, there is no indication as to how the store CASH BOOK is held. Where it is desired to also include physical information on the diagram, this can be done with the aid of a 'bottom stripe' on the boxes and a parenthetic statement for the flows (Figure 29). The process of obtaining cash from a bank account is fundamentally the same whether or not the process is automated. In the simple description in Figure 29 it is only the bottom stripes and parenthesis which signify that the task is not performed by a bank clerk.

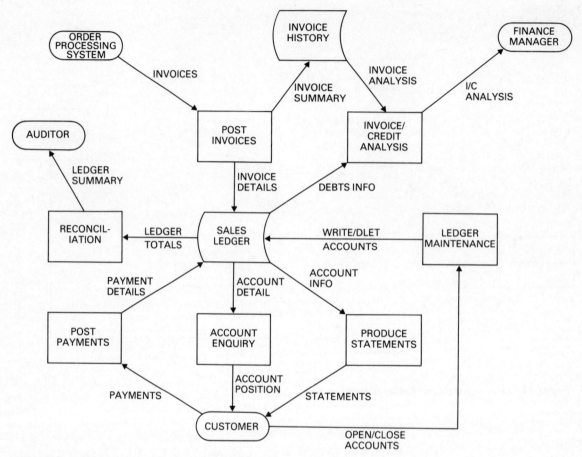

Figure 25   *Sales ledger system: final flow diagram*

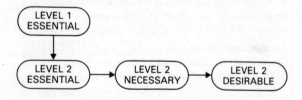

Figure 26   *Requirement levels: relationships of Figures 22–25*

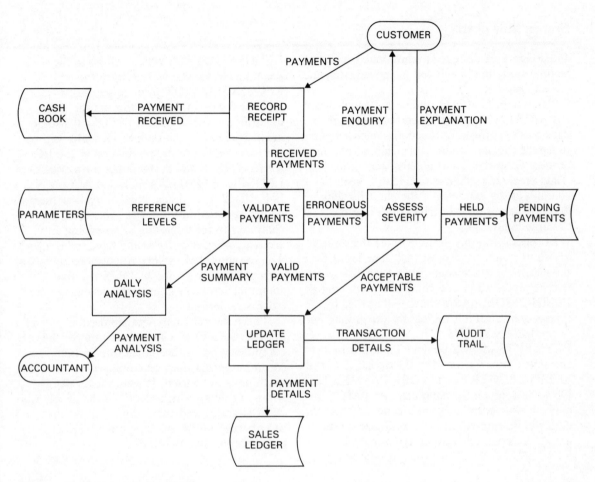

Figure 27   *Posting payments function*

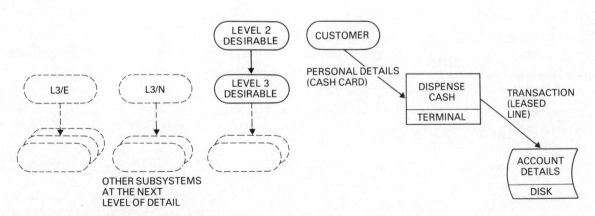

Figure 28   *Relationship between Figures 25 and 27*        Figure 29   *Bottom stripes and parentheses*

## System flow charts

These charts are designed to show where data is to be processed, and how it will be moved from one place to another.

The system flow chart divides a sheet of paper into several columns which correspond to the departments, offices, or functions which are going to handle the data; there is typically a column headed 'Computer', and possibly one headed 'Data prep'. It is often convenient to keep the columns at the extremes of the chart for data flows, to and from external entities (see for example Figure 30).

In considering this diagram, note the design decisions which are represented. The input from the sales order processing system is on disk which will be processed on the computer producing an INVOICE SUMMARY which will be filed by the finance staff until it is needed for the production of the I/C ANALYSIS. The VALIDATE PAYMENTS job will be done manually by the accounts clerks leaving only the updating of the SALES LEDGER by the POST PAYMENTS job to be done on the computer. As there is no explicit 'Data prep.' column it is implied that the data will be entered into the computer by the accounts clerks. On a monthly basis the STATEMENTS will be produced and also the LEDGER TOTALS which will go to the accounts clerks who will perform the RECONCILIATION prior to sending a LEDGER SUMMARY to the auditor. On a monthly basis the DEBTS INFO will also be made available to the finance staff who will use this information in the production of the I/C ANALYSIS. It was decided that the processes of LEDGER MAINTENANCE and ACCOUNT ENQUIRY were similar enough to allow them to be incorporated into a single process on the computer (prior to closing or amending an account, when enquiry would have to be made). The accounts clerks will be responsible for liaising with the customers and will then use the computer to obtain information or change the ledgers as desired.

Where several computers are used as part of a system, the idea of a special column for the computer is not sufficient and the 'bottom stripe' (denoting media) may be employed to say which machine is to be used. It would naturally go within a column which described the people who were operating and controlling the machine, and links between different computers represented as input/output data flows.

Figure 30   *System flow chart: order processing*

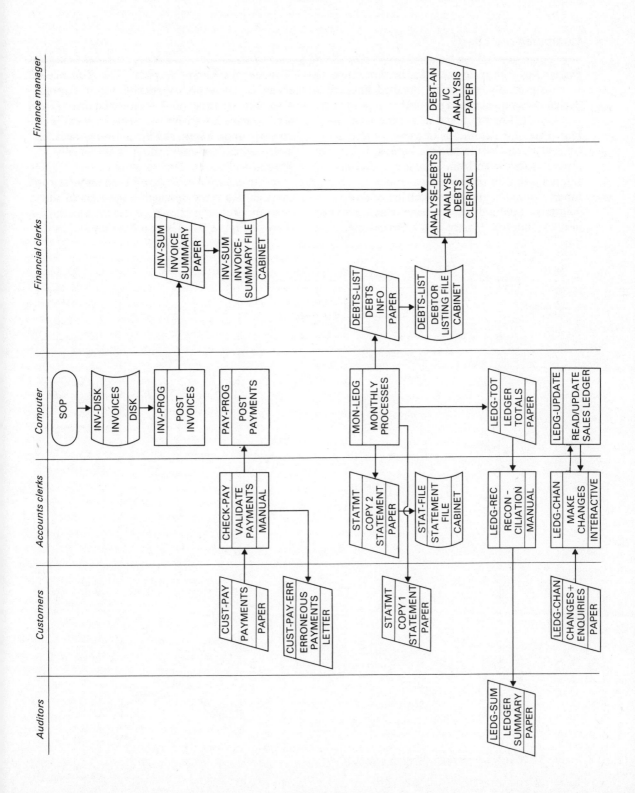

## Computer run charts

System flow charts do not describe the computer systems precisely enough for detailed physical design to commence, and so another type of chart is required. For batch and near-time jobs (see Part Three for definitions of these terms), a computer run chart is suitable because a series of processes follow on from a trigger (either an external event or reaching a particular point in time). Computer run charts consist of five columns running down the page which may be headed 'Inputs', 'Master files', 'Processes',

'Transfer files' and 'Outputs'. The sequence of events is represented vertically, top to bottom. Two processes may not be connected directly and need to have a transfer file between them if one depends upon another. This is simply because interprogram communication is not usually allowed within this type of system.

In the example of Figure 31 a computer run chart gives a more detailed description of the monthly processes shown on the systems flow chart of Figure 30. There are no inputs, as the

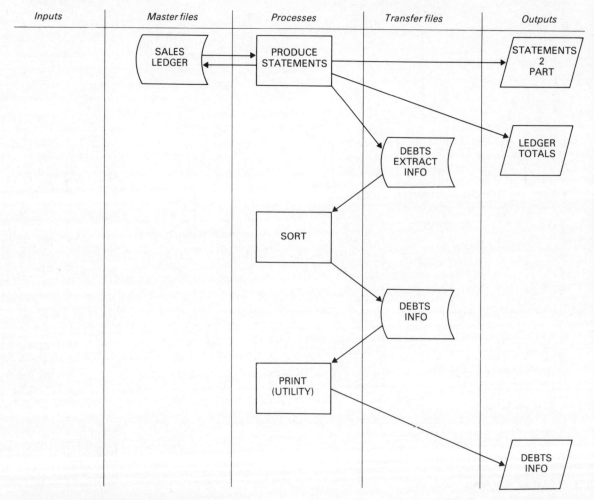

Figure 31  *Computer run chart: monthly processes*

processes are triggered by time, i.e. the end of a trading month, rather than being triggered by an event which might involve an input. The SALES LEDGER is on a direct access device which allows it to be both read from and written to at the same time. Further detail could be given by a 'bottom stripe' containing, for example, DISK.

## Interactive system flow charts

These charts (e.g. Figure 32) are used to describe the flow of data and control between a terminal operator, shown on the left-hand side of the page, and a program, shown to the right. The input/output symbols in the middle identify the data items and format of the interaction. Within the left- or right-hand columns the arrows indicate passing control from one job to another.

This type of chart needs to be supported by detail, which could be held in a data dictionary as described in Chapter 2.

## Network charts

These charts show not only the flow of data, but also the flow of control. Lines with small arrows at the destination end represent movement of data, detail again being held elsewhere such as in a data dictionary. The large arrowheads in the middle of lines show that control is being passed from one process to another. The control may be temporarily passed, as between UPDATE BOOK FILE and ERROR ROUTINE, and could be implemented with a COBOL PERFORM. If the large arrowhead has a straight line behind it, control is permanently passed. This is equivalent to a COBOL GOTO and is shown between INPUT BOOK LOAN and UPDATE BORROWER FILE.

Within information systems control and data often flow together.

However, in real-time systems this is not true, and it is imperative that the events which trigger an operation can be explicitly shown. Network charts attempt to meet both needs.

Figure 33 shows how a simplified library issue/discharge system could be designed with terminals to enter and validate the loans and returns. Once the data is entered and any reservation for the book shown on the discharge screen, these input programs pass any necessary data to two other jobs which will update the appropriate files, immediately freeing the terminals to process another transaction. In such a system the data to be passed from one program to another needs careful definition, and so too do the circumstances under which it will be passed. Frequently such systems employ specialized systems software which may involve its own standards for design and documentation.

All these system charting techniques have their advantages which can be exploited in the right circumstances. Data flow diagrams are very flexible and useful for logical as well as physical designs. Computer run charts are specific to batch processing and describe a run ideally. System flow charts emphasize the movement of data across boundaries which the data may not recognize but which can cause the downfall of a system. Again the designer needs to match the tool against the subject matter and the objectives of the exercise.

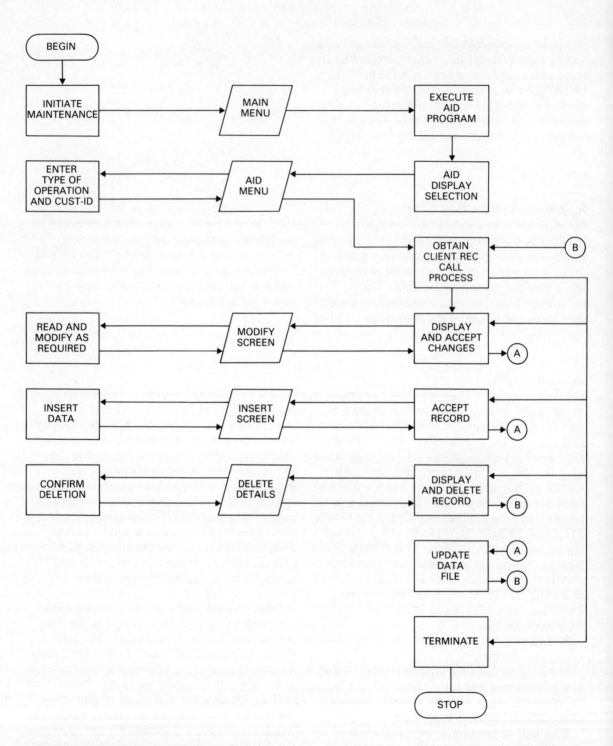

Figure 32   *Interactive system flow chart*

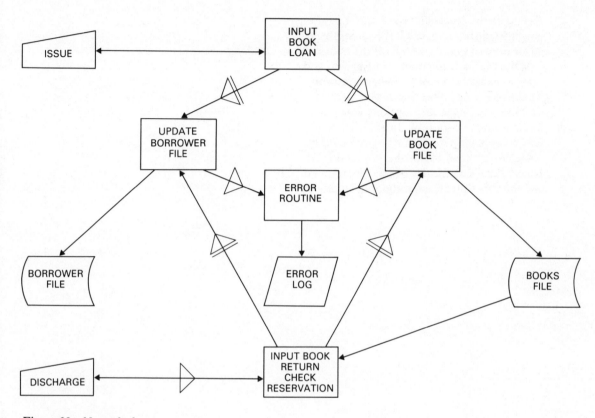

Figure 33 *Network chart*

## Exercises for Part One

**1.1** What do you understand by *good* systems design?

**1.2** Briefly discuss the relationship between a system designer and a shop owner for whom a system is being designed.

**1.3** To what extent would achievement of systems which are flexible be made easier by using a bottom-up approach to design? What would be an example of this?

**1.4** What are the most likely reasons for a system not to be considered a success?

**1.5** Compare DM/1 with any other description of project development.

**1.6** Draw a diagram which shows how the different types of entry in an extended data dictionary are related to each other, and which fields are used to allow the cross-referencing.

**1.7** 'For temperature data types, whenever the reading is less than 40°C switch on the pumps. Some readings will be in Fahrenheit and must be converted to centigrade units.

As long as the process is type 2 and the value is over 40, do nothing, but if the value is over 40 for process type 1, switch off the pumps.'

Write this logic in structured English, and draw a decision tree of it. What questions would you need answering if you were to avoid making logic assumptions yourself?

1.8   Draw a simple data flow diagram to show how an appointment with a doctor could be made, which then led to the production of patient details on the day of the appointment and the subsequent updating of the medical records.

Part Two

# Logical design

# 5 Overview

## Introduction

Part Two is concerned with logical application modelling in five stages (objectives, outputs, stores, processes and maintenance) (Chapter 6) and logical data modelling in two stages (normalization and courting) (Chapter 7). These are then brought back together by a review stage, and finally a summary of the system designed is presented (Chapter 8).

The purpose of the logical design stage of a project is to create a detailed description of the new system which is completely independent of any hardware, software, or other physical considerations and is derived directly from the objectives of the system. In fact, several alternative systems will be designed each corresponding to different types of system objectives, as will be illustrated by the design of an order processing system.

To emphasize what is meant by 'logical' in this context, consider the simple data flow diagram of Figure 34. The diagram states that customers will be given information called ACCOUNT POSITION and this will come from a function called ACCOUNT ENQUIRY. In order to be able to perform the function the ACCOUNT ENQUIRY process will need ACCOUNT DETAIL from the SALES LEDGER. This function could be performed by looking through a card sales ledger and speaking to a customer, by looking through a printed report and writing to the customer, or even directly by the customer using a VDU and communications link. All the diagram says is that somehow the designer will need to incorporate this function into the final design.

There are two aspects to the designer's work. First, there is the production of the logical application model which describes the messages which must flow to and from the users or to and from the stored data, together with a description of the tasks which need to be performed to support these message flows. This is designed with the objective of meeting the requirements of the users in as efficient a method as possible. The second aspect is the design of a logical data model to represent the stored data which will be used by the application area. The objective here is a design which will be stable in the face of change, providing a firm base which this and other applications can use.

If an organization uses data management software such that all its stored data is organized independently of specific applications, it will require a global logical data model. The description of the stored data developed here is application specific and may be termed the local logical data model. The global model is an extension beyond the local model and may be derived from all the local models of the organization. If a global model already exists the local model is developed and then the two are compared, the global model being modified to support the local model if it does not already do so.

The final part of logical design is a review of the application design in the light of the data design. The purpose of this is not to stop the designer thinking about processes and flows while looking at the data, but rather to leave the review of the application model until the whole data model is known.

Figure 34  *Design illustration*

## DM/1 logical design

DM/1 includes five stages through which the designer can work in order to produce a logical application model. Each of the five stages is subdivided into three priority classes – essential, necessary, desirable. These classifications lead to the development of alternative systems corresponding to E, E + N, and E + N + D Desirable objectives can be ranked in terms of their importance and a greater number of alternative systems developed. The logical data model is then developed by normalizing and then courting the data stores developed in the application model. The impact of the data model on the application is the final stage of logical design, the review. The association of the stored data with the objectives which gave rise to it is maintained throughout the data modelling. A sequence is shown in Figure 35.

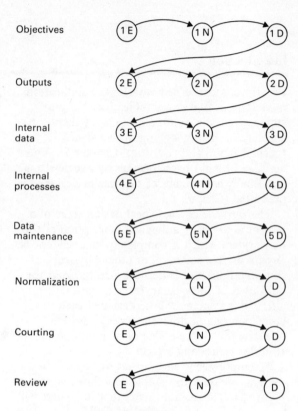

Figure 35   *Logical design sequence*

## Logical application modelling

The five stages of application modelling take the system from the high-level objectives to the detail of field maintenance, in that order. Briefly:

### Stage 1   *Objectives*
The system is described in terms of its objectives and the major components are identified by the functions they will perform. Simple data flow diagrams are used.

Obtain primary objectives.
For each class of objectives:
(a) Produce a simple data flow diagram (which only has one process box).
(b) Create skeleton entries in a data dictionary for each entity and flow, stating their functions.

### Stage 2   *Outputs*
The data flows out of the system are defined at element level.

For each class of objectives:
For each outgoing data flow:
(a) Identify the data items which compose the flow and their organization.
(b) Enter details of items, structures and flows in the data dictionary.

### Stage 3   *Internal data*
The origin of the data which is to flow out of the system is considered by asking: can it be derived from something, can it be stored, and can it be input? This is followed by a summary of the

processing implication of the derivation of data.

For each class of objectives:
For each outgoing data flow:
(a) Identify the items which can be derived, stored and input using application knowledge.
(b) Identify the processing needed to support this (the secondary objectives), the required contents of incoming data flows and the provisional contents of the data stores.
(c) Store all detail in the data dictionary.

### Stage 4   Internal processes
Turns attention to the design of processes to support all the data flows described in the preceding stages. Portions of data flow diagrams are developed followed by a composite diagram for each priority classification.

For each class of objectives:
(a) For each primary objective:
    Draw a data flow diagram to describe what must be done to achieve it.
    Specify the data flows to and from store.
    Describe the functions of each process as a structured list.
(b) Check secondary objectives have been designed in.
(c) Draw a composite data flow diagram for that class of objectives.

### Stage 5   Data maintenance
This is the review of the stored data elements to assess how they are amended, inserted, and deleted.

For each class of objectives:
For each data store:
(a) For each item: identify the cause(s) of its creation, amendment and deletion.
(b) Design any extra processes and data flows, such that the stored data is kept as up to date as necessary.
(c) Store all detail in the data dictionary.

These five stages start at the level of general objectives and then jump down to the detail of outputs from the system. If the system is sufficiently large, as for example a real-life order processing system could be, then several iterations of stage 1 might be needed. This would allow the specification of subsystems which could then be progressed through stages 2 to 5. The stages are not one way. The designer needs to go back to previous work, and check and possibly modify it. Stages 2 and 3, about data, have implications for the processes. Similarly in stages 4 and 5 new data flows and stores may be introduced to the design. The separation of the stages helps to divide the job into more manageable tasks – to help to divide and conquer. It does *not* create extra work, because all the jobs need doing at some stage in the design; it does offer a framework to guide the design. However, it is a tool, and therefore needs to be adapted and used with thought (Golden Rule 11).

The use of three classes, according to the level of importance of the objectives, can create work compared with a design where no such classification is used. The extra work is involved in maintaining these three separate streams. This is seen as well worthwhile because it provides the basis for honest and rational decision-making during outline design.

Every component in the final system is associated with an objective. This alone means that such general goals as data integrity and data privacy need to be specified as objectives if they are to be designed into the system. This is right and proper: if a system needs validation of data at input, or password protection, this needs to be designed into the system from the beginning and its effects properly allocated to this objective. Only in this way can the value of these general objectives be truly assessed. A second purpose is that, by maintaining the three streams, the designer is building in fall-back positions which may be used during outline design or during operation of the system.

System reliability, together with archiving and recovery techniques, need to be specified as objectives for the system or for the whole organization. These physical aspects of security are built into the system during outline design. This emphasis upon objectives does *not* imply that all objectives can be known at the outset of a project. Objectives will change and new ones arise throughout the lives of both the project and the system. It does mean that new or changed objectives should be rationally considered. Flexibility to cope with these changes is built into the design process, particularly by the separation of logical from physical design, and the explicit nature of the basis for decisions taken.

A major source of work in any systems design effort is the documentation of the decisions. This method of design produces various versions of the system depending upon the stage of design, or the class of objectives. It therefore requires a method of documentation which exploits the fact that the same name can be used for two data flows which contain different data because one is version 2E and the other 2N. A data dictionary is appropriate.

The reader's attention is drawn to the fact that even in the rather simplified system used to illustrate the method, a great deal of supporting documentation has been missed out, e.g. nowhere are data elements defined.

## Logical data modelling

Data modelling is derived from the formal methods of data analysis and design used by large organizations having itegrated data bases. The original objectives of data base management systems included the need to eliminate unnecessary duplication of data and the need to reduce the impact of change on the system. These objectives led to the development of data base software, but the data used by this software needed to be structured in such a way as to help software achieve these objectives. It is these data design techniques which are now being used widely in both data base and non-data base sites.

> Data models help in achieving some understanding of the data and information needs of an organization and by extension the way in which an organization functions. . . . It seems, therefore, that data modelling is an important activity for information integration regardless of the use of a data base management system. Data modelling is needed even if we use file systems. . . the area is very important, not merely fashionable.
>
> *Tsichritzis and Lochovsky*

Duplication, or redundancy, of data can be reduced by storing the information once and once only. If there is something of interest to the organization in the environment, such as an employee who has a name and address, then this information is held in one place only, all users of this name and address being provided with access to it.

Data base software helps the system to cope with change by confining each user to just the data items they use, and so changes in other items are not seen by the user. Data design helps by keeping different types of data separate from each other. For example, if information about employees, their banks and their training is held together, a change in the format of say the training information will mean that processes just looking at the bank details will also need to be modified. A flexible design would hold information about the three things – employees, banks and training – separate, and cross-reference one to another. In this way changes in one area are limited to users who use that specific area.

These two major objectives may be summarized by saying that the purpose of data design is a one-to-one relationship between stored data and the real things it represents. One data store does only contain information about one type of thing, and the information about one thing is only stored in one place. Data structured in such a way is also very easy to understand by both DP staff and users. There are also a growing number of non-procedural, fourth-generation languages being devised to make processing of this type of data a relatively simple task.

The logical data modelling stage of the design methodology presented here employs only a subset of the techniques used in data analysis and design. The intention is to produce a structuring of the stored data as defined during logical application modelling.

Therefore, because the data model follows on from the application modelling (with its emphasis upon the data flows to the users), if the data model designed here supports the stored data then it will also support the user views as specified in the objectives.

There are, however, several differences between the data design as performed for large-scale data base systems and the methods described here for this part of the design. Here the data which is to be structured has already been specified down to field level and is all used by a single application area. Following on from this is the fact that the grouping of data items will be done by first looking at these items and working upwards from these, i.e. bottom-up design. Furthermore, many data design methodologies involve the proof of the correctness of the model, whereas here the theoretical aspects of data design are played down.

Data modelling as presented here could almost be considered as stage 6 of the logical application modelling, as it follows from the work done in the five stages described. This has not been done because the data design performed here and formal top-down data analysis and design are compatible. The full methods aim to produce a logical model of the data for the whole organization, starting with an identification of the major objects and relationships between objects, as found in the environment of the organization. This global model will be able to support several application areas and the uses to which data is put within them. These full data design methods often include a stage called functional analysis. This is approximately equivalent to the logical data modelling presented here, and looks at how a subset of the global model will support a particular application area.

It is possible to combine several application-specific models into a larger more global data model. This should be quite straightforward because each model should represent an area of the environment. If two areas overlap, so should the models. For example, a personnel system holds data about employees and training courses, and a payroll system has data about employees and their banks. In the real world, real employees attend courses and have bank accounts, and this can easily be shown in a combined data model. It is the real world which provides the common basis for joining the models. In this way a global model can be developed in a bottom-up manner.

In summary, the method used here is specific to the application area, and proceeds in a bottom-up manner from fields which have been specified during application modelling. It is compatible with top-down data analysis and the design of global data models, as they both share the goal of simple and accurate modelling of reality.

Note that data modelling proceeds very largely independent of the application model, referring to it only as necessary to understand exactly what is meant by the data items. This knowledge of the way in which an organization uses and interprets its data, which must be gained by thorough system analysis, is sometimes referred to as the enterprise rules.

**Normalization and courting**

The method employed here to produce the logical data model involves two phases. First, each of the data stores identified during the application modelling is subjected to the process of normalization. This produces an increased number of very simple data structures.

*Normalization*

For each class of objectives:

For each data store:
(a) Ensure that each store has a key which uniquely identifies something, splitting the store if required.
(b) Ensure that only key fields determine the values of other fields, splitting the store if required.
(c) Record all changes in the data dictionary.

Second, courting is the identification of relationships between the simple structures defined during normalization. Where overlap occurs and two structures describe the same thing, these structures are merged together.

*Courting*

For each class of objectives:

(a) Identify any data stores which describe the same entities and join them together.
(b) Identify and name any useful relationships between stores.
(c) Update the data dictionary.

# Review

The final part of logical design is to ensure that the application and data models are fully integrated.

*Review*

For each class of objectives:

(a) Check that the flows into store can support the model.
(b) Check that the model supports the flows out of it.
(c) Look for improvements in the design of the flows or processes to take advantage of the data model.

# Conclusion

DM/1 therefore describes logical modelling as a sequence of some twenty-four operations (eight stages × three priority classes). This is most definitely *not* the only way to produce a logical systems design. The same operations could be performed in a different sequence, for example by fully designing a system for each level of objective before moving on to the next level. In some circumstances certain functions need not be performed, and on other occasions additional operations may well need to be performed. Remember Golden Rule 11. What follows is a detailed description of these operations in the design of an order processing system, trying to make every decision explicit and justified.

# 6 Application modelling

Application modelling is described here in the five stages outlined in Chapter 5:

1 Objectives
2 Outputs
3 Internal data
4 Internal processes
5 Data maintenance.

## Stage 1  Objectives: essential/necessary/desirable

This stage is summarized as:

Obtain primary objectives.
For each class of objectives:
(a) Produce a simple data flow diagram (which only has one process box).
(b) Create skeleton entries in a data dictionary for each entity and flow, stating their functions.

At the highest level the system is described in terms of its objectives and functions. In designing a system at this level the first question must be 'What are the logical objectives of this system?', and a clear answer to this is essential. This is not to underestimate the difficulty in defining requirements (see Chapter 1), but it is useful to know the destination prior to beginning a journey. The systems investigation takes place and produces a set of requirements for the new system. This includes both logical and physical requirements, i.e. both what needs to be done and how fast/cheaply it must be done. In producing the logical application model only the logical requirements are considered; the physical requirements are used during outline and detailed physical design.

In order that priority in resource allocation can be given to the most important jobs, during both the design and the subsequent operation of the system, the objectives need to be classified:

1 Essential objectives are the complete reason or purpose for the system as seen in the context of the organization as a whole. If these objectives cannot be met, the system is not worth designing or running.

2 Necessary objectives exist in order to support the essential objectives, and they must be achieved in order that the system functions smoothly and precisely. They must be designed into the system; however, if during operation these objectives are not met there will be a time lag before a live system becomes worthless.

3 Desirable objectives may be omitted from the design or operation of the system, and the essential objectives still met. However, this omission may well reduce the viability of the whole system, and so any such omission should be carefully reviewed.

These objectives are all termed the primary objectives, to distinguish them from secondary objectives which will be described in more detail later but which are, in effect, means by which to achieve the ends of the primary objectives.

The categories essential, necessary and desirable represent one possible way of structuring and organizing the system objectives. They will not be the best categories to use for all projects, e.g. some systems may benefit from separating update transactions from information retrievals, or alternatively the design may be organized around functional areas. Likewise even when essential, necessary and desirable are used to structure the design, their precise meaning and how they will be interpreted will need to be determined by the designer, the analyst, and the users, in a way that is meaningful to the organization and all concerned.

### Example: order processing

Just imagine that the terms of reference for a project stated 'the objective is to reduce the despatch time for 95 per cent of orders to three days or less'. An investigation into the existing sales order processing systems took place and found that only 60 per cent of orders were despatched within three days, the average time being 4.3 days. The investigation also identified the major cause of the delay as being the existing order processing system. This system is a batch system using key-to-disk data preparation, with a daily processing cycle; orders received after 2 p.m. miss that day's cycle.

The investigation produced the following logical requirements of any new sales order processing system:

### Essential

E1   Receive orders from customers.
E2   Send picking notes to the warehouse.
E3   Store invoice details.

The system must include a means by which customers' orders are converted into picking notes, which the warehouse staff will use to assemble and despatch goods. There must also be a means for remembering who owes how much for what, by sending details to an external entity, the sales ledger.

### Necessary

N1   Send invoices to customers.
N2   Report stockouts to stock control.

If the system is to function for any length of time, customers need to be kept informed of the detailed costs of their orders and stock control need to know when an item urgently needs purchasing.

### Desirable

D1   Control customer's credit.
D2   Produce sales analysis for sales
       management.
D3   Produce despatch statistics for general
       management.

Credit control is seen as desirable but not essential or necessary. It will obviously have benefits for the organization, but if it costs too much to implement then the system can go ahead without it. The desired effect of credit control is the reduction of the total debt of the customers as well as limiting the risk taken with any one customer. There will be a need to reject whole orders if enough credit is not available.

The reports analysing sales over a period and informing general management of the performance of the new systems, need to be justified in terms of costs and benefits if they are to be included in the final system. It is possible to rank the desirable objectives in terms of their importance within this classification. This is most easily done by using a financial guide measuring the anticipated benefits compared with the anticipated costs.

It would be possible to define this system purely in terms of the output it had to produce, i.e. what information it provided to the organization. Thus if objective E1 had not been specified for this system, the items which need to be provided would still have been identified during stage 3 of the design when the origin of data going out of the systems is considered. In some systems data is stored so that unplanned enquiries can be made against it, so there is no general rule saying that only the output objectives are used as the starting point of design. Stage 2 looks at outputs, but for information retrieval systems this would need amending (DM/2?). Refer also to Exercise 2.2.

The eight points (E1–3, N1, 2, D1–3) answer the question 'What are the logical objectives of the system?' The design proceeds by taking each group of objectives in turn and producing a high-level data flow diagram for them. At this level all the processing is shown as a single box.

### Essential

The essential objectives are achieved through the relationships illustrated in Figure 36.

In the supporting documentation there would need to be a description of the objectives or function of every component of the diagram. This could be held in an extended data dictionary which had entries for data flows, stores and processes, as described earlier. The dictionary

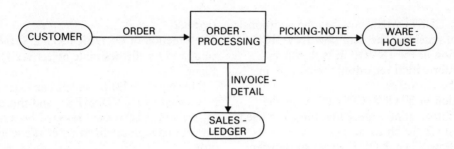

Figure 36 *Order processing: essential objectives*

could be further extended to store the function of the external entities, in relation to this system.

The description of the process ORDER-PROCESSING would consist of objectives E1–3.
The function of the CUSTOMER would be to send an order requesting goods.
The function of the data flow ORDER would be to convey details of the goods required by a particular customer to the order processing system.
The function of the PICKING-NOTE would be to inform the warehouse of which items should be collected together and despatched to a particular customer.
The function of the WAREHOUSE, as far as this part of the system is concerned, is the receipt of picking notes.
The function of the SALES-LEDGER is to store the details of how much a particular customer

owes for a particular order, and the INVOICE-DETAIL data flow has the function of getting this information from the order processing system to the external entity.

These functions need to be specified precisely and carefully because they will guide the design work and can be subsequently be used as a guide to review the design.

*Necessary*
The next stage of the design is the addition of the necessary objectives to the essential data flow diagram (Figure 37). The processing is shown as a single box because this diagram is still at the top level of stage 1. The supporting documentation needs to account for the following:

The ORDER-PROCESSING process now has the additional objectives N1 and N2 as specified previously.

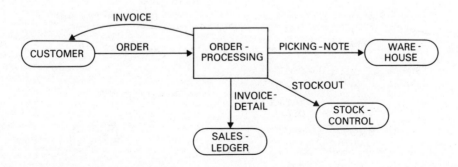

Figure 37 *Order processing: necessary objectives*

The entity CUSTOMER now has the additional function of receiving the data flow INVOICE. The function of the INVOICE is to convey detailed information regarding the cost of an order to the customer.

The function of STOCK-CONTROL is the receipt of information stating that there is a need to obtain stock for an item.

The data flow STOCKOUT serves to transfer out-of-stock information from the order processing to the stock control and facilitate purchasing, by giving information on supplier and previous purchases. In this organization the storage and processing of back orders is done within the warehouse. All orders are eventually fully despatched although this may involve several shipments on different dates. If back orders were handled in this system it would make the example more complex than be necessary in order to illustrate the design method.

Where new entries are made in the documentation, or existing ones enhanced, it is most important that the priority classification of the objective is noted. For example, the CUSTOMER now serves two functions; sending an order is essential but receiving an invoice is only necessary.

*Desirable*

The function of ORDER-PROCESSING is enhanced by the desirable objectives D1–3 in Figure 38.

The objective D1 means that an extra data flow is received by CUSTOMERs, and this consists of orders which have been rejected because there was not enough credit to cover the whole order.

The function of SALES-MGMT is to receive the data flow S-ANAL which serves to convey an analysis of sales from the order processing system to the sales management.

The WAREHOUSE now has the extra function of sending the data flow DESPATCH-CONFIRM to the order processing system. This data flow serves to provide information on the date of despatch of orders which will form the basis of the data flow DESPATCH-STATS, which functions to transfer a summary of the performance of the system in despatching goods to the general management. The function of the external entity GENERAL-MGMT as regards this system is solely the receipt of the DESPATCH-STATS data flow.

The general management, together with all the other external entities, do more than is described

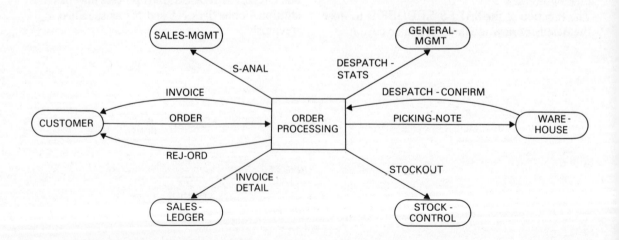

Figure 38 *Order processing: desirable objectives*

by the functional descriptions given here. It is only those functions which help meet the system objectives that are relevant, and worth definition. Activities which lie beyond the boundary of the system under consideration should be ignored.

At this point stage 1 of the design is complete as the new system has been described in terms of its objectives and functions. The objectives, and the design, have been classified under three headings according to importance. There is a diagram to illustrate each part of the design, and the details of how each component serves the overall system are recorded in the documentation.

## Stage 2   Outputs

This stage is summarized as:

For each class of objectives:
For each outgoing data flow:
(a)   Identify the data items which compose the flow and their organization.
(b)   Enter details of items, structures and flows in the data dictionary.

At this stage the design is expanded to include more detail of the outgoing data flows. Subsequently stores, processes, and inputs will need to be designed, but these only have a purpose in that they support the outgoing data flows to the users. It is therefore appropriate that the outputs are considered first. It is also easier to derive outputs from stage 1 than from the other stages.

Adding detail to the functional descriptions of the data flows requires knowledge of the data which the users will need. This needs to be complete and unambiguous, avoiding such problems as synonyms and homonyms. There are many problems involved with the precise definition of data, particularly where multiuser systems are concerned. To adapt an example from Kent (1978): if a library identifies a book by a unique number and then a publisher issues it in two volumes, do both volumes have the same number or different numbers, and is it the same book or a different one? These problems need to be ironed out with the users of a system, who are the only people who can say how the data is interpreted and how it relates to the real world.

In defining the data items which constitute a data flow it is important to include only (and all) the data which is relevant to the user's job. If an existing system provides payroll staff with a person's training record, on an employee file printout, then just because it is a print of the whole record (which is also used by a personnel department) this does not mean that a data flow to these users should include it. An appraisal of the findings of the systems investigation should lead to a definition of the data as the user would like to see it.

The detailed description of the data flows is added to the documentation which supports the data flow diagrams. The notation used earlier to describe data structures will be employed here.

### Example: order processing

*Essential*
Consider the PICKING-NOTE first. In order that it can 'inform the warehouse of which items should be collected together and despatched to a particular customer', it will need to contain item and customer information:

PICKING-NOTE
(CUST-NAME, DELIV-ADRS,
PICK-LINE* (ITEM-NO, QTY))

This is all the information that must be present in order that goods can be picked and despatched to customers. Several other fields are seen as important by the warehouse, in particular the location of the items in the warehouse as given by BIN-NO, and a description of the item, ITEM-DESCRIP, so as to reduce the chances of despatching the wrong goods. It is also important to be able to identify one picking note from another for the same customer, which may be being processed at the same time. To this end the data flow needs to include a unique identifier, PICK-NO:

PICKING-NOTE
    (PICK-NO, CUST-NAME, DELIV-ADRS,
    PICK-LINE* (BIN-NO, ITEM-NO,
    ITEM-DESCRIP, QTY))

Now consider the function of the INVOICE-DETAIL data flow, which is conveying details of particular customer's debts on particular orders:

INVOICE-DETAIL
    (CUST-NO, [PURCH-NO], INV-DATE,
    TOTAL-VALUE, DISCOUNT %,
    TOTAL-TAX, INV-NO)

This data flow specifies which customer the invoice relates to by means of a CUST-NO, which acts as a unique identifier for the customer, and acts as an abbreviation for the whole name and address, which is the alternative. Another item of customer information which is seen as important by those representing the sales ledger is the customer's own purchase order number, PURCH-NO. Details of the debt are conveyed such that there is no unnecessary redundancy. The amount of discount or the net value of the order may be required and either can be calculated if needed. Note that this applies to a data flow into a data store or process, but *not* to data flows to users of the system. The principle is that users should get the information in the form which is useful to them, with all processing already done. If the flow is 'internal' to the system

then redundancy should be reduced and controlled. The data flow also includes the INV-NO, which uniquely identifies the invoice. The combination of CUST-NO and PURCH-NO could do this if each customer could be guaranteed to provide a purchase order number, and use it once only. This potential uncertainty leads to the use of INV-NO.

*Necessary*
The necessary outputs consist of the INVOICE sent to the CUSTOMER and the STOCKOUT sent to STOCK-CONTROL.

INVOICE
    (INV-NO, CUST-NAME, INV-ADRS,
    DELIV-ADRS, [PURCH-NO],
    ORDER-DATE, INV-DATE,
    TOTAL-VALUE, DISCOUNT %,
    DISCOUNT-AMT, TOTAL-TAX,
    NET-VALUE, INV-LINE* (ITEM-NO,
    ITEM-DESCRIP, QTY, LINE-VAL,
    ITEM-DISCOUNT %, ITEM-TAX %,
    LINE-NET))

There is redundancy in this data flow; for example, the TOTAL-VALUE is the sum of all the LINE-NET fields each of which is calculated invidually. The NET-VALUE for the whole order is the result of a calculation using the TOTAL-VALUE and applying a DISCOUNT %, for the whole order, to it. This is, however, the data which the users wish to see, and so it should be provided. The INV-NO is added to give the INVOICE a unique identifier, as with INVOICE-DETAIL.

STOCKOUT
    (ITEM-NO, ITEM-DESCRIP,
    RE-ORD-QTY, SUPLS* (SUPL-NAME,
    SUPL-ADRS, SUPL-CONTACT,
    LAST-PURCH-DATE, LAST-COST))

The stock control department require only the ITEM-NO in order to identify which items have zero stock. The remainder of the information serves to 'facilitate purchasing'.

*Desirable*

If an order fails the credit check, then the customer needs to have the details of the rejected order returned to him at the invoice address. The total value and the credit limit are included:

REJ-ORD
  (CUST-NAME, INV-ADRS, DELIV-ADRS, [PURCH-NO], ORD-LINE* (ITEM-NO, ITEM-DESCRIP, QTY) CREDIT-LIM, NET-VALUE)

Other desirable data flows out of the system are to management in the form of summary information:

S-ANAL
  (SCUR-DATE, SDETAIL* (ANAL-CLASS, CUR-MONTH, CUR-MONTH-TARGET, YTD, YTD-TARGET))

This information is sent to sales management; it is an analysis of the sales broken down into current month and year-to-date figures, together with the targets for these periods. The analysis class consists of either the customer group or the product group.

DESPATCH-STATS
  (DCUR-DATE, NO-LINES-PERIOD, VAL-LINES-PERIOD, DETAIL* (DAYS, NUM-LINES, NUM %, VALU-LINES, VALU %))

GENERAL-MGMT receive information which shows how many order lines have been despatched (and their value), broken down by the number of working days since the receipt of the order. The figures are also sent as percentages of all order lines received over a period. The report is based around order lines because the warehouse may despatch the order over several days.

## Stage 3  Internal data

This stage is summarized as:
For each class of objectives:
For each outgoing data flow:
(a)  Identify the items which can be derived, stored and input using application knowledge.
(b)  Identify the processing needed to support this (the secondary objectives), the required contents of incoming data flows and the provisional contents of the data stores.
(c)  Store all detail in the data dictionary.

In the third stage of the design, the origin of the data which will flow out of the system is considered. The output may come from stored data, may be input to the system, or may be derived or calculated from other data.

All data held by the system must come from input at some time, but the origin of the reference data held in data stores will be considered during stage 5 of the design rather than here. Data which is in some way derived or the result of calculation implies the existence of a process to do the derivation. In preparation for the next stage, these extra jobs are added to the functional description of the order processing system. These supporting processes are termed the secondary objectives.

As in other stages of design, detailed information is being generated, and it is important that this is recorded in the documentation. This needs to include a reference to the classification of the objective (E/N/D) which gave rise to it.

There are basically two approaches which could be used to establish the origin of the output data and where necessary add to the list of functions for the system. Each output field could be taken in turn and allocated to the input, stored or derived classes of data and then the new functions considered. Alternatively each of these classes may be looked at in turn for all the data output. The latter method of looking at all the data for each class will be used here, primarily because it is easier to describe and illustrate given the sequential nature of a book.

Thus, for each class of objectives, the derived, stored, input and then functional areas will be focused upon in turn. Another term for derived or calculated data is virtual data. To all intents and purposes the data exists, because it can be derived from more basic data which is stored.

The input of data at the operational (i.e. transaction) level, and the storage of data, also need to be considered together, because in many cases if the data is already stored it need not be input. Golden Rule 14 applies in this situation and shows the interdependence of input and storage.

*Golden Rule 14* Once you've got it in, keep it in.

This rule is designed to emphasize the savings which follow from using stored data rather than reinput data. The savings are in terms of less input effort and less chance of inconsistency between the two versions of the same data. A good example of this is the storage of incorrect data awaiting its correction rather than complete re-entry.

Stored information is only kept in the hope that it will prove useful, being the most efficient (if not the only) source of information at some future time. A typical type of stored information is static data such as name and address, which do not frequently change. If a system stores these it then removes the need for their input every time a person is to be identified, and an abbreviated code may be used in their place. The other major type of stored data is that which constitutes a record of things which have taken place in the real world, e.g. tax paid this year, or training courses attended.

The design of the data stores is the subject of the logical data modelling. The purpose here is simply to identify what data needs to be stored. For the sake of convenience during this stage, and also because it will be a preliminary to data modelling, the stored data will be described as records, and where possible will use the suffix -DATA.

**Example: order processing**
*Essential*
Consider the two data flows PICKING-NOTE and INVOICE-DETAIL:

PICKING-NOTE
(PICK-NO, CUST-NAME, DELIV-ADRS, PICK-LINE* (BIN-NO, ITEM-NO, ITEM-DESCRIP, QTY) )

INVOICE-DETAIL
(CUST-NO, [PURCH-NO], INV-DATE, TOTAL-VALUE, DISCOUNT %, TOTAL-TAX, INV-NO)

There are some fields on the INVOICE-DETAIL data flow which could be calculated by the order processing system. The INV-DATE, which is the date on which the invoice amount was calculated, is the calendar date of the system, and is kept as TODAY'S-DATE by the system. The TOTAL-VALUE field could be calculated by adding up the net values of the lines, i.e. LINE-NET, on the order. This in turn means that the value of the item, and any discount or tax relating just to that item, would need to be stored, and the order quantity for each item input. The data to be stored can be defined as ITEM-PRICE, ITEM-DISCOUNT %, and ITEM-TAX %. (Note that this type of detailed information regarding exactly what is meant by a field like TOTAL-VALUE and how it is calculated must be collected during the systems investigation, as there is no other source for it.)

In a similar manner the field TOTAL-TAX can be calculated, using the same stored data and the order quantity.

We now move on to data which can be stored. Data items referring to the customer include CUST-NO, CUST-NAME and DELIV-ADRS. These fields all contain information referring to a unique customer as defined by CUST-NO. The delivery address may vary with the order, and in that case the stored delivery address needs to be overridden. The customer's purchase number will change with each order and it is not worth storing PURCH-NO. The DISCOUNT % is a discount which is given to a customer and does not change frequently.

A second group of data refers to products and includes ITEM-NO, ITEM-DESCRIP and BIN-NO, all stable fields. There are also the fields necessary for the calculations, ITEM-PRICE, ITEM-DISCOUNT %, and ITEM-TAX %, which are likewise relatively static.

At this point the stored data would include:

CUSTOMER-DATA
  (CUST-NO, CUST-NAME, DELIV-ADRS, DISCOUNT %)

and

ITEM-DATA
  (ITEM-NO, ITEM-DESCRIP, BIN-NO, ITEM-PRICE, ITEM-DISCOUNT % ITEM-TAX %)

and for the whole system,

SYSTEM-DATA
  (TODAY'S-DATE)

Given that the information which can be stored or derived has been established, then the information which needs to be input with each order can now be defined.

The ORDER is a flow from an external entity which is beyond the control of the order processing system in any but a marginal way. Orders may arrive as text rather than on a form and a great variety in content is possible. The designer is left with the job of defining the minimum possible data content which will allow processing, together with the specification of the range of possible data which is considered relevant:

ORDER
([CUST-NO/CNDA(CUST-NAME +
  DELIV-ADRS)], [DELIV-ADRS],
  [PURCH-NO], ORDER-LINE*
  ([ITEM-NO/ITEM-DESCRIP], QTY))

There must be some way of identifying the customer, and this may be done by the CUST-NO or by the CUST-NAME concatenated with the delivery address (see Chapter 2 for notation). The delivery address and the purchase order number are optional and may be included. There must be details of what is required by the customer, and these details are held in the ORDER-LINE. ITEM-NO or ITEM-DESCRIP need to be present, as does the quantity ordered.

The only input data which has not been accounted for is PICK-NO and INV-NO. These fields both act as unique identifiers for data flows which are triggered by the presence of an order in the system. It would appear to be logical if they both used a common identifier, called say ORDER-NO. INV-NO, PICK-NO and ORDER-NO are therefore all synonyms, and the designer may decide to choose one name by which to refer to the identifier, thus standardizing the terminology. The question now exists regarding the origin of ORDER-NO. If a unique identifier is to be given to each order, then it is best done as soon as it enters the system, and if allocated sequentially the stored data needs to hold a field for LAST-ORDNO-USED. This field, which is part of the system rather than being a reflection of some feature of the world, may be kept as part of the system's data.

SYSTEM-DATA
  (TODAY'S-DATE, LAST-ORDNO-USED)

The implications of the derivation of data now need to be spelt out explicitly in order that they may be included in the functional description of the system. These are the secondary objectives or functions which serve as a means to achieving those defined in stage 1:

**Essential**

E(a)  Obtain LAST-ORDNO-USED and assign ORDER-NO to orders.

E(b)  Calculate order LINE-NET and then TOTAL-VALUE and TOTAL-TAX using ORDER and ITEM-DATA.

E(c)  Derive INV-DATE, PICK-NO and INV-NO using TODAY'S-DATE and ORDR-NO.

It is not necessary to specifically state that data should be read from store if it will be needed for a calculation or for an outgoing data flow, e.g.

obtaining the BIN-NO to go on to the
PICKING-NOTE. In designing processes the
first place to look for data which is not on the
transaction is the store, and it may be assumed
that this will be done in stage 4.

*Necessary*
The two necessary outward data flows are:

INVOICE
(INV-NO, CUST-NAME, INV-ADRS,
DELIV-ADRS, [PURCH-NO],
ORDER-DATE, INV-DATE,
TOTAL-VALUE, DISCOUNT %,
DISCOUNT-AMT, TOTAL-TAX,
NET-VALUE, INV-LINE* (ITEM-NO,
ITEM-DESCRIP, QTY, LINE-VAL,
ITEM-DISCOUNT %, ITEM-TAX %,
LINE-NET))

and

STOCKOUT
(ITEM-NO, ITEM-DESCRIP,
RE-ORD-QTY, SUPLS* (SUPL-NAME,
SUPL-ADRS, SUPL-CONTACT,
LAST-PURCH-DATE, LAST-COST))

The first area to be considered is the
derived/calculated data. The ORDER-DATE can
be derived from the SYSTEM-DATA when an
order enters the system. The fields INV-NO,
INV-DATE, TOTAL-VALUE, TOTAL-TAX
and LINE-NET may be derived by the same
means as for INVOICE-DETAIL.
DISCOUNT-AMT can be calculated from
TOTAL-VALUE and DISCOUNT %, and
NET-VALUE from TOTAL-VALUE.
DISCOUNT-AMT, and TOTAL-TAX
LINE-VAL is an intermediate field in the
calculation of LINE-NET. None of the data
needed for the STOCKOUT data flow appears to
be derivable from other data.

Next consider the data which could be stored,
in addition to that already established as essential
to the system.

The only data item associated with customers
which is stable enough to store, but is not already
in the customer group of stored data, is the

invoice address:

CUSTOMER-DATA
(CUST-NO, CUST-NAME, DELIV-ADRS,
DISCOUNT %, INV-ADRS)

Considering the data which could be stored to do
with items; this leaves ITEM-DATA unchanged
after looking at the INVOICE, but all the data in
the flow STOCKOUT is to do with items and
could be stored. It also follows that in order to
know if there is no stock of an item, the quantity
on hand must be stored. This is most definitely
not static. It does however constitute a record of a
real-world phenomenon, the level of stock, which
is changing.

ITEM-DATA
(ITEM-NO, ITEM-DESCRIP, BIN-NO,
ITEM-PRICE, ITEM-DISCOUNT %,
ITEM-TAX %, RE-ORD-QTY, SUPL*
(SUPL-NAME, SUPL-ADRS,
SUPL-CONTACT, LAST-PURCH-DATE,
LAST-COST), QOH)

Now that attention has been given to the
derivation and storage of data which is required to
support the outgoing necessary data flows, the
next step would be to look for data items which
needed to be input with each transaction. In this
example, however, there are none over and above
those already deemed essential and in the
ORDER.

The final step is the expansion of the functional
description of the system to cover the processes of
calculation and derivation:

**Necessary**
N(a) Assign ORDER-DATE to an ORDER
when it enters the system, using
TODAY'S-DATE.
N(b) Calculate DISCOUNT-AMT and
NET-VALUE using TOTAL-VALUE,
DISCOUNT % and TOTAL-TAX.

*Desirable*
An output data flow which arises from this class of
objectives is:

REJ-ORD
    (CUST-NAME, INV-ADRS, DELIV-ADRS,
    [PURCH-NO], ORD-LINE* (ITEM-NO,
    ITEM-DESCRIP, QTY) CREDIT-LIM,
    NET-VALUE)

The fields which are not given on the original order are already present in either CUST-DATA or ITEM-DATA, with two exceptions.

The NET-VALUE may be derived as for the invoice production. The CREDIT-LIM itself is however not yet available. The organization desires a very simple credit control system based upon a maximum value for any order, for a particular customer. (If any other methods were to be employed, more integration of the sales ledger entity and the order processing system would be needed.) It is therefore possible to store the field CREDIT-LIM with the CUSTOMER-DATA for use in this data flow:

CUSTOMER-DATA
    (CUST-NO, CUST-NAME, DELIV-ADRS,
    DISCOUNT %, INV-ADRS, CREDIT-LIM)

The other desirable outgoing data flows are:

S-ANAL
    (SCUR-DATE, SDETAIL* (ANAL-CLASS,
    CUR-MONTH, CUR-MONTH-TARGET,
    YTD, YTD-TARGET))

and

DESPATCH-STATS
    (DCUR-DATE, NO-LINES-PERIOD,
    VAL-LINES-PERIOD, DDETAIL* (DAYS,
    NUM-LINES, NUM %, VALU-LINES,
    VALU %))

The last two data flows are different from all the preceding ones in that they contain summarized information. This information is based upon the operational level information of day-to-day transactions taking place in the organization. It is then processed to produce this summary information used by management in overall control and tactical decision-making. The question for the designer is at what point this summarizing should be done. Is it better to store the detailed operational level information and summarize only when the output is required, or should the detail be summarized and then stored in its final form ready for output? The problem with summarizing is that as soon as this is done and some detail lost, there are questions which can no longer be answered from the stored data.

In order to produce the S-ANAL data flow the system needs to either (1) store the value of sales in the current month and year to date for each analysis class (customer group and product group) or (2) store details of each sale so that this information can be derived.

If option (1) is chosen it is not possible to produce statitics referring to customer group within product group or vice versa. This would be possible if option (2) was taken.

*Golden Rule 15*
Keep the data as raw as possible as long as possible.

This emphasizes the advantages in terms of future flexibility of the system which follow from holding the data in its detailed raw form.

During this part of the systems design the optimistic approach may be taken and the detailed form of the data stored. Whether or not this can be justified in terms of costs and benefits will be reviewed during the outline design, because it is not until the physical aspects are included that well-founded decisions can be made.

In the S-ANAL data flow the field SCUR-DATE can be derived from TODAY'S-DATE. The fields for the sales values for the current month and this year to date would be derived from the sales details for the year to date.

As the prices, discounts and tax percentage held in the data stores may change between an order being processed and S-ANAL being required, the figures relevant to a particular order need to be available. It is assumed that no significant changes take place while an order is in the system. The value of sales used for analysis purposes excludes tax but includes both the item and customer discounts. The relevant fields are ITEM-PRICE, ITEM-DISCOUNT % and DISCOUNT %, and all three will be stored to enhance flexibility:

SALES-DETAIL-DATA
(CUST-GROUP, PROD-GROUP, ORDER-DATE, ITEM-PRICE, ITEM-DISCOUNT %, DISCOUNT %, QTY)

Note that because there will be a SALES-DETAIL-DATA entry for every line on every order received, the same data values can theoretically occur more than once.

The customer and product data stores would need to hold the analysis group if this objective were to be achieved:

CUSTOMER-DATA
(CUST-NO, CUST-NAME, DELIV-ADRS, DISCOUNT %, INV-ADRS CREDIT-LIM, CUST-GROUP)

ITEM-DATA
(ITEM-NO, ITEM-DESCRIP, BIN-NO, ITEM-PRICE, ITEM-DISCOUNT %, ITEM-TAX %, RE-ORD-QTY, SUPLR* (SUPL-NAME, SUPL-ADRS, SUPL-CONTACT, LAST-PURCH-DATE, LAST-COST), QOH, PROD-GROUP)

The targets for sales are relatively stable and can be stored:

SALES-TARGETS-DATA
(ANAL-CLASS, MONTH, TARGET)

This enables the CUR-MONTH-TARGET field to be extracted and the YTD-TARGET to be calculated by adding up to monthly targets for the year to date.

The DESPATCH-STATS is a flow of summarized data and will be based, at least until outline design, on storage of the raw data where possible. The DESPATCH-STATS are an analysis of the time between orders being received and goods being despatched:

DESPATCH-DETAIL-DATA
(ORDER-DATE, DESPATCH-DATE, ITEM-PRICE, ITEM-DISCOUNT %, ITEM-TAX %, DISCOUNT %, QTY)

If this data is stored for every order line despatched, then for any given period the two total figures NO-LINES-PERIOD and VALU-LINES-PERIOD can be derived.

Again it is assumed that ITEM-PRICE etc. may change between receiving the order and a flow of DESPATCH-STATS, but that changes while an order is being processed are insignificant.

Within this defined period the number and value of lines despatched within a certain number of days can be derived. The two percentage figures can then be calculated from these totals. The field DAYS would take on values representing the range of days it actually did take to despatch products. Finally, the DCUR-DATE can be taken from TODAY'S-DATE.

In order that the details of which order line was despatched and when can be stored, they need to be input, and this is already included on the data flow diagram (Figure 38) as the flow DESPATCH-CONFIRM. Unlike the flow ORDER the designer may specify exactly what the flow will consist of:

DESPATCH-CONFIRM
(PICK-NO, DESPATCH-DATE, ITEM-NO, QTY)

All these fields are present in the warehouse from the PICKING-NOTE data flow, and from them the DESPATCH-DETAIL-DATA can be derived or obtained by using the data stores.

We now turn to the processing which needs to be done to support these desirable outputs. The following would need to be included in the systems functional description:

**Desirable**
D(a)   Calculate NET-VALUE of an order, to compare with CREDIT-LIM.
D(b)   Allocate SCUR-DATE and DCUR-DATE from TODAY'S-DATE.
D(c)   Calculate CUR-MONTH and YTD for S-ANAL using SALES-DETAIL-DATA.
D(d)   Derive the number and value of order lines despatched in a period, broken down by DAYS taken to despatch, using DESPATCH-DETAIL-DATA.

## Stage 4   Internal processes

This stage is summarized as:

For each class of objectives:
(a) For each primary objective:
   Draw a data flow diagram to describe what must be done to achieve it.
   Specify the data flows to and from store.
   Describe the functions of each process as a structured list.
(b) Check secondary objectives have been designed in.
(c) Draw a composite data flow diagram for that class of objectives.

At this stage in the design of the logical application model, attention is turned to the processes. The single process box which existed in the early data flow diagrams has had secondary functions added to it. These new functions, together with the use of the data stores, needs to be incorporated into the design and the diagrams.

Again, detailed knowledge of what is required of the new system, together with how any existing system operates, is essential. This should be based upon the results of the systems investigation, whether it was completed before design began or is seen as ongoing.

The obvious starting place for the detailed processing is the primary objectives as described in stage 1, and the data flow diagrams. The data flows do not just magically enter and leave the system; they need to be sent and received. In performing these tasks the processes will use the data stores and calculations described in stage 3, incorporating all the secondary objectives defined there.

The outputs from stage 4 are detailed data flow diagrams and definition of each process, which will be found in the supporting documentation. the diagram may specify new data flows which need to be documented. It is worth emphasizing that data flows from data stores are specified at the field level. This may seem to be much too detailed for the designer who has already decided that standard files and a record-based programming language like COBOL will be used.

Designers who specify the detail allow for the use of non-record languages and field level I/O from a data base management system.

**Example: order processing**

*Essential*
There are three data flows which need to be received or sent: ORDER, PICKING-NOTE, and INVOICE-DETAIL.

*E1   RECEIVE-ORDER*

ORDER
   ([CUST-NO/CNDA(CUST-NAME +
   DELIV-ADRS)], [DELIV-ADRS],
   [PURCH-NO], ORDER-LINE*
   ([ITEM-NO/ITEM-DESCRIP], QTY))

This process needs to receive orders from customers and pass them on for further processing. As noted in stage 3 the format of the ORDER is very variable and so consideration needs to be given to standardizing the data once it enters the system. Most organizations do standardize input, by transcribing it on to forms (on paper or on a VDU). This has the advantage of being able to check all data is present and correct before passing it on to be dealt with by comparatively simple tasks. If the data is unstructured its processing is more complex but this flexibility can be of benefit, e.g. most order forms do not allow the purchaser to specify that item X is only required if item Y is available. There is also the disadvantage of the extra work involved in standardizing the data.

In the order processing system being designed here, the decision is in favour of standardization. The reader is reminded that although this is the common choice in the 1980s, computing developments such as fifth-generation architecture with natural language input and knowledge bases may swing the balance in favour of textual data. The designer needs to question the traditional as well as the novel methods of processing data.

This process then needs to receive the order and to put it into a standard form. The requirements are for a customer identifier. The field CUST-NO will be used, and where a customer name and delivery address are the only identifier the process will need to perform a conversion.

This necessitates a search being made of the CUSTOMER-DATA, using CUST-NAME and DELIV-ADRS as the search argument and obtaining the CUST-NO as the reply. The DELIV-ADRS and PURCH-NO need to be kept if they exist as they will be used for output if given on input. The item description will be converted to the ITEM-NO, if it is the only identifier of the product wanted. To do this the ITEM-DATA will be searched on ITEM-DESCRIP to retrieve the ITEM-NO.

From the secondary function E(a) there is the need for an ORDER-NO to be given to the ORDER on entry to the system. This involves reference to the SYSTEM-DATA field LAST-ORDNO-USED, and then its updating, as shown in Figure 39.

The four new data flows may be described as:

STD-ORDER
(ORDER-NO, ORDER-DATE, CUST-NO,
[DELIV-ADRS], [PURCH-NO],
ORDER-LINE* (ITEM-NO, QTY))
CUST-ID, SA = CUST-NAME + DELIV-ADRS
(CUST-NO)
ITEM-ID, SA = ITEM-DESCRIP
(ITEM-NO)

Where a data flow is a retrieval of data from store to a process, the search argument used to select the data needs to be specified. This needs recording in the documentation and will be given here with the 'SA = ' clause, as above.

ORDAT
(LAST-ORDNO-USED, TODAY'S-DATE)

This data flow is shown as bidirectional because the field which is received by the process will subsequently be replaced in the data store. This contrasts with data retrieval, which is shown as one way because the search arguments do not change the data stored in any way.

The functions that the process RECEIVE-ORDER must perform need to be specified:

RECEIVE-ORDER
For each ORDER received:
(a) Obtain CUST-ID if CUST-NO not already present.
(b) Obtain ORDAT for ORDER-NO and ORDER-DATE.
(c) For each ORDER-LINE: obtain ITEM-ID if ITEM-NO not already present.
(d) Send STD-ORDER.
(e) Replace ORDAT.

In specifying the functions, the designer needs to avoid stating how the results will be achieved. The procedures for performing a task will vary depending upon whether or not it is automated and, if automated, the type of language used. The functions therefore are described by means of a structured list of tasks.

The second of the essential objectives, E2, was to send data out of the system.

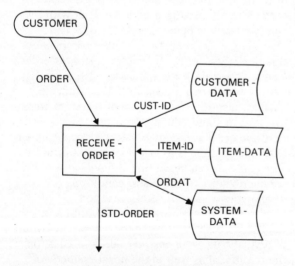

Figure 39  *RECEIVE-ORDER: objective E1*

### E2  SEND-PICKING-NOTE

PICKING-NOTE
(PICK-NO, CUST-NAME, DELIV-ADRS,
PICK-LINE* (BIN-NO, ITEM-NO,
ITEM-DESCRIP, QTY))

A picking note is a special version of an order for use in a warehouse. As stated in stage 3, production of the picking note depends upon access to the orders, which are available in standard form as STD-ORDER. The PICK-NO is then taken as the ORDER-NO, and the CUST-NAME obtained using the CUST-NO. If a DELIV-ADRS is present on the STD-ORDER it will be used; if not then the DELIV-ADRS will be obtained from the store of CUSTOMER-DATA. The BIN-NO and ITEM-DESCRIP will be taken from the ITEM-DATA using ITEM-NO as the search argument.

If more data was provided to this process with the STD-ORDER, such as CUST-NAME and ITEM-DESCRIP, the work involved here would be less. The reason why this has not been done is because of the redundancy of data which would follow, customers' names and item descriptions being duplicated on every STD-ORDER (Figure 40).

The two new flows can be defined as:

CUST-DAT, SA = CUST-NO
(CUST-NAME, [DELIV-ADRS])
ITEM-DAT, SA = ITEM-NO
(BIN-NO, ITEM-DESCRIP)

The function of the process would then be:

SEND-PICKING-NOTE
For each STD-ORDER received:
(a) Obtain CUST-DAT including DELIV-ADRS if not already present.
(b) For each ORDER-LINE: obtain ITEM-DAT.
(c) Assign ORDER-NO to PICK-NO.
(d) Send PICKING-NOTE.

### E3  SEND-INVOICE-DETAIL

INVOICE-DETAIL
(CUST-NO, [PURCH-NO], INV-DATE,
TOTAL-VALUE, DISCOUNT %.
TOTAL-TAX, INV-NO)

This process needs the STD-ORDER data flow which contains the INV-NO (as ORDER-NO), CUST-NO and the optional PURCH-NO. The invoice amounts can be calculated using the ITEM-NO and ITEM-DATA, as specified in stage 3, with DISCOUNT % coming from CUSTOMER-DATA. INV-DATE is taken from the SYSTEM-DATA (Figure 41).

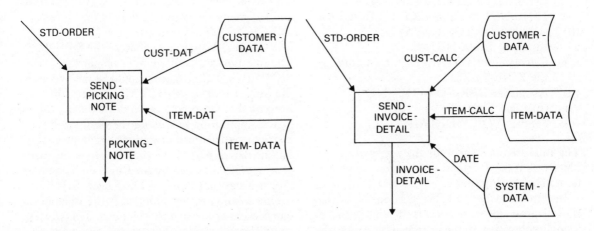

Figure 40   *SEND-PICKING-NOTE: objective E2*          Figure 41   *SEND-INVOICE-DETAIL: objective E3*

The flows are:

CUST-CALC, SA = CUST-NO
(DISCOUNT %)
ITEM-CALC, SA = ITEM-NO
(ITEM-PRICE, ITEM-DISCOUNT %,
ITEM-TAX %)
DATE
(TODAYS-DATE)

and the functions (following the function E(b)) are:

SEND-INVOICE-DETAIL
For each STD-ORDER:

(a) For each ORDER-LINE:
Obtain ITEM-CALC.
Calculate the discounted extended value DISC-EXT as

$$DISC\text{-}EXT = QTY \times ITEM\text{-}PRICE \times \left(1 - \frac{ITEM\text{-}DISCOUNT\ \%}{100}\right)$$

Calculate the LINE TAX as

$$LINE\text{-}TAX = DISC\text{-}EXT \times \frac{ITEM\text{-}TAX\ \%}{100}$$

Calculate the net value LINE-NET as
LINE-NET = DISC-EXT + LINE-TAX
(b) Calculate the TOTAL-VALUE by summing LINE-NETs.
(c) Calculate the TOTAL-TAX by summing the LINE-TAXs.
(d) Assign ORDER-NO to INV-NO (function E(c)).
(e) Send INVOICE DETAIL.

The final step in stage 4 for the essential objectives is the development of a composite data flow diagram (Figure 42).

In contrast to the individual portions of the data flow diagram, the stored data is shown together as a single component in the system. This makes the diagram easier to draw and read, and has no effect on the processes which either store or retrieve data without concern for the structuring of that data. It follows from this that two or more flows may be shown as a single line from the store to a process, with individual flow names alongside.

Note in the diagram that STD-ORDER is shown twice. The information must be passed to both processes from RECEIVE-ORDER and there are no sequence constraints. The information could therefore be passed via a shared file or via a common area in memory, or each flow sent separately. The diagram shows that the information needs to get to two places without limiting later choices.

*Necessary*
The two data flows which need to be sent are the INVOICE and the STOCKOUT.

*N1 SEND-INVOICE*

INVOICE
(INV-NO, CUST-NAME, INV-ADRS,
DELIV-ADRS, [PURCH-NO],
ORDER-DATE, INV-DATE,
TOTAL-VALUE, DISCOUNT %,
DISCOUNT-AMT, TOTAL-TAX,
NET-VALUE, INV-LINE* (ITEM-NO,
ITEM-DESCRIP, QTY, LINE-VAL,
ITEM-DISCOUNT %, ITEM-TAX %,
LINE-NET))

This data flow is based upon the STD-ORDER and has many fields in common with INVOICE-DETAIL. In Fact INVOICE-DETAIL is a subset of the INVOICE. The question arises of whether or not the SEND-INVOICE process should be merged with the SEND-INVOICE-DETAIL process. In keeping the two processes separate during the logical application modelling the designer is not restricting the choice of options available at the outline design part of the project. However, both processes need to be designed into the system as they are classed as essential and necessary.

One solution to the problem is the isolation in one process of the shared functions. This process could then send data flows to the two other processes which perform the different tasks, as shown in Figure 43. The flows are:

CUST-IC, SA = CUST-NO
  (DISCOUNT %)
ITEM-IC, SA = ITEM-NO
  (ITEM-PRICE, ITEM-DISCOUNT %,
  ITEM-TAX %)
SYS-IC
  (TODAY'S-DATE)
CAL-DET
  (CUST-NO, [PURCH-NO], INV-DATE,
  TOTAL-VALUE, DISCOUNT %,
  TOTAL-TAX, INV-NO)
CAL-INV
  (INV-NO, CUST-NO, [PURCH-NO],
  ORDER-DATE, INV-DATE,
  TOTAL-VALUE, DISCOUNT %,
  DISCOUNT-AMT, TOTAL-TAX,

NET-VALUE, INV-LINE* (ITEM-NO,
QTY, LINE-VAL, ITEM-DISCOUNT %,
ITEM-TAX %, LINE-NET))

The function of INVOICE-CALC would be:

INVOICE-CALC
For each STD-ORDER:
(a)  Obtain CUST-IC.
(b)  For each ORDER-LINE:
     Obtain ITEM-IC.
     Calculate LINE-VAL, LINE-TAX and
     LINE-NET:

$$LINE\text{-}VAL = ITEM\text{-}PRICE \times QTY$$
$$DISC\text{-}EXT = LINE\text{-}VAL \times \left(1 - \frac{ITEM\text{-}DISCOUNT \%}{100}\right)$$

$$LINE\text{-}TAX = DISC\text{-}EXT \times \frac{ITEM\text{-}TAX \%}{100}$$

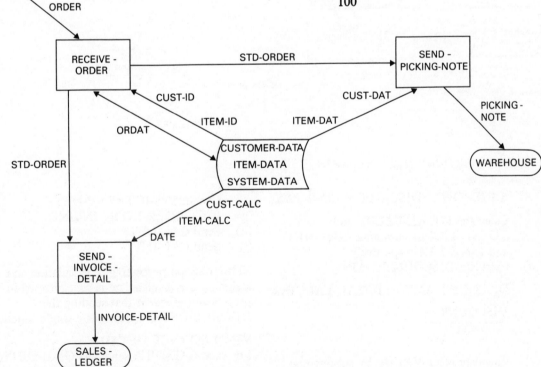

Figure 42  *Composite data flow diagram for essential objectives*

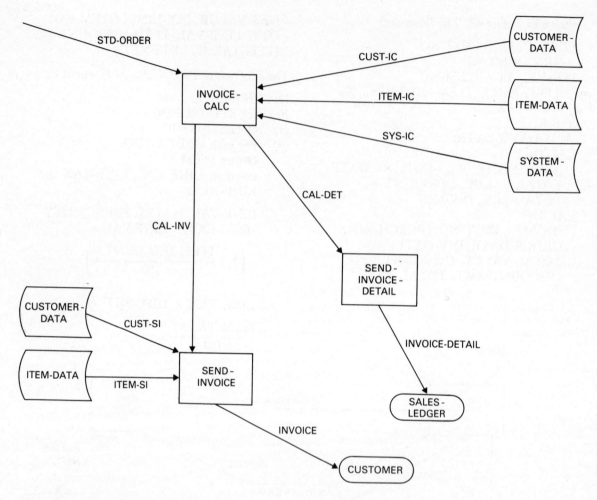

Figure 43 *SEND-INVOICE*: objective N1

LINE-NET = DISC-EXT + LINE-TAX

(c) Calculate TOTAL-VALUE and TOTAL-TAX by summing LINE-NET and LINE-TAX respectively.

(d) Calculate DISCOUNT-AMT:

$$DISCOUNT\text{-}AMT = TOTAL\text{-}VALUE \times \frac{DISCOUNT\ \%}{100}$$

(e) Calculate NET-VALUE by subtracting DISCOUNT-AMT from TOTAL-VALUE.

(f) Obtain SYS-IC for INV-DATE.
(g) Use ORDER-NO for INV-NO.
(h) Send CAL-DET.
(i) Send CAL-INV.

The common processing of calculation and assigning the invoice date is concentrated in this process to the extent that sending the INVOICE-DETAIL becomes a single function:

SEND-INVOICE-DETAIL
For each CAL-DET: send INVOICE-DETAIL.

Sending the INVOICE itself is slightly more complex, as static data is required from store:

CUST-SI, SA = CUST-NO
  (CUST-NAME, INV-ADRS,
  DELIV-ADRS)
ITEM-SI, SA = ITEM-NO
  (ITEM-DESCRIP)

Again the functional description is brief:

SEND-INVOICE
  For each CAL-INV:
(a) obtain CUST-SI.
(b) for each INV-LINE: obtain ITEM-SI.
(c) Send INVOICE.

## N2  SEND-STOCKOUT

STOCKOUT
  (ITEM-NO, ITEM-DESCRIP,
  RE-ORD-QTY, SUPLS* (SUPL-NAME,
  SUPL-ADRS, SUPL-CONTACT,
  LAST-PURCH-DATE, LAST-COST))

The event which gives rise to this data flow is a stock level, as known by the system, falling to zero. In order that the system can have knowledge of stock levels, the field QOH (quantity on hand) was introduced during stage 3. This field needs to be kept up to date by the system, as well as being checked every time it is reduced to see if zero has been reached.

The real-world stock levels, which QOH is modelling, are changed by the production of a picking note; therefore a process to maintain QOH also needs to follow the SEND-PICKING-NOTE process. In order to allow for future flexibiltiy the interaction will be seen as a data flow. This flow from SEND-PICKING-NOTE to SEND-STOCKOUT need only contain the ITEM-NO and the quantity ordered; SEND-STOCKOUT will do all the remaining work.

A data flow diagram for this section of the processing is given in Figure 44. The data flows are:

PICK-STK
  (ITEM-NO, QTY)

QUANT, SA = ITEM-NO
  (QOH)
PURCH-INF, SA = ITEM-NO
  (RE-ORD-QTY, SUPLS* (SUPL-NAME,
  SUPL-ADRS, SUPL-CONTACT,
  LAST-PURCH-DATE, LAST-COST),
  ITEM-DESCRIP)

The description of the processing functions would then be:

SEND-STOCKOUT

For each PICK-STK:
(a) Obtain QUANT
(b) For QOH-QTY ≤ 0
  Obtain PURCH-INF
  Send STOCKOUT
(c) Replace QUANT

The functions of SEND-PICKING-NOTE would need to be increased:

SEND-PICKING-NOTE
For each STD-ORDER received:
(a) . . . .
(b) . . . .
(c) . . . .
(d) . . . .
(e) Send PICK-STK

A composite data flow diagram for the essential and necessary objectives is shown in Figure 45.

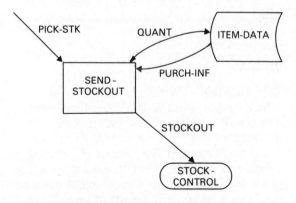

Figure 44  *SEND-STOCKOUT: objective N2*

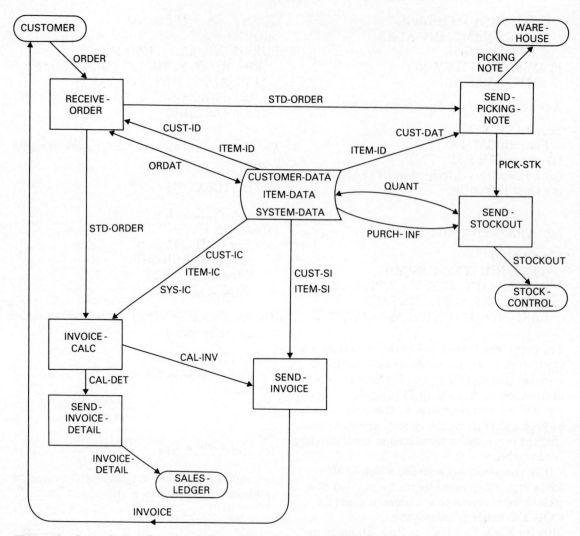

Figure 45   *Composite data flow diagram for essential and necessary objectives*

## Desirable

### D1   CREDIT-CHECK

The desirable objective D1, controlling credit, has a great deal in common with invoice production, and yet needs to be done as soon as the order is received. The impact of including credit control in the system designed so far will be quite considerable. This does not mean that what has been done so far is a waste of time. If the designer is to make honest and rational decisions about whether or not desirable objectives can be justified, she needs to know what the system would look like without them.

As soon as an order has been received and standardized it needs to be priced. Following this a decision on whether or not to reject the order can be made. If the order is accepted, then data must be sent for invoicing and picking note production.

The process INVOICE-CALC is necessary for the system and may be employed for credit

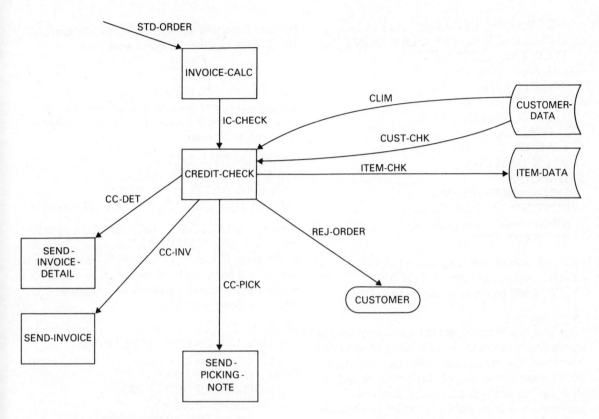

Figure 46 *CREDIT-CHECK: objective D1*

control purposes. It will send data to the CREDIT-CHECK process which will then assess credit. It may accept the order in which case the data flows to the SEND-PICKING-NOTE, SEND-INVOICE and SEND-INVOICE-DETAIL will originate from the CREDIT-CHECK. If the order is rejected then a REJ-ORDER will be sent to the customer after obtaining necessary information from the data stores.

Figure 46 shows the relevant part of a data flow diagram.

The functions of the CREDIT-CHECK will be:

CREDIT-CHECK
For each IC-CHECK:
(a)   Obtain CLIM.
(b)   If CREDIT-LIM < NET-VALUE
       Obtain CUST-CHK.

Obtain ITEM-CHK.
Send REJ-ORDER
Else (credit is good):
Send CC-DET.
Send CC-INV.
Send CC-PICK.

The flows are:

REJ-ORDER
   (CUST-NAME, INV-ADRS, DELIV-ADRS,
   [PURCH-NO], ORD-LINE* (ITEM-NO,
   ITEM-DESCRIP, QTY) CREDIT-LIM,
   NET-VALUE)
IC-CHECK
   (INV-NO, CUST-NO [PURCH-NO],
   [DELIV-ADRS], ORDER-DATE,
   INV-DATE, TOTAL-VALUE, DISCOUNT
   %, DISCOUNT-AMT, TOTAL-TAX,

NET-VALUE, INV-LINE* (ITEM-NO,
QTY, LINE-VAL, ITEM-DISCOUNT %,
ITEM-TAX %, LINE-NET))
CLIM, SA = CUST-NO
(CREDIT-LIM)
CUST-CHK, SA = CUST-NO
(CUST-NAME, INV-ADRS,
DELIV-ADRS)
ITEM-CHK, SA = ITEM-NO
(ITEM-DESCRIP)
STD-ORDER
(ORDER-NO, ORDER-DATE,
CUST-NO, [DELIV-ADRS],
[PURCH-NO], ORDER-LINE*
(ITEM-NO, QTY))

CC-DET will be the same as CAL-DET
CC-INV will be the same as CAL-INV
CC-PICK will be the same as STD-ORDER.

Note that data is being passed from one process to another rather than the results being recalculated whenever they are needed. Although this does increase the complexity of the interfaces and therefore make the system more costly to maintain, it is kept within intuitively acceptable limits. The data that is needed from the stores is obtained only when needed, which is correct. For example, the flow CUST-CHK is only obtained if a credit check fails and not automatically with CLIM. This may appear inefficient if the reader is thinking of CUST-DATA as a file of records all of the same type, but the file structure has not yet been considered, and names and addresses may end up somewhere distant from the figure for the credit limit. The precision of the design in this way enhances the flexibility.

The data flow STD-ORDER will no longer move from RECEIVE-ORDER to SEND-PICKING-NOTE and INVOICE-CALC. The documentation will have to be modified to send STD-ORDER to INVOICE-CALC only.

The process INVOICE-CALC will need to be modified such that it does not send CAL-DET or CAL-INV; rather, functions (h) and (i) (see under 'Necessary') are replaced by a new (h): (h) Send IC-CHECK.

In this way the decision about credit limits, and the data flows which originate from that decision, are all kept together in a single process.

## D2   SALES ANALYSIS

Objective D2 requires the production of a sales analysis, and the data on which this is to be based is described in stage 3.

SALES-DETAIL-DATA
(CUST-GROUP, PROD-GROUP,
ORDER-DATE, ITEM-PRICE,
ITEM-DISCOUNT%, DISCOUNT%, QTY)

An entry in SALES-DETAIL-DATA needs to be made for every ORDER-LINE received. This can be achieved if RECEIVE-ORDER sends a data flow of the basic order information, to a process which then stores the analysis data (Figure 47). The data flows would be:

RO-SANAL
(CUST-NO, ORDER-DATE, LINE*
(ITEM-NO, QTY) )
PGRP, SA = ITEM-NO
(PROD-GROUP, ITEM-PRICE,
ITEM-DISCOUNT%)
CGRP, SA = CUST-NO
(CUST-GROUP, DISCOUNT%)
STOR-SANAL
(CUST-GROUP, PROD-GROUP,
ORDER-DATE, ITEM-PRICE,
ITEM-DISCOUNT%, DISCOUNT%, QTY

There would need to be a change of the functional description of RECEIVE-ORDER (see under 'Essential') such that function (c) now reads:

(c) For each order line:
Obtain ITEM-ID if ITEM-NO not already present.
Send RO-SANAL.

The process STORE-SALES-DETAIL would be relatively simple:

For each RO-SANAL:
(a) Obtain CGRP.
(b) For each LINE:
   Obtain PGRP.
   Send STOR-SANAL.

The other aspect of this objective is the S-ANAL data flow, as shown in Figure 48.

It is assumed that the trigger which causes the production of S-ANAL is a request from the SALES-MGMT for the analysis. The trigger is not shown on the data flow diagram because it is a flow of control and not of data. Flow charts, precedence charts or some other means would need to be used to describe this graphically. This trigger would always be recorded in the data dictionary entry.

SANAL-DETL
   (CUST-GROUP, PROD-GROUP,
   ORDER-DATE, ITEM-PRICE,
   ITEM-DISCOUNT%, DISCOUNT%, QTY)
TARGETS
   (ANAL-CLASS, MONTH, TARGET)
S-ANAL
   (SCUR-DATE, SDETAIL* (ANAL-CLASS,
   CUR-MONTH, CUR-MONTH-TARGET,
   YTD, YTD-TARGET) )
DATE
   (TODAYS-DATE)

The functions of GENERATE-SANAL would be:

For each request for S-ANAL:

(a) Obtain DATE.
(b) For each SANAL-DETL obtained:
   Calculate sales value:

   SALE-VALU =

$$\left( QTY \times \text{ITEM-PRICE} \times \left(1 - \frac{\text{ITEM-DISCOUNT \%}}{100}\right) \right) \times$$

$$\left(1 - \frac{\text{DISCOUNT \%}}{100}\right)$$

Accumulate SALE-VALU for relevant ANAL-CLASS, i.e. PROD-GROUP and CUST-GROUP.
(c) Obtain TARGETS.
(d) Send S-ANAL.

Given the date, the current month and year-to-date sales values for each analysis class can be calculated and then totalled, being output alongside the targets.

### D3  DESPATCH-STATS
Production of DESPATCH-STATS for the general management will be based upon:

DESPATCH-DETAIL-DATA
   (ORDER-DATE, DESPATCH-DATE,
   ITEM-PRICE, ITEM-DISCOUNT%,
   ITEM-TAX%, DISCOUNT%, QTY)

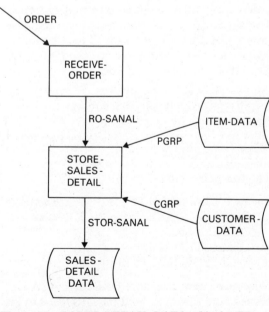

Figure 47  *SALES-DETAIL-DATA: objective D2*

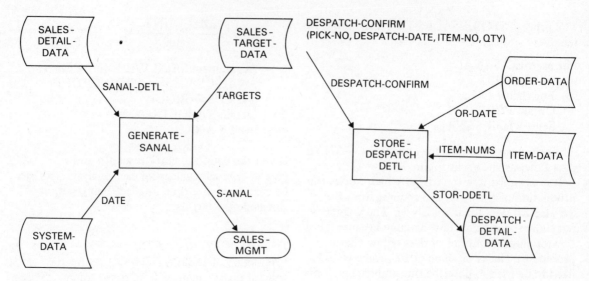

Figure 48   *S-ANAL: objective D2*

Figure 49   *DESPATCH-DETAIL-DATA: objective D3*

In stage 3 the DESPATCH-CONFIRM data flow was designed to support this data store. Owing to the fact that the warehouse is not informed of the ORDER-DATE or any financial aspects of the order, these must be obtained from data stores. The alternative would be to send the warehouse information they did not want so that it could later be sent back to the system. See Figure 49. The other data flows would be:

OR-DATE, SA = ORDER-NO
  (ORDER-DATE, DISCOUNT %)
ITEM-NUMS, SA = ITEM-NO
  (ITEM-PRICE, ITEM-DISCOUNT%,
  ITEM-TAX%)

The functions could then be:

For each DESPATCH-CONFIRM received:
(a) Obtain OR-DATE, using PICK-NO as ORDER-NO.
(b) Obtain ITEM-NUMS.
(c) Send STOR-DDETL.

Note that a new data store ORDER-DATA is needed, and this must hold the ORDER-DATE and DISCOUNT% as well as the ORDER-NO to

be used for access:

ORDER-DATA
  (ORDER-NO, ORDER-DATE, DISCOUNT %)

The origin of this store needs now to be considered. A process which has all the fields available to it can create the store. Such a process is INVOICE-CALC, which has the ORDER-NO and ORDER-DATE from the STD-ORDER flow and obtains the DISCOUNT% from CUST-DATA (Figure 50). There would need to be the modification to the functional description of INVOICE-CALC to include the job: send STOR-ORD.

We turn our attention now to the generation of the DESPATCH-STATS from the data now stored (Figure 51). The flows are:

DESP-DAT
  (ORDER-DATE, DESPATCH-DATE,
  ITEM-PRICE, ITEM-DISCOUNT%,
  ITEM-TAX%, DISCOUNT%, QTY)
DESPATCH-STATS
  (DCUR-DATE, NO-LINES-PERIOD,

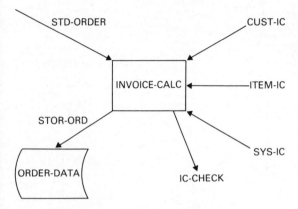

Figure 50 *INVOICE-CALC: objective D3*

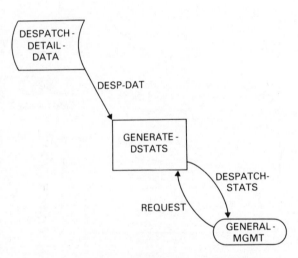

Figure 51 *DESPATCH-STATS: objective D3*

VAL-LINES-PERIOD, DETAIL* (DAYS, NUM-LINES, NUM%, VALU-LINES, VALU%))
REQUEST
 (BEGIN-DATE, END-DATE)

The trigger for this processing is again a request for the outgoing data flow, although on this occasion this does appear on the diagram because there is data transferred. The begin and end dates

describe the period over which the statistics will range, and refer to the DESPATCH DATE; orders not being despatched are therefore excluded.
The functions are:

GENERATE-DSTATS
For each REQUEST received:
(a) Obtain DESP-DAT.
(b) If despatched in right period: calculate DESP-VAL:

$$DESP\text{-}VAL = QTY \times ITEM\text{-}PRICE \times$$

$$\left(1 - \frac{ITEM\text{-}DISCOUNT\,\%}{100}\right) \times$$

$$\left(1 + \frac{ITEM\text{-}TAX\,\%}{100}\right) \times$$

$$\left(1 - \frac{DISCOUNT\,\%}{100}\right)$$

Calculate despatch delay, DAYS:

$$DAYS = DESPATCH\text{-}DATE - ORDER\text{-}DATE$$

Accumulate total number of lines and value of lines for the period.
Accumulate number of lines and value of lines for the DAYS.
(c) For each DAYS: calculate NUM% and VALU%.
(d) Send DESPATCH STATS.

As with S-ANAL, the information is calculated and accumulated when it is requested and then sent out of the system.
 The reader's attention is drawn to the fact that the source of data for ORDER-DATA, SALES-DETAIL-DATA and DESPATCH-DETAIL-DATA has been considered in some detail. This is not true of the other data stores. These three stores are the by-product of processing at the operational level. Data is stored in them for each order entering the system. The more stable and static data stores will

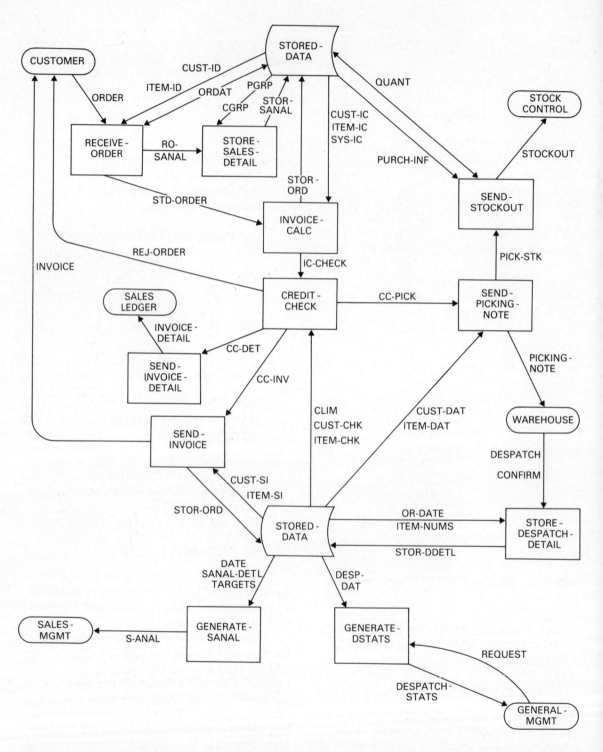

Figure 52   *Composite data flow diagram for essential, necessary and desirable objectives*

be considered in the next stage, together with the deletion of information from all the data stores. It is intended that, by separating out those aspects of logical design which are not immediately involved with the operational tasks, these second-level tasks will receive adequate attention.

There are eight possible data flow diagrams that could be drawn to show the new system with or without any of the objectives D1–3. If none was developed the necessary diagram could be used.

Shown in Figure 52 is the composite diagram with all these objectives included. Note the central role of CREDIT-CHECK. Note also the duplication of the data stores for clarity:

STORED-DATA
   (SYSTEM-DATA, ITEM-DATA,
   CUSTOMER-DATA,
   SALES-DETAIL-DATA,
   SALES-TARGET-DATA, ORDER-DATA,
   DESPATCH-DETAIL-DATA)

## Stage 5   Data maintenance

This stage is summarized as:

For each class of objectives:
For each data store:
(a) For each item identify the cause(s) of its creation, amendment and deletion.
(b) Design any extra processes and data flows, such that the stored data is kept as up to date as necessary.
(c) Store all detail in the data dictionary.

The object of systems design is the modelling of the 'real' world, and this can clearly be seen here. Consider a payroll system. When an employee starts with the firm, data needs to be inserted into storage. If the employee changes his name or tax code, the system needs to be aware of this in order to carry on functioning. When the person leaves, the payroll system needs to know. In this way the system follows reality as closely as it can.

The purpose of this stage of the design is the maintenance of all the stored data. Maintenance here is used to mean the amendment, insertion and deletion (A/I/D) of stored data, and the system must make provision for this.

This stage corresponds closely to the idea of modelling the entity life cycle or history. Effort is focused upon the way in which an entity, e.g. a customer or order, comes into being, changes, and is destroyed. The design can then be checked to ensure that these processes have been catered

for. This information can be shown in a data dictionary. Figure 5 shows this incorporated into an element's description.

One approach to this stage of the design is to look at each data item for each data store, answering the questions of what causes the field to exist, change, and disappear.

Stage 5 may be prioritized such that the stored data is considered in the sequence essential, necessary, and desirable. In this way any additional effort required to maintain a field can be identified and apportioned to the relevant objective. The priority class of these processes and flows will be necessary if the stored data is either essential or necessary, and desirable if the data stores derive from desirable objectives.

It is possible to set up a flow for the changes not already defined. The flow is designed to take information about the world from those people best able to provide it, and in this way keep the systems data accurately up to date.

**Example: order processing**
In the order processing example, the essential stored data about customers can be seen to originate from two distinct sources:

CUSTOMER-DATA
   (CUST-NO, CUST-NAME, DELIV-ADRS,
   DISCOUNT %)

The fields CUST-NAME and DELIV-ADRS

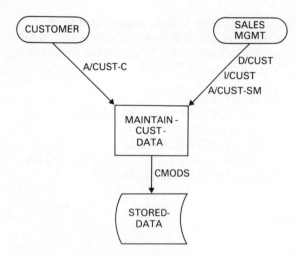

Figure 53  *MAINTAIN-CUST-DATA*

may be changed by existing customers. Both the remaining fields are allocated by the organization itself. The CUST-NO is given to new customers according to set rules and the DISCOUNT % is determined by SALES-MGMT. Figure 53 depicts the situation.

When a customer wishes to open or close an account, it contacts the sales management directly, and they in turn can generate the data flows:

D/CUST
  (CUST-NO)
I/CUST
  (CUST-NAME, DELIV-ADRS, DISCOUNT
  %)

They may also generate an amendment flow:

A/CUST-SM
  (CUST-NO, [DISCOUNT %])

The customer flow is:

A/CUST-C
  ([CUST-NO/CNDA(CUST-NAME +
  DELIV-ADRS)], [NEW-NAME],
  [NEW-DELIV-ADRS])
CMODS
  ([CUST-NO/CNDA(CUST-NAME +
  DELIV-ADRS)], [CUST-NAME],
  [DELIV-ADRS], [DISCOUNT %])

The functions of the MAINTAIN-CUST-DATA process would be:

For each:
(a) D/CUST, identify the relevant customer data and delete it;
(b) I/CUST:
    Calculate CUST-NO algorithmically;
    Insert customer data in store;
(c) A/CUST-SM, identify the relevant customer data and modify where required;
(d) A/CUST-C, identify the relevant customer data and modify as necessary.

The major part of data A/I/D is purely physical and relatively simple, even when the contents of several data fields need to be checked before an entry can be deleted.

It is particularly important to bear in mind the fact that the structure of the stored data is yet to be determined. All that can be said at this stage is that somehow these fields will be stored, and will need maintaining.

The major concern for the designer is that formal channels exist by which the system is kept up to date. In the example, imagine the problems which could be caused if the roles of CUSTOMER and SALES-MGMT were not defined with respect to the A/I/D of the CUSTOMER-DATA.

The non-essential customer fields INV-ADRS, CREDIT-LIM, PROD-GROUP are maintained by the same people as the essential fields. The purpose here is not to describe every stored field given in the example, but rather to briefly indicate how the question of maintaining the data can be tackled with the tools and methods described in the preceding stages.

The SALES-TARGET-DATA stores the sales target for a product or item group, for a particular month. Sales management are responsible for all the A/I/D on this data store.

The position with the ITEM-DATA is again simple, as all the data (except QOH) originates from and is controlled by STOCK-CONTROL. The field QOH is reduced by the ORDER-PROCESSING system. The designer needs to ensure that somewhere this field is incremented by goods received or manufactured.

If this is not done by another system which shares the data store (the assumption made here) then provision needs to be made for this data to flow from either the WAREHOUSE or STOCK-CONTROL.

Of the fields in SYSTEM-DATA, the field LAST-ORDNO-USED is amended by the system itself, and will not be deleted without change to the system. The designer needs to give consideration to the initialization of this field. There is also the process of assigning a value to TODAYS-DATE and allowing its amendment; again, its deletion will involve system change and need not be planned. The date used by a system, mechanized or manual, may be controlled by an operator who informs the machine of the date to be used, or changes the calendar. These fields may be handled in a similar manner to CUSTOMER-DATA, by a maintenance process with external inputs.

The data stores which collect data from the operational system have need only for deletion procedures. It is rare to build into the system a facility to modify the accumulated data that will be used for statistics. Deletion may be performed on all the data or on a subset, and it will follow an event in the world.

The designer needs to know precisely what event will cause the deletion of the data. All of SALES-DETAIL-DATA, ORDER-DATA and DESPATCH-DETAIL-DATA contain the field ORDER-DATE. This could be used to delete all records before a certain date or over a certain age. The date or age to be used would need to be entered on to the system. Alternatively, deletion could take place following a request from management.

We now turn our attention to the store:

ORDER-DATA
(ORDER-NO, ORDER-DATE, DISCOUNT %)

Any of the fields in it could be used for selective deletion. A further useful possibility exists and that is deletion following an operational event. A field could be added to the store by INVOICE-CALC, which creates it to say how many ORDER-LINEs there were on the original order. (This field is an example of transparent data, i.e. data which is used by the system but is never seen by the users of the system.) The process STORE-DESPATCH-DETL could then decrement this field when an order line had been despatched, eventually deleting the information stored for a particular order. It will be assumed here that this option is not chosen and that deletion is based upon selection by ORDER-DATE.

The description of this stage of the design is deliberately brief because the problems can be tackled by the methods described in stage 4. Most important of all is the need for the designer to consider every field stored, and answer the questions about the circumstances which will give rise to change. How will that field keep up to date with a changing world? From this the requirements for A/I/D can be specified, possibly modifying the work done in earlier stages to support them.

# 7 Data modelling

Data modelling takes place in two phases. First, the provisional data stores of the application modelling are analysed using normalization. Second, the final data model is synthesized using courting.

## Normalization

This is summarized as:

For each class of objectives:
For each data store:
(a) Ensure that each store has a key which uniquely identifies something, splitting the store if required.
(b) Ensure that only key fields determine the values of other fields, splitting the store if required.
(c) Record all changes in the data dictionary.

The first technique used in the structuring of the data is normalization. This is a set of operations through which a group of data items are put. Normalization separates out the items which are independent of each other into simple groupings.

As well as the fields to be structured, two other types of information are needed. First, the keys must be identified, i.e. which field or group of fields is able to uniquely identify the one thing in the real world which the data describes. Second, any relationships between fields needs to be known. One such relationship is between the key and other fields, because given the value of the key field you could determine the value of the other fields, if necessary, by going to the real-world object which is being described. In general terms, if a given value of field A can determine a value of field B then it can be said that field B depends upon field A. Given these two types of information, it is possible to automate the normalization process.

Consider the following distortion of the legal oath as a description of normalization:

1  No repeating,
2  The fields depend upon the key,
3  The whole key,
4  And nothing but the keys,
5  So help me Codd.

The explanation starts with line five because these techniques were first developed by E. F. Codd in the early 1970s.

Line two states that the fields will depend upon a key. This means that keys need to be identified and data grouped about them. For example:

EMPLOYEE-DATA
(EMPL-NO, EMPL-NAME,
SALARY, MTHLY-PAY, BANK-NO,
BANK-NADRS, TRAINING*
(COURSE-NO, COURSE-DESCRIPT,
DATE-COMPLTD, RESULT))

Data items are grouped around the key EMPL-NO which uniquely identifies the real-world employee which the other fields describe. The EMPL-NAME is marked as an alternative key because it also uniquely identifies the employee (using a numeric suffix for duplicate Smiths, Kahn etc.). Given either of these two keys, all the other fields could be determined, say by talking to the employee, and so the fields are said to depend upon the key.

The stage of checking that all keys have been identified and that the fields are determined by them is usually regarded as a preliminary to the normalization proper.

Moving on to line one does necessitate a change to EMPLOYEE-DATA. 'No repeating' means that there will be no repeating groups of data in the structure. The reason for this step in normalization is that wherever there are repeating fields then something more specific than defined by the key is being described, and it should be able to stand alone. In the example it can be seen that the repeating group TRAINING is 'training done by an employee' and is more specific than the general employee information. EMPLOYEE-DATA is therefore split into EMPL-BASIC-DATA and EMPL-TRAIN-DATA:

EMPL-BASIC-DATA
  (EMPL-NO, EMPL-NAME,
  SALARY, MTHLY-PAY, BANK-NO,
  BANK-NADRS)

The operation here is simply the removal of the TRAINING group of data.

In creating the EMPL-TRAIN-DATA care has to be taken not to violate line two, i.e. the data needs to have a key which will uniquely identify it. The fields in the group TRAINING are not able to do this alone because they depend for their meaning upon the fact that they were placed within EMPLOYEE-DATA. The training fields depended on EMPL-NO. The way out of this problem is simply to copy the key of the original group into each new group (it is already in EMPL-BASIC-DATA):

EMPL-TRAIN-DATA
  (EMPL-NO, COURSE-NO,
  COURSE-DESCRIP,
  DATE-COMPLTD, RESULT)

If it is assumed that an employee is only ever allowed to attend a course once, pass or fail, then a combination of EMPL-NO and COURSE-NO will uniquely identify the other fields. The key is composite, in that it is composed of two or more fields. Alternatively the EMPL-NO could be combined with COURSE-DESCRIP, which is the composite alternative key. If an employee had attended three training courses, the original one record would now be replaced by four – one EMPL-BASIC-DATA, and three EMPL-TRAIN-DATAs all having the same value for EMPL-NO. The benefits of normalization can be seen at this stage. For example, adding a digit to the SALARY field would not involve a change to processes which just used the training data,

whereas in the former structure every process which used EMPLOYEE-DATA would need modification.

The structures EMPL-BASIC-DATA and EMPL-TRAIN-DATA are said to be in first normal form (1NF) because they do not contain repeating groups.

The meaning of line three is that the fields must depend upon the whole of the key and not just a part of it. It follows then that line three will only need to apply to data structures with composite keys. EMPL-BASIC-DATA does not need to be changed because it has a single key field. It is already in second normal form (2NF).

Each field in EMPL-TRAIN-DATA needs to be considered in conjunction with the whole key to see if it is possible to determine the value of a field using only a part of the composite key. Looking at COURSE-DESCRIP and the key it can be seen that if you know the COURSE-NO you could determine the COURSE-DESCRIP independent of the EMPL-NO. COURSE-DESCRIP, therefore, does not depend upon the whole key. The two other fields both need the whole key to determine them, e.g. if either the employee or the course to which we are referring are unknown, the DATE-COMPLTD and RESULT cannot be specified.

The solution is again to split the structure, this time taking out the part(s) which does not need the whole key:

EMPL-TRAINING-DATA
  (EMPL-NO, COURSE-NO,
  DATE-COMPLTD, RESULT)
COURSE-DATA
  (COURSE-NO,
  COURSE-DESCRIP)

Alternatively, the COURSE-DESCRIP could have been left in EMPL-TRAINING-DATA. It is necessary to have a common field so that no data is lost, and the original EMPLOYEE-DATA could be reconstructed if necessary.

The benefits here include the fact that course information can be stored prior to an employee attending the course, which was not previously possible. Physically, 2NF structures will occupy less space than 1NF structures in general, because

whereas the COURSE-DESCRIP occurred in
1NF for each employee that attended the course,
now it will only be held once. There will be more
occurrences of COURSE-NO, as there were of
EMPL-NO in the earlier stage, but rarely is this a
significant use of storage.

In moving the structures into third normal
form (3NF), line 4 applies. The fields must
depend upon the key or alternative keys. This is
why the plural 'keys' is used in line four. The
inclusion of alternative keys is simply because if
both the key and the alternative can uniquely
identify some one thing in the world, then it
follows that any fields which can be determined
by the key can also be determined by the
alternative key.

The procedure used here is to consider all the
non-key fields to see if there are (1) any
dependencies which can be split into a separate
data structure and (2) fields which can be derived
from other fields.

There are no non-key fields in
COURSE-DATA and so it must be in 3NF
already. In EMPL-TRAINING-DATA,
DATE-COMPLTD and RESULT
are independent of each other. In
EMPL-BASIC-DATA, there are relationships
between non-key fields. SALARY and
MTHLY-PAY are related by the fact that
SALARY is simply twelve times MTHLY pay.
One can be derived from the other and is
therefore redundant. There is also a relationship
between BANK-NO and BANK-NADRS. Given
the bank's code number, its name and address
could be determined and vice versa. A separate
data structure is set up to contain the bank
information:

EMPL-BASE-DATA
(EMPL-NO, EMPL-NAME,
SALARY, BANK-NO)
BANK-DATA
(BANK-NO, BANK-NADRS)

MTHLY-PAY has been dropped altogether,
and physical space savings could result from the
non-repetition of BANK-NADRS. This also has
the benefit that bank information is independent

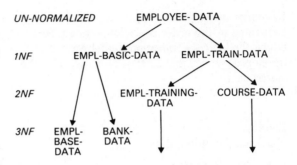

Figure 54 *Normalization: employee data*

of employee information. One may exist without
the other, and changes in one do not affect the
other. Figure 54 summarizes this.

Normalization of the EMPLOYEE-DATA
showed that it contained four separate groups of
data. It identified the fields which belonged to
each group and established simple structures with
a minimum of redundancy. These separate
structures make the system very flexible because
each may be processed independently of the
others, e.g. it would be relatively simple to obtain
a list of banks used. If a new application wishes to
use the COURSE-DATA, it already exists
separately from employees, and any changes to
the layout of fields would only have impact upon
processes using COURSE-DATA.

In retrospect, these four components may well
appear obvious. Possibly they did at the outset.
After all, normalization has been described as a
set of rules for making all designers do what good
designers have been doing intuitively.

Once a store is in 1NF an alternative approach
to normalization can be taken. This is the
application of the Boyce-Codd rule, which states
that every determinant in a structure must be
either a primary or an alternative key. If this rule
is applied to all structures, splitting where
necessary, the final stores are said to be in
Boyce-Codd normal form, BCNF. This is a
slightly 'higher' form than 3NF. There are fourth
and fifth normal forms where the problems of one
field determining a group of values for another
field are handled. However, the practical need for
these forms is very limited and for the present
purposes they will be disregarded.

**Example: order processing**
Returning to the order processing system for which the logical application model was developed, we can make a start on structuring the stored data.

*Essential*
The essential stored data was:

CUSTOMER-DATA
  (CUST-NO, CUST-NAME,
  DELIV-ADRS, DISCOUNT %)
ITEM-DATA
  (ITEM-NO, ITEM-DESCRIP,
  BIN-NO, ITEM-PRICE,
  ITEM-DISCOUNT %, ITEM-TAX %)
SYSTEM-DATA
  (TODAYS-DATE, LAST-ORDNO-USED)

The SYSTEM-DATA will not be considered for restructuring because it is basically a list of working values or parameters which the system uses on a regular basis. The fields held are independent of each other and depend upon the whole system at a particular point in its operation.

Apply normalization to the customer and item data:

Q  Have the keys been identified?
A  Yes.
Q  Given the key, can all fields be determined?
A  Yes (this assumes that ITEM-TAX % does vary with the item and is not completely independent of it).
Q  Are there any repeating groups of data?
A  No, so they are already in 1NF.
Q  Do the fields depend upon the whole key?
A  There are no composite keys, so the data structures are already in 2NF.
Q  Are there any non-key relationships?
A  No, so the data is in 3NF.

*Necessary*
The necessary data to be stored adds INV-ADRS to the CUSTOMER-DATA:

CUSTOMER-DATA
  (CUST-NO, CUST-NAME,
  DELIV-ADRS, DISCOUNT %,
  INV-ADRS)

The invoice and delivery addresses can vary independently of each other, e.g. a company with a central accounting department and several depots. It is because each depot could have its own account that CUST-NAME and INV-ADRS are not candidate keys. The addition of this field does not alter the fact that CUSTOMER-DATA is already in 3NF. The reader can check this by going through the proceding questions again.

The necessary objectives lead to a large increase in the product information:

ITEM-DATA
  (ITEM-NO, ITEM-DESCRIP,
  BIN-NO, ITEM-PRICE, ITEM DISCOUNT
  %, ITEM-TAX %, RE-ORD-QTY, SUPLR*
  (SUPL-NAME, SUPL-ADRS,
  SUPL-CONTACT, LAST-PURCH-DATE,
  LAST-COST), QOH)

All the keys have been identified. All the fields can be determined by the key. There is a repeating group, and so the SUPLR data needs to be split out from ITEM-DATA, but will have to take the ITEM-NO with it:

ITEM-BASIC-DATA
  (ITEM-NO, ITEM-DESCRIP,
  BIN-NO, ITEM-PRICE, ITEM-DISCOUNT
  %, ITEM-TAX %, RE-ORD-QTY, QOH)
SUPLR-DATA
  (ITEM-NO, SUPL-NAME, SUPL-ADRS,
  SUPL-CONTACT, LAST-PURCH-DATE,
  LAST-COST)

These data structures are in 1NF; ITEM-BASIC-DATA, having only a single field key, is also in 2NF. Do the fields in SUPLR-DATA depend upon the whole of their composite key? The answer here is 'no'. Although the person with whom the purchase was made, and the date and cost of the last purchase, are specific to a combination of the item and the supplier, the SUPL-ADRS depends only upon the SUPL-NAME.

LAST-BUY-DATA
   (ITEM-NO, SUPL-NAME,
   SUPL-CONTACT, LAST-PURCH-DATE,
   LAST-COST)
SUPPLIER-DATA
   (SUPL-NAME, SUPL-ADRS)

The final operation ensures that there are no non-key dependencies, and so these structures are also in 3NF.

*Desirable*
As a result of the desirable objectives, the CUSTOMER-DATA has the credit limit and customer group added to it. The product group was added to the original ITEM-DATA and can now be put with the ITEM-BASIC-DATA. The addition of these three fields leaves the data still in 3NF.

Objective D2 for sales analysis adds to the list of stored data with:

SALES-TARGET-DATA
   (ANAL-CLASS, MONTH, TARGET)
SALES-DETAIL-DATA
   (CUST-GROUP, PROD-GROUP,
   ORDER-DATE, ITEM-PRICE,
   ITEM-DISCOUNT %, DISCOUNT %, QTY)

The SALES-TARGET-DATA is in 3NF because the non-key field TARGET needs both the other fields to determine it. The SALES-DETAIL-DATA presents some problems, however, because it is not unique. There are no fields in this data store which can form a unique key, and so normalization cannot proceed. It would be possible to regard the SALES-DETAIL-DATA as some type of special case and therefore exempt from normalization. Better, however, to look at exactly what the data stored does represent, with a view to adding a key to it. This approach is in line with the overall aim of keeping the data model and the real world closely related. The real-world things which SALES-DETAIL-DATA represents are order lines received. The data which could uniquely identify an order line is ORDER-NO and ITEM-NO. Assuming this data is added to the store, the real-world thing which is being described can be identified:

SALE-LINE DATA
   (ORDER-NO, ITEM-NO, CUST-GROUP,
   PRODUCT-GROUP, ORDER-DATE,
   ITEM-PRICE, ITEM-DISCOUNT %,
   DISCOUNT %, QTY)

This data store may now be normalized. There are no repeating groups. Do the fields depend upon the whole key? The fields ORDER-DATE, CUST-GROUP and DISCOUNT % apply to the whole order and not just one line of it. The fields PRODUCT-GROUP, ITEM-PRICE and ITEM-DISCOUNT % are not dependent just upon ITEM-NO because the values for these items could change between one order for an item and a subsequent order for that same item. These fields cannot therefore be determined by the ITEM-NO alone, and do need the ORDER-NO, which places them in their historical context. A similar argument would apply to the CUST-GROUP and DISCOUNT % if CUST-NO were in the store. The reader should note that a detailed knowledge of exactly what the data represents is required, and that apparent dependencies between say an ITEM-NO and an ITEM-PRICE may not be valid.

SOLD-ORDER-DATA
   (ORDER-NO, ORDER-DATE,
   CUST-GROUP, DISCOUNT %)
SOLD-ORDLIN-DATA
   (ORDER-NO, ITEM-NO, PROD-GROUP,
   ITEM-PRICE, ITEM-DISCOUNT %, QTY)

These stores are then in 2NF. They are also in 3NF because there are no relationships between non-key fields.

We turn our attention to objective D3 and the DESPATCH-STATS; the data stores involved are:

DESPATCH-DETAIL-DATA
   (ORDER-DATE, DESPATCH-DATE,
   ITEM-PRICE, ITEM-DISCOUNT %,
   ITEM-TAX %, DISCOUNT %, QTY)
ORDER-DATA
   (ORDER-NO, ORDER-DATE, DISCOUNT
   %)

The ORDER-DATA is already in 3NF, but as with the SALES-DETAIL-DATA there is no key for the detail data, and reference needs to be made to the underlying real thing being represented in the model. This approach leads to the inclusion of ORDER-NO and ITEM-NO because the data refers to order lines which have been despatched:

DESPATCH-LINE-DATA
(ORDER-NO, ITEM-NO, ORDER-DATE,
DESPATCH-DATE, ITEM-PRICE,
ITEM-DISCOUNT %, ITEM-TAX %,
DISCOUNT %, QTY)

As with the sales analysis data, this can be broken down into that which refers to the whole order and that which is specific to a line, again noting that the ITEM-DATA and CUSTOMER-DATA cannot be used because the data used in this part of the system is historical.

DESP-ORDER-DATA
(ORDER-NO, ORDER-DATE, DISCOUNT %)
DESP-LINE-DATA
(ORDER-NO, ITEM-NO,
DESPATCH-DATE, ITEM-PRICE,
ITEM-DISCOUNT %, ITEM TAX %, QTY)

The ten underlined data structures in Figure 55 are capable of holding the stored data for all the E, N and D objectives.

As a result of normalization, CUSTOMER-DATA, SALES-TARGET-DATA and ORDER-DATA have remained the same.

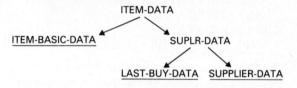

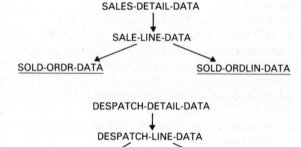

Figure 55   *Normalization: order processing*

## Courting

This is summarized as:

For each class of objectives:
(a) Identify any data stores which describe the same entities and join them together.
(b) Identify and name any useful relationships between stores.
(c) Update the data dictionary.

This step of the design is concerned with finding data which will be held twice, and eliminating this redundancy. This is important because the normalization is only applied to single data stores and it is quite possible that overlapping data existed in the stores. In normalizing the EMPLOYEE-DATA of Chapter 6, stage 2, four separate structures were identified (see previous section):

EMPL-TRAINING-DATA
(EMPL-NO, COURSE-NO,
DATE-COMPLTD, RESULT)
COURSE-DATA

```
    (COURSE-NO,
     COURSE-DESCRIP)
EMPL-BASE-DATA
    (EMPL-NO, EMPL-NAME,
     SALARY, BANK-NO)
BANK-DATA
    (BANK NO, BANK-NADRS)
```

If another part of the design included the training department, a store for lecturers could have been defined:

```
LECTURER-DATA
    (LECT-NAME, DATE-JOINED, TAUGHT*
    (COURSE-NO, COURSE-DESCRIPT),
    PREPARED* (COURSE-NO,
COURSE-TITLE))
```

In 3NF this could be:

```
LECT-DATA
    (LECT-NAME, DATE-JOINED)
TAUGHT-DATA
    (LECT-NAME, COURSE-NO)

PREPARED-DATA
    (LECT-NAME, COURSE-NO)
COURSE-DATA
    (COURSE-NO, COURSE-TITLE)
```

Intuitively it can be seen that there are many overlaps between the employee and training data. A good guideline to use is to check to see if two structures share a common identifier or candidate identifier. Wherever common keys occur there is a good chance that the same real-world object is being described and that the structures can be merged. For example, two groups of data both having the employee name M. Gandhi as the value of that identifier probably contain data about the same real-world person. The designer needs to know of any synonyms or homonyms, as well as to distinguish between stores which hold the same data items to represent transactions in different states, e.g. satisfied orders, back orders, or forward orders.

In the example here, LECT-DATA and EMPL-BASE-DATA could be merged. The new data store would be able to support both views of this data while adhering to the general principle that a single real-world entity has data stored

about it, and only it, in one place only. Likewise the two COURSE-DATA structures could be merged together. The structures TAUGHT-DATA and PREPARED-DATA would not be merged because they represent different things. The addition of an extra field would allow a merger. This is not necessary at this stage, and should not be done because it limits future flexibility. For example, if the number of students taught on a course by a lecturer were to be added to the store, any processes which just used PREPARED-DATA would also need their data definitions amending.

### Example: order processing

*Essential*
At the essential level, there are just two data stores which are independent of each other, and there is no overlap of data between them (Figure 56).
*Necessary*
At the necessary level, not only are new fields added to the CUSTOMER-DATA store, but three new structures are introduced as a result of additions to the original ITEM-DATA which normalization split out. The new structures – ITEM-BASIC-DATA, LAST-BUY-DATA and SUPPLIER-DATA – are related to each other (Figure 57).

The relationships between the data structure, as shown by the arrows on the diagram, need to be given names. (This helps to avoid the ambiguity which could arise if two structures are related in a complex way; for example, STUDENT and STAFF structures could be related by lines representing teachers, supervisors, tutors or counsellors.) In this case the ITEM-BOUGHT relationship links data about items with a record of purchases of items. The SUPPLIED-ITEM links the supplier data with a record of items

Figure 56 *Courting: essential*

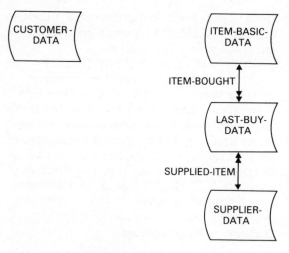

Figure 57   *Courting: necessary*

supplied by them. In the former case the relationship is possible because of the shared field ITEM-NO, and in the latter case SUPL-NAME supports the relationship.

The arrowheads show that one item can have a relationship with many LAST-BUY-DATA entries, but that each LAST-BUY-DATA entry can only be related to one item. A similar one-to-many relationship exists between the SUPPLIER-DATA and LAST-BUY-DATA.

### Desirable

In the consideration of the desirable objectives, the impact of each one will be taken in turn.

*Credit control* involves only the addition of the field CREDIT-LIM to the CUSTOMER-DATA,

which still stands alone.

For *sales analysis*, the analysis classes are included in the customer and product data, and also there is the addition of three new structures (Figure 58).

The SOLD-ORDERED-LINES relationship links the order header information with the detailed line information. Both structures contain the field ORDER-NO. Note that not all possible links are shown. SOLD-ORDLIN-DATA holds the ITEM-NO, as does ITEM-BASIC-DATA, but a link between the two could be very misleading as explained earlier. A link between SOLD-ORDR-DATA (which contains DISCOUNT %) and CUSTOMER-DATA (which also contains DISCOUNT %) is possible but is not very meaningful.

For *despatch statistics*, three new structures are encountered which have keys that overlap with each other and existing keys. Consider the identical structures ORDER-DATA and DESP-ORDR-DATA. They both contain information describing an order, and identify it by the key ORDER-NO. In the data model these two can be merged into one, say DESP-ORDER-DATA. This will have a one-to-many relationship with DESP-LINE-DATA, as one order may own many lines but one line may belong to only one order (Figure 59).

There is obviously a great deal of overlap between the data held for objectives D2 and D3. If both objectives are considered together, the first point to note is that they keys are the same, being ORDER-NO and ORDER-NO with

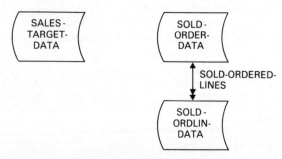

Figure 58   *Courting: desirable: sales analysis*

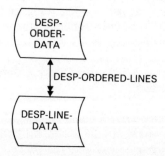

Figure 59   *Courting: desirable: despatch statistics*

ITEM-NO. Are both data stores describing the same thing? In answering this question the designer needs to consider time: When are the stores created? What might happen between the creation of an entry in SOLD-ORDLIN-DATA and the creation of an entry in DESP-LINE-DATA, both referring to the same real-world order line? The only way of answering these questions about what exactly the data means is through intimate knowledge of the system. In this case an order may be rejected by the CREDIT-CHECK if this objective is incorporated in the final design. If this were not included the stores could be simply merged, because every ORDER received is despatched in full eventually.

When allowance is made for the credit control, either two sets of data can be held, or the structures can be merged and some extra non-key field introduced. This extra data would be transparent to the user but will be based upon the real order. The real difference between the two types of orders is whether or not credit was available. If the CREDIT-LIM is held with the order header then the distinction can be recreated as and when necessary. Alternatively, the presence or absence of the DESPATCH-DATE can be used in the present case. This would be practical for the GENERATE-DSTATS as non-despatched orders, either rejected or still awaiting despatch, are ignored by this process. This option has not been selected because, although it meets the existing objectives in

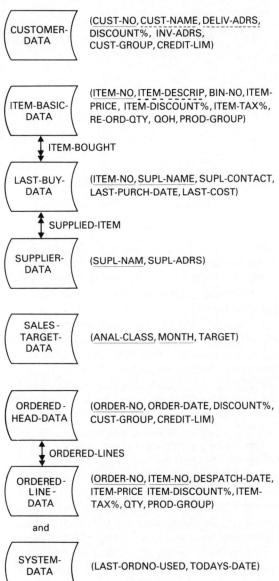

Figure 61 *Courting: all objectives*

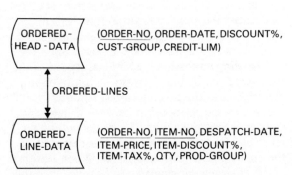

Figure 60 *Courting: desirable: stores statistics*

making rejected and awaiting despatch orders inseparable, it is making the system less flexible than it could be. If the designer was confident that these two types of order would not need separating, so as to meet some future demand

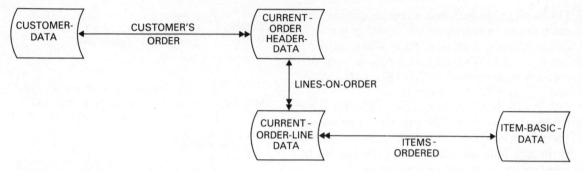

Figure 62   *Relation of customers and orders*

made of the system, the DESPATCH-DATE could be used. The key data should not be changed otherwise the new data structure would be identifying something different from the old structures.

Joining the structures involves simple concatenation and elimination of redundancy, as shown in Figure 60. Note that the names of these data stores are kept in the past tense – ORDERED – to signify that they are historical and may contain information which is not the same as that currently used by the system, e.g. ITEM-PRICE or DISCOUNT %.

The reader's attention is drawn to the fact that unless the ORDER-NO and ITEM-NO were included in the stored data for the sales and despatch details, the joining of the stores would not have been possible. It is because both sales and despatch data identify the precise real-world object they represent that joining can take place.

The inclusion of the stored data for all the objectives gives the data model of Figure 61. It represents the seven things in the real world which the system needs to know about, together with the parameters used by the system itself.

As an example of how the data modelling has brought the system closer to the real world, consider the reorganization of SALES-DETAIL-DATA and DESPATCH-DETAIL-DATA. If both objectives are implemented they can be based upon shared data structures, as they are both derived from the same things – orders. If either objective is implemented alone then the original detailed data has been restructured into header and line levels. This is a more accurate reflection of reality than the data stores developed in the application modelling, which were designed for a single purpose only.

There are relationships between the data which are not shown, for example: relate customers to items by current orders. This involves storing the current order data which represents the relationship (Figure 62).

If enquiries were made on the state of *current* orders by either CUSTOMERs or STOCK-CONTROL, then this model may need to be supported in the data store. The relationships shown in Figure 62 do exist whether or not they are held in the data store. In the example system, these relationships are represented in data flows and processes when needed, e.g. the flow STD-ORDER, or the process INVOICE-CALC (which adds order line information to create order header totals). If there was a need for enquiry facilities into current orders, then the data stores could be introduced then. Because the data model is based upon the reality being represented, additional aspects of the real world can be incorporated with minimum disturbance to the existing stores. It follows from the one-to-one relationship between things, and the data about them, that the model will be no more and no less complex than those aspects of the environment being described. When features of the environment change significantly, then the model will need to change.

# 8 Review and summary

When the data modelling is completed, the application model is reviewed. A summary of the logical design is then presented.

## Review

This is summarized as:

For each class of objectives:
(a) Check that the flows into store can support the model.
(b) Check that the model supports the flows out of it.
(c) Look for improvements in the design of the flows or processes to take advantage of the data model.

The final step is to review the application modelling in the light of the data modelling.
    Each class of objectives is taken in turn and the following topics considered:

1  Are the data flows into store sufficient to support the model?
2  Can the data model support all the flows out of it?
3  Are any improvements in the design of the flows or processes possible to take advantage of the data model?

### Example: order processing

*Essential*
At the level of essential objectives no changes were made by the data modelling to the stored data as originally envisaged. This means that the essential logical application model already matches the data model.

*Necessary*
As a result of the necessary objectives the ITEM-DATA was expanded and then split into three groups. In answer to the above questions:

1  Yes, the data flows into store will be sufficient because all that has happened is that the details previously to be stored in ITEM-DATA have been split up; there are no new fields stored, and so the flows in will be adequate.
2  Yes, the stores out can be supported because there is no reduction in the data being stored, just a reorganization.
3  A review of stage 4 of the application modelling does not suggest any areas of improvement. Only the process SEND-STOCKOUT will use the LAST-BUY-DATA and SUPPLIER-DATA, and the structuring of data in the flows seems quite appropriate. Similarly, no changes to INVOICE production is envisaged, with all the item data coming from ITEM-BASIC-DATA.

*Desirable*
The desirable objective of *credit control* had a profound effect upon the process model but only a slight impact upon the data model. The CUSTOMER-DATA has a field added to it (CREDIT-LIM). This field is also carried over for use in the analysis systems to distinguish accepted from rejected orders. The flows do not need changing and improvements cannot be seen to follow on from the data model, which has had no impact upon CUSTOMER-DATA.
    In contrast to credit control, the data stores for the *sales analysis* objective have been significantly changed. First, the normalization process required there to be a flow of ORDER-NO and ITEM-NO into store along with the sales details. This suggests a change to the process RECEIVE-ORDER to include the ORDER-NO on the RO-SANAL data flow. The process which receives this flow, STORE-SALES-DETAIL, can then include the ORDER-NO on the flow STOR-SANAL data flow into storage (Figure 63).

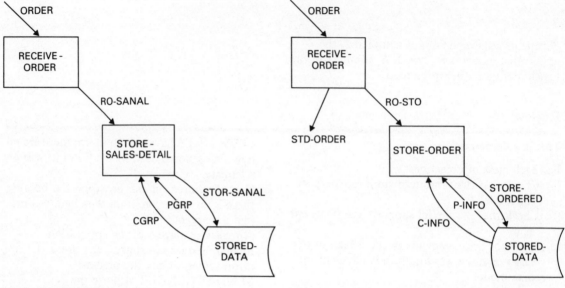

Figure 63   *Review: desirable:*
*STORE-SALES-DETAIL*

Figure 64   *Review: desirable: STORE-ORDER*

The changed flows are:

RO-SANAL
  (ORDER-NO, ORDER-DATE, CUST-NO,
  LINE* (ITEM-NO, QTY))

and

STOR-SANAL
  (ORDER-NO, CUST-GROUP,
  ORDER-DATE, DISCOUNT %, OLINE*
  (ITEM-NO, PROD-GROUP, ITEM-PRICE,
  ITEM-DISCOUNT%, QTY))

Previously STORE-SALES-DETAIL had
transferred one entry for every LINE being
received; this revision sends the order header and
lines information together which is somewhat
more compact, and better represents the true
nature of the order. Similarly, the process
GENERATE-SANAL may be amended so that
rather than being driven by the receipt of
information at an order line level, data can be
obtained which is in the same form as the real
order, i.e. with an order header followed by one
or more detail lines. The flow SANAL-DETL

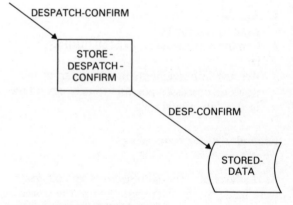

Figure 65   *Review: desirable:*
*DESPATCH-CONFIRM*

from store to the process would also need to be
modified.

Note also that in Figure 63 the data model is
shown as the single symbol STORED-DATA.
The reason for the separateness in the original
application modelling was as a preliminary to the
data modelling. This is no longer necessary.

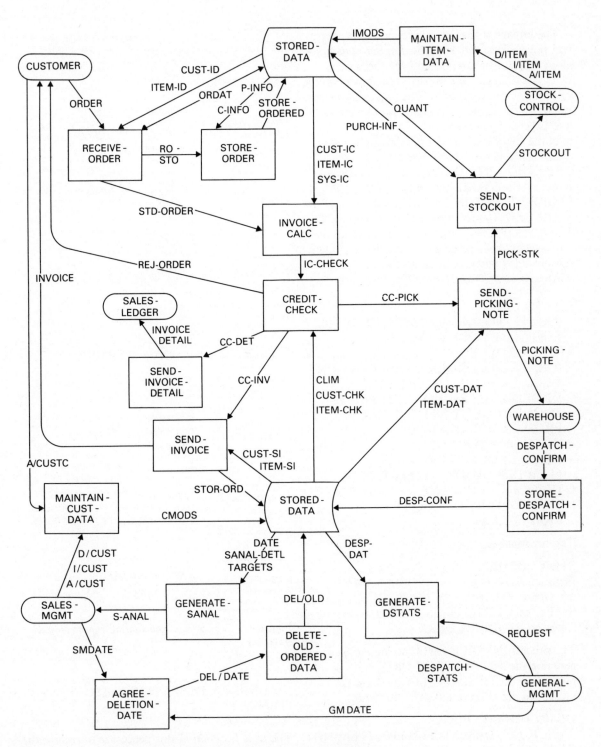

Figure 66 *Logical application model for all objectives: order processing*

The impact of the data model on the processes and flows associated with the *despatch statistics* alone will not be considered here, because it would be similar to the impact of the model on the sales analysis objective D2. The impact of the data model on the application model for objectives D2 *and* D3 will be considered.

In the application model the data to be held in ORDERED-HEAD-DATA and ORDERED-LINE-DATA is sent from three sources – the STORE-SALES-DETAIL the STORE-DESPATCH-DETAIL and, as the flow STOR-ORD, the INVOICE-CALC process. The data model will store the details of an order as soon as it has been received and the despatch date can be added when notified by the WAREHOUSE (Figure 64). The flows are:

RO-STO
    (ORDER-NO, ORDER-DATE, CUST-NO, LINE* (ITEM-NO, QTY))
STORE-ORDERED
    (ORDER-NO, ORDER-DATE, DISCOUNT %, CUST-GROUP, CREDIT-LIM, ORDLINE* (ITEM-NO, ITEM-PRICE, ITEM-DISCOUNT %, ITEM-TAX %, PROD-GROUP, QTY))
P-INFO, SA = ITEM-NO
    (PROD-GROUP, ITEM-PRICE, ITEM-DISCOUNT %, ITEM-TAX %)
C-INFO, SA = CUST-NO
    (CUST-GROUP, DISCOUNT %, CREDIT-LIM)

The functions are:

STORE-ORDER
For each RO-STO:
(a)  Obtain C-INFO.
(b)  For each LINE: obtain P-INFO.
(c)  Send STORE-ORDER.

The process INVOICE-CALC no longer needs to generate the data flow STOR-ORD, and processing the DESPATCH-CONFIRM is much simpler (Figure 65). The flows are:

DESPATCH-CONFIRM
    (PICK-NO, DESPATCH-DATE, ITEM-NO)
DESP-CONFIRM

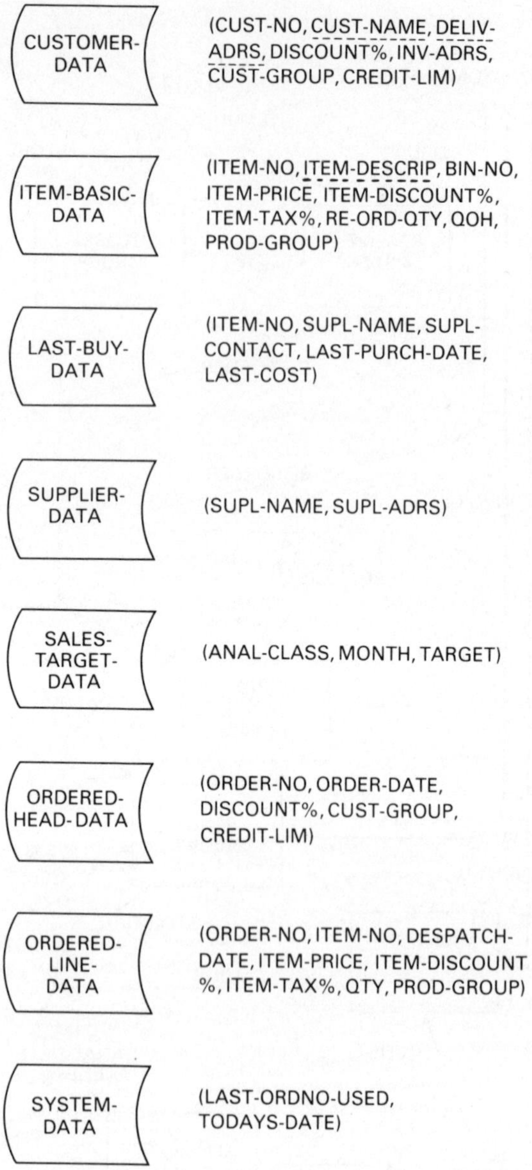

CUSTOMER-DATA — (CUST-NO, CUST-NAME, DELIV-ADRS, DISCOUNT%, INV-ADRS, CUST-GROUP, CREDIT-LIM)

ITEM-BASIC-DATA — (ITEM-NO, ITEM-DESCRIP, BIN-NO, ITEM-PRICE, ITEM-DISCOUNT%, ITEM-TAX%, RE-ORD-QTY, QOH, PROD-GROUP)

LAST-BUY-DATA — (ITEM-NO, SUPL-NAME, SUPL-CONTACT, LAST-PURCH-DATE, LAST-COST)

SUPPLIER-DATA — (SUPL-NAME, SUPL-ADRS)

SALES-TARGET-DATA — (ANAL-CLASS, MONTH, TARGET)

ORDERED-HEAD-DATA — (ORDER-NO, ORDER-DATE, DISCOUNT%, CUST-GROUP, CREDIT-LIM)

ORDERED-LINE-DATA — (ORDER-NO, ITEM-NO, DESPATCH-DATE, ITEM-PRICE, ITEM-DISCOUNT%, ITEM-TAX%, QTY, PROD-GROUP)

SYSTEM-DATA — (LAST-ORDNO-USED, TODAYS-DATE)

Figure 67   *Logical data model for all objectives: order processing*

(ORDER-NO, DESPATCH-DATE, ITEM-NO)

The only function of this process is to receive the DESPATCH-CONFIRM and send the details into store where they will be added into ORDERED-LINE-DATA.

The data flow out of store to the process GENERATE-SANAL can be in the same form as described previously, based upon the data model. The process GENERATE-DSTATS would need modification to include an accumulation of the NET-VALUE of the order from the lines despatch values, which are already calculated. If the CREDIT-LIM is $<$ NET-VALUE then the data is not included in the despatch statistics. This process could also receive data structured with a header and lines rather than all data being at the line level.

## Summary

A series of models of the application area, its processes and data have been developed and described with the use of data flow diagrams. It has been assumed that documentation, in the form of a data dictionary, held all the supporting detail. These models were categorized (E, E + N, E + N + D) according to the design objectives from which they were developed. The definition of outputs prior to consideration of the internal aspects of data, processes and maintenance also emphasized the application area rather than the data processing system. These models do not contain any presumptions about how they will physically be implemented, and as such are independent of hardware or software changes. This high-level system description provides a standard which the physical implementations are required to meet.

The data model was developed so as to reflect the parts of the world which the enterprize sees as relevant to this application area. It was derived from the data stores of the application model using normalization and then courting. Again, the model provides a high-level description which will transcend specific data storage systems, be they filing cabinets, file management software, or relational data base machines.

The review of the design ensured that the two models were consistent with each other. This process will normally be ongoing but the presence of an explicit review stage forces this co-ordination. It would be possible to keep the two models separate from each other and allow some software to act as an intermediary. Specifically, this would be a data base management system which based its conceptual schema on the data model and its external schema around the data stores, as described in the application model. (In fact the external schema would be derived from the flows to and from storage, but would in total describe the application models data stores.)

The design at this high level is complete, and it is possible to move on to develop a physical implementation of (some of) the objectives. The logical application model is shown in Figure 66, followed by its logical data model (Figure 67). The presumption is that all the essential supporting detail is held elsewhere in the documentation.

## Exercises for Part Two

2.1 An improved understanding of, and skill in, logical design will follow from doing the work. The best example for learning purposes is one that is simple enough not to obscure the design process in its own detail, and yet allows scope for the derivation of both processes and stores from some objectives. You are encouraged to find your own sample problem and work out a design for it. There is no outline solution for this exercise!

2.2 It has been suggested that DM/1 would need

modifying to make it suitable for the design of information retrieval systems. What modifications would be needed?

2.3  In stage 3 the designer needs to distinguish between data which will be stored and data which will be input. Why is this not always simple?

2.4  In what circumstances could stage 5 be redundant?

2.5  A car park management company stores data on parking permits issued. A person has an annual permit which is for a specific car in a specific car park. The information held is currently in the form:

(NAME, ADDRESS, CAR-NO, COLOUR, TYPE, CAR-PARK, PAID)

Normalize this data, identifying keys. What would the data model be if a person could have several permits at the same time for which they were billed separately?

# Part Three

# Physical design

# 9 Outline design

Once a rigorous definition of what is required of the new system has been developed during the stage of logical design, the job of deciding in broad terms how the system will work must be undertaken. The essence of this is the drawing of boundaries based upon physical units, i.e. people, components, disks, filing cabinets etc.

The first part of this chapter will describe the major factors which influence the selection of how data will be processed in a system. This covers the areas of response times and volumes, distributed processing, computing aspects, and the drawing of man/machine boundaries. By considering these areas the designer is able to generate a 'first sketch' of the physical system which will subsequently be checked and refined. The uniqueness of each situation means that it is difficult to give useful suggestions on how this sketch is created. The novice may find hope in the fact that many designers feel that this stage does not exist as such. Instead, the processing methods are either prescribed or have evolved with the design so far to the state where it appears the only viable option.

Even when the hardware and software, together with design standards, are determined in advance of the project or during an initial feasibility study, there are still decisions to be made. The availability of sophisticated software and cheap processing power means that few designs are completely unworkable, but there is a great deal of difference between systems which are well known as troublesome and those which continue for years almost unnoticed with simple maintenance. The decisions made during physical design are about how to make optimum use of available resources (where optimum includes such aspects as flexibility and portability).

The sequence then is the production of a first sketch of the physical system, based upon the logical design. This will incorporate knowledge about the physical capacities and requirements of the system as collected during systems analysis. This will be done for a logical system

essential + necessary, or
essential + necessary + desirable. The first sketch is then checked to make sure that the new system will fit within any design constraints such as volume of stored data, run times and implementation times. This is initially done for the first sketch, which is either expanded towards the desirable objectives or contracted, depending upon the fit of the system to the constraints. By this means the first sketch is refined and developed into the single outline design.

A profitable use of prototypes may take place at the end of outline design. The outline design should be presented to the users prior to commencing detail design, and then a prototype can provide a demonstration of the final system. The users need to be satisfied that their requirements will be met by the new system and much of their concern lies with the input and output as well as with a description of the system objectives, constraints and general design. At this stage in the design the top has been followed down to the point where the data items which will flow in and out of the system are known, and the media for this flow is selected. The prototype can then generate these flows and users can be asked to confirm that the output is what they need and that they can provide the input. The prototype does not replace the need for confirmation of the system at a top level, but rather makes it much easier for users to appraise the detail of the system. If the design is accepted then the use of application generator software means that it is relatively easy for end users to become involved in designing their own input and output, which can then be mocked up with the prototype and seen by the users prior to final detail design.

If the users do not accept the design, further work may need to be done at the logical or the outline stages. The most likely outcome is qualified approval for the outline design, such that some modifications need to be made. A reminder is given that live projects tend to be iterative, in contrast to the sequential nature of books.

# First sketch

Under the following headings are described some of the major factors which influence the physical design of a system; each individual system will need the factors which are significant for it.

## Response times

The major factor in selecting the processing media is speed. How quickly does the job need to be done? The usual starting-point here is the consideration of the timing requirements of the output data flows to external entities. The systems analyst should have obtained information on the timing of these output data flows, e.g. a report to be produced by 9 a.m. the next day, or a customer's account status to be available while the customer is still on the telephone. This information should be recorded in the documentation and is essential for this stage of the design.

It is often useful to categorize the required speed of processing as the implications of this timing constraint are reasonably well established. The following categories are suggested:

### Immediate processing

This is the nearest to true real-time processing. It consists of an event in the environment causing an interrupt to any current processing activities so that the information regarding this event can be processed immediately. In this way the computer system can respond to changes within a fraction of a second. Typical examples are process control, robotics and machine control systems.

### Real-time processing

This is better termed 'relevant time' or conversational. Here the computer system responds to changes in the environment in a matter of seconds (typically between 1 and 15). The precise speed depends upon the needs of the users of the system. For example, if orders are being taken over the telephone and immediately entered into a computer via a VDU, each item of information must be accepted and validated very quickly (possibly within 1 second). However, at the end of the order a delay of around 30 seconds may be acceptable while files are updated and the preliminary part of the next telephone conversation takes place.

### Near time processing

This is an intermediate level where jobs are processed as soon as it is convenient to do so, and are usually put in a queue and allotted a priority level. The results may be available within minutes or hours, and will depend upon the other work being done by the computer at the time of the request and the priority given to the job. Examples include remote job entry systems, and *ad hoc* management report production.

### Batch processing

Batch processing is periodic and usually predictable. Jobs may be run daily, weekly, monthly or even annually, and the results are available some time after the events to which they relate have occurred. In many cases this delay is wholly acceptable, e.g. sales analysis reports which refer to a data collected over a period.

If immediate processing is excluded from consideration as being beyond the scope of this book and what is usually understood by data processing systems, then the other three categories are often found working together within an institution. It would be most unusual for any organization to require only one speed of response; if a system handles mainly real-time enquiries, sooner or later file reorganization programs will need to be run and monthly statistical reports on usage may be necessary. Similarly, many users of purely batch systems would be glad to be able to obtain immediate answers to some questions, and happy to pay for this privilege.

If we turn now to the question of costs of the system designed, it can be said that the cost of the system (or part of it) is inversely proportional to the response time required:

$$\text{cost} \propto (\text{response requirements})^{-1}$$

Thus batch systems are cheaper than near-time

systems, which in turn are cheaper than real-time systems. Some of the reasons for this are:

1  The faster the response, the more sophisticated the software needs to be, in that it must schedule the requests, allocate resources and keep jobs separate and may need to allow interjob communication, i.e. support multiprogramming. (Figures suggest that system software for real-time systems may involve a CPU overhead in excess of 50 per cent, whereas for batch systems 25 per cent is more usual.)
2  The hardware may need to provide fast access to data, which will involve direct access devices and possibly communications equipment for faster input and output.
3  If the system is responding to events in the environment the demand for resources will vary and, although allowance for maximum demand may be necessary in some cases, most of the time it will be extremely wasteful.
4  Allowing users devices for remote input and output increases security problems and puts greater importance on the design of user-friendly interfaces, as well as making any system failures and down time more directly felt.

This is not to suggest that real-time systems are uneconomic – rather that wherever possible their use should be carefully considered, and only jobs which can justify the need for real-time processing should be so designed. Similarly, jobs which can be performed on a regular periodic batch basis do not need to be queued for processing during peak time. Even if an 'all terminal' system is in operation, this does not mean that high-priority real-time processing of the data needs to be performed for all jobs. The level of response provided needs to be a match between the needs of the job and a conservation of available resources. Many organizations operate a real-time system during the normal working hours, with a relatively low priority queue system running in conjunction with it. At the end of the working day any jobs still on the queue are processed and then the batch jobs run. It is this type of arrangement which allows optimum use of resources to be had, while at the same time providing the services required of the system.

The designer must consider the timing information collected by the analyst in conjunction with the logical design to establish how quickly each process needs to be performed, and this information is included in the description of the process. Similarly, the media on which the data is stored will be affected by these considerations, as well as the media which supports the data flows. By working inwards from the outputs, the first part of this categorization can be achieved.

For illustration, consider Figure 68 (given earlier as Figure 25). The data flow ACCOUNT POSITION may need to follow the request for an account enquiry within seconds. Similarly, the I/C ANALYSIS data flow may be needed on demanded. As for the inputs there may be a need to process payments as they are received so that receipts can be issued.

The next stage of this categorization is to consider what implications for other processes within the system follow on from the established response requirements, in particular the freshness of the data. Freshness refers to the up-to-dateness of the data upon which the output is based, e.g. the value of real-time enquiries would be somewhat dubious if the files which were being enquired upon were only updated monthly. Again, information defining the freshness of the data flowing out from the system should have been collected by the analyst, and the designer can now use this. If the ACCOUNT POSITION data flow needs to have fresh or real-time data, then it follows that the POST PAYMENTS, VALIDATE PAYMENTS and POST INVOICES processes will all need to be done in real time, thus keeping the sales ledger as accurate as possible short of having immediate processing facilities typical of process control systems. The designer is now in a position to identify those sections of the data flow diagram which need to be performed in real time, in near time and in batch.

A further factor to consider in this context is the volume of data being processed. If there are only twenty customers on the sales ledger and say

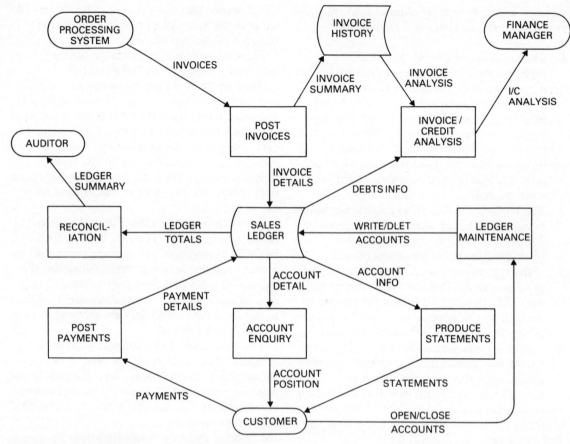

Figure 68    *Sales ledger system: final flow diagram*

five invoices per day, then a manual system will be capable of real-time processing with only one operator. As the amount of data increases, and with it the amount of repetitive work, machines become more worth while. Once on a computer, relatively small volumes of data will be processed very quickly. For example if the sales ledger now has 500 accounts stored on disk, serial processing should be able to retrieve a specified account in a matter of seconds. With small volumes of data, performance and storage criteria will almost inevitably be achieved irrespective of how the equipment is used.

The term 'hit rate' is used to describe the percentage of records in a file which will be accessed for an average run of a program. This only has meaning where transactions are collected together to be processed sequentially so as to take advantage of the fact that the position of the next master record is known as soon as the last one has been read; also double buffering to reduce I/O time could then be employed. Conversely, a low hit rate suggests processing by direct access.

The value of high and low in this context can be calculated and will vary with the hardware and the design of the system. The following variables would need to be taken into account. To process transactions against a sequential master file, they need to be sorted, and the time taken to do this needs to be included in an assessment of high or low. Similarly, the amount of buffering and possibly overflow on the sequential file can have an impact on the small amount of seek time incurred. Access directly to records does in fact mean that a whole block is physically moved from disk, and the time taken to find and retrieve the block needs calculating. Finding records will take longer if indexes are used rather than hashing, and again overflow will have an effect.

## Distributed processing

The availability of hardware and software which allows economic linking together of several processors and data stores leads to an increased likelihood of the designer building a distributed system. In the same way that real-time systems are more complex than batch systems, so distributed systems are more complex than their centralized equivalents. This is simply because of the extra hardware and software to pass data and control, over distances, as well as the usual facilities required at each processing node in the system. The fact that nearly every piece of hardware is becoming increasingly intelligent suggests that there will soon be no such thing as a truly centralized system. Designing systems which take advantage of the benefits of distributed processing without incurring too many of the penalties is a specialist topic. This brief treatment concerns itself with the general principles of which the designer should be aware.

The logical design should be capable of being implemented on one central system or on a distributed system. It is only at the stage of outline design that the choice needs to be made. Distributing a system may be done by partitioning it in a variety of ways.

Timing requirements may be such that enquiry and data entry need to be done in real time while there are several large jobs to be done in batch mode. Possibly a small computer could do the real time work, passing the data to a large machine (possibly at a bureau) for periodic processing.

A further partition may be made on the basis of a business function: each department could have its own machine. This leads to the obvious dangers of underuse of equipment, lack of standardization, and empire building. Properly managed this partitioning can be very effective, e.g. in obtaining users' involvement in their systems and developing systems geared to users'

needs. The danger lies in the possible duplication of effort and data, which was a major problem with the traditional application-oriented systems. The use of a central data base was seen as an aid to sharing data between application areas. Distributed data base systems do exist, and need to identify exactly what data is needed in one location only and what data needs to be shared between several locations. The data is then sited so as to reduce transmission traffic by keeping it as close to its users as possible. In order to achieve this a thorough analysis and design of local and global data models must have been made. Similarly, the processing to be done at each node needs to be carefully allocated to reduce redundancy.

The guideline here, as throughout the logical design, is to keep close to reality. If the logical data model and application model closely resemble the activites that are happening in the real world, then the computer system may be partitioned to take advantage of real-world divisions. If there are real boundaries in the business operations and environment, they can be incorporated into the system. The designer needs, however, to distinguish these from historical accidents, e.g. an organization may have two companies, one dealing in small tools and the other in large tools. If the markets they serve and the methods of processing the data are very different, each could have its own system. Alternatively the distinction could be the result of a merger and there could be very little real difference between the needs of the companies.

Natural geographic boundaries may be important, even if the information needs are identical. Before designing a system which distributed the processing to each geographical area, the designer needs to assess their stability. Are the operations going to continue to be performed in these diverse locations for a time sufficiently long to justify the design of a distributed system?

In conclusion, distributed systems need to have a rational division of processing and data to the nodes of the system. The location, either centrally or remotely, of the data or processes needs to be justified, on the basis of real and stable boundaries. However, the logical design should be able to support all the various physical designs without modification.

## Computing aspects

The processing may be divided along lines which are convenient to the data processors. In the past the nature of the available hardware and software has determined the nature of the processing; the modern equivalent is the need to use the latest software purchased, or possibly the need to follow some system design standards that determine the mode of processing to be used. The most obvious example here occurs for sequential file processing systems, where a large number of separate tasks are put together so that only one pass through a large file is required in order to achieve all these tasks. If the system is designed in this way, there is the obvious limitation that if and when direct access files replaced the sequential files, unless the system was redesigned it could not take advantage of the new facilities. Many systems running today were designed to be very efficient with a particular set of hardware, but unfortunately now run on more powerful hardware without being able to use the additional features, or even with worse performance than originally achieved. An alternative to this is designing the system around transactions rather than stores. With this approach, tasks which process a particular transaction type are put together so that, once a package of data has entered the system, it is fully processed before attention is turned to the next piece of data. To illustrate this transaction orientation, consider the enrolment of a student; this requires validation, file updating, and the production of a letter to the body sponsoring the student. In this case, all these jobs could be done by a single program as soon as the student was enrolled. This is in contrast to a system which, say, validated on-line and then passed the data to other tasks which ran in the background waiting for enough data to make it worth updating the files or using the printer.

The reader is referred back to the section 'Design objectives and contraints' in Chapter 1, which describes other factors (such as project funding) and their impact on design.

## Human/machine partition

We now turn specifically to the man/machine boundary. The general guide here is that whereas computers are good at solving algorithmic problems (those for which a set of rules can be devised which will always lead to a solution), people are good at solving heuristic problems (where the information may be ill defined; there may be several alternative goals and many routes to them.) Thus for the current state of the art of computer systems, where knowledge-based systems capable of solving 'fuzzy' problems are not commonplace, there are some jobs which must be done by people. Frequently heuristic problems arise where contact with other people occurs, and the job is to convert the requirements of the external person into a format which is structured enough to allow standardized processing. (A good example of a heuristic problem solver is the systems designer him/herself.) It is in these areas that the use of judgment, initiative and understanding are required, and help towards job satisfaction.

The algorithmic problems may be solved by either machines or people, and the decision is usually based upon a combination of social, economic and technical factors. Generally this includes such considerations as:

The quantity and quality of available staff
The long-term economic efficiency of the system
The short-term costs of implementing a computer-based system and/or training staff
The volume, speed, and accuracy of the work to be done.

As the cost of computer systems, particularly hardware, continues to fall and applications software is becoming increasingly more packaged and available, at relatively low cost, there are decreasing economic or technical requirements for people to do algorithmic work. Most usually, people are needed when the computer system does not fully meet the organization's requirements and neither the organization nor the system are capable of change. To make any more general statements regarding the allocation of work to people or computers would be unprofitable, as in reality each specific situation is so unique as to make the exceptions outweigh almost any guidelines that could be suggested. Intuition, common sense, an understanding of the power and limitations of both machines and human beings, and good luck, are necessary here. Generally, the designer needs to turn to the line management regarding the deployment of their staff.

## Reliability

The extent to which one can rely upon a system is influenced by a great many factors, only some of which will be dealt with here. The identification of assets and the sources of threats to such assets is the area of risk management. The terms 'mean time between failure' (MTBF) and 'mean time to repair' (MTTR) have been developed to quantify the degree of reliability required and the probability of achieving it. The emphasis here will be upon provision for failure of processing or data integrity as it most commonly occurs, and in regard to which the designer of a system may have some influence. Note that reliability is not the same thing as validity. The concern here is that the system is consistent: whether or not the data being manipulated is a valid representation of reality is a different topic.

For both processing and data integrity failures the sequence for handling errors is the same. First the error needs to be identified, and the sooner this can be done the less damage the error will have caused. The designer needs to build a system which will report all errors in such a way that attention is paid to them. Those operating the system must inspect, and act upon, the hardware error log which the operating system will produce. Once a problem has been identified its impact needs to be minimized. The design of the whole system into self-contained modules will do much to isolate errors within the directly affected area. The designer must specify precisely what action needs to be taken whenever an error is identified. This will usually be in the form of operating instructions or programmed error routines, depending upon the type of error. Good error handling instructions can go a long way towards isolating the impact of an error by eliminating the panic/random action which might

otherwise be taken. The impact of failure can also be reduced by allowing processing to continue wherever possible, i.e. by adopting a fall-back position. For example, if a payroll system will fail when new starters are encountered, the system may be operated for existing staff and the data for all new staff handled manually until the fault is corrected.

The next area of concern is the recovery of the system, which will be greatly assisted by documentation regarding what was happening at the time of the error. This is necessary so as to discover the cause(s) of the error, and fix such cause(s). Procedures for obtaining this information should be part of the error handling routines. After the hardware engineers or system maintenance staff have corrected the fault, then processing needs to be resumed from the point of failure. This involves two problems; first, knowing at which point the system stopped, precisely; and second, getting to that point. Knowledge of where the processing stopped can be improved if all operators are aware of their current position, e.g. messages confirming acceptance of transactions or stating what is happening during a screen-quiet period of processing will assist this. If the hardware gets a warning of imminent failure it may be able to dump its entire memory contents to disk, and then recovery is relatively simple once the fault is cleared. This is done by some systems when power failure is detected.

'Polymorphic' is a term used to describe systems which consist of several small parts rather than one large part. For example, 512 Kb of memory exists in eight 64 Kb modules. A failure in one module could still leave the machine working with 87 per cent of its memory. Distributed processing systems are in effect polymorphic with respect to processing. Network systems which allow a task to be processed at one of several sites also exemplify this idea. One possible danger here is dependence upon any single component. If a network operates within a factory and has its own clean power supply, then a failure of the power supply will take out the whole system. Similarly, if a network depends upon software which only runs from one node, or the operating system must have memory locations 0–64 K, then there is still vulnerability to complete failure. Wherever a system relies upon a single unit, be it a front-end or back-end machine, a communications link or a person, the realiability suffers.

Hardware failure is most likely to occur where moving parts are involved, primarily in keyboards, printers and disk drives. Keyboards can usually be interchanged, and printer data spooled, until a fault is corrected. Serious problems arise with disk failure because without the data some processing cannot be performed, and whereas back-up copies of programs or an operating system can be reloaded, file recovery is much more complex because of the constant updating. Dual recording of the live data is rarely worth while.

The separation of the design objectives into the priority classes (E/N/D) provides the designer with a basis for a fall-back position. As long as the physical design maintains the separation between processes in each class it will be possible for a 'graceful degradation' of processing through D to N and finally to E prior to halting the system. Each of these fall-back positions may involve the use of temporary stores to keep data which will later be used by a suspended job. In this way necessary processing does not just involve not running the desirable jobs; interfaces will need to be established. The classification of objectives thus forms the basis for handling partial hardware failure and as such will need to be incorporated into both manual and computer error handling routines. In the event of a complete hardware failure the system will, not surprisingly, stop. Once the hardware is working again the essential jobs can receive priority in recovery and operation until the backlog of work is reduced and necessary or desirable jobs can be processed. Polymorphism and the classification of objectives provides the theory with which the designer can work. The detailed stages of fall-back, handover to these stages and interfaces between them, still need to be designed and justified in terms of costs and benefits. If complete failure of the system for one day a year can be tolerated, is the development effort of two fall-back positions cost effective?

We now turn our attention to the integrity of the data. The first problem is the identification of errors. If this follows a disk crash then the problem will have been identified. The most common source of the identification is with the user, who finds that the output is wrong or inconsistent. This is followed by an investigation which leads back to corruption of the stored data. This lamentable situation could be eliminated by constant checking of the data, but the cost would be prohibitive in most cases. A compromise in which checks are conducted periodically is frequently best. Such checks could be done when whole files were processed, e.g. performing a record count, or accumulating a hash total, for comparison with a header value. Alternatively, when files were copied all pointers between indexes and data or from one record to another can be usefully matched, if there is enough data at either end of the chain to check for matches. These checks help in particular to identify errors in data which is infrequently processed – the cause of many 'intermittent' failures.

If there is a minimum of data redundancy and data stores are able to exist independently of one another, as in the logical design, then data corruption will be isolated to the area of the data store directly affected.

In batch processing, recovery from data failure is relatively simple. After each processing cycle the input to that cycle is archived, i.e. transaction files together with the original master files. When recovery is needed, the transactions are again processed against the master files to regenerate the up-to-date master file. By holding archive copies of these files for several processing cycles, recovery can be started from a much earlier time. Frequently three cycles are held – grandfather, father and son – for each processing run. If back-up copies of the whole of the end-of-day data are taken, to facilitate this type of recovery, a greater number of copies will need to be kept, such that three days after a month end run the only back-up copy of that work is not lost. In this situation daily, weekly and monthly archives are usually kept separate.

Real-time processing complicates archiving and recovery because there is not necessarily a file of transactions. This can be overcome simply by logging every transaction which causes a change to the contents of the data stores. Such a system involves the programs in writing to the transaction log and in being able to be driven by the log. More sophisticated than this simple log is one which also includes before and after images of modified master records and is maintained as a module of the system software. The program must notify the archiving module of the beginning and end of each transaction, together with details of it. This module automatically takes a copy of every record read from or written to master data stores. If a 'clean' failure occurs, such as a power cut to a disk drive, it is known that most of the data is good and only the transactions actually being processed at the point of failure will lead to corrupt or inconsistent data. Transactions which have not been fully processed can be identified from the log, and any changes to the data store for such transactions can be backed out by overwriting stored values with those held on the log as before images for that transaction. Where the data stores are not in essence good, e.g. following a disk crash, recovery will involve the use of a back-up copy of the store. The back-up copy is loaded and the after images on the log need to overwrite their back-up equivalents until most of the data is correct. Half-finished transactions may then be backed out. In either event it is important for operators to know exactly which was the last transaction entered and accepted by the system, so as to avoid lost or duplicate transactions. This may be achieved by displaying to the operator a message saying that the transaction was accepted straight after the log was told that the transaction was complete. All unconfirmed transactions would then need to be re-entered. (An alternative is for the recovery program to tell each operator which of their transactions was the last one to be recovered. This is more complex for the machine but easier for the operator.) The programs will also need to know what data to send to the log and, more particularly, when to send it. The interface between the application system and an archiving/recovery system needs to be specified precisely and in line with installation standards.

One further comment upon system reliability is necessary. Many failures remain unexplained, but the bulk of the explained failures are the result of software errors. If the logic is wrong the only way of correcting the data may be to go back and run the old data with a new program. Such terms as quality assurance, proveable programs and software engineering are used to emphasize the need for and methods of achieving reliable software. The errors here are both program and system errors. If each processing unit in a system checks the data it is receiving, e.g. by validating transactions against data stores, then any errors will be more easily identified and their source located. This presupposes that the error is a result of an inconsistency, not a misconception, and that the extra work involved in performing this check is justifiable. The implementation of structured modular systems, together with good system testing, can help produce better software. This is yet another specialist area which the reader may wish to pursue.

### Example: order processing

As an example of initial physical design work (first sketch), consider the necessary (E + N) system as defined for the logical application and data models (Figure 69).

We take the original purpose behind the order processing project to be the speeding up of the despatch of goods from the organization. The investigation showed that the batch system introduced too many delays. Orders had to be batched, transcribed, keyed on to disk and verified prior to awaiting the late afternoon processing run. This meant that orders received before 2 p.m. arrived as picking notes in the warehouse the next morning (average 22 hour delay) and any arriving after 2 p.m. did not reach the warehouse until a day later (average 42 hour delay). This system meant that the warehouse staff tended to be very busy in the mornings and relatively slack in the late afternoons.

When response time is considered, there is seen to be a need to reduce the time between the arrival of an order and the sending of its corresponding

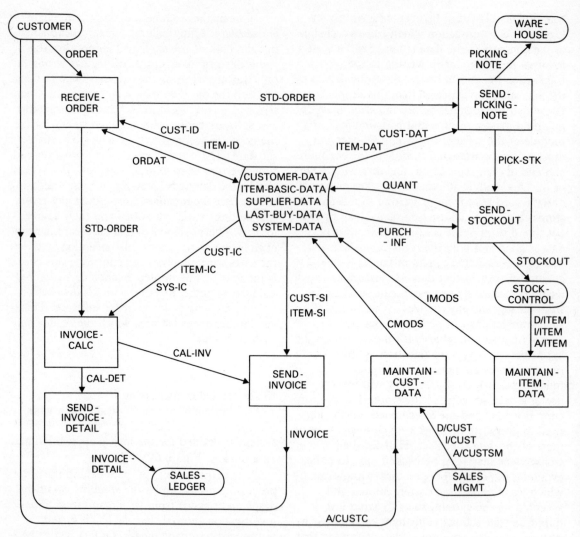

Figure 69  *First sketch: order processing, essential and necessary*

picking note. The SEND-PICKING-NOTE process also passes data to the SEND-STOCKOUT process. If an item does become out of stock some action needs to be taken quickly. This adds weight to the need for fast response times in this area of the system. The warehouse already operates a back-order system for goods which cannot be despatched immediately, and have considered buying a microcomputer to automate this system. The warehouse manager is hoping that picking notes will be available in magnetic form, so that her new system becomes viable.

The processes which produce the invoices for the customers and the sales ledger can afford to have a delay between the order arriving and the output. These activities are not time critical. The system appears to have divided itself into two halves according to the required response times. What may be termed the stock subsystem needs to operate to real time, or at least near time, whereas the invoicing subsystem can be batch.

Is near-time processing sufficient for picking note production? To answer this question requires knowledge of the distribution of orders received over the day and the work patterns of warehouse staff. (A relatively simple analysis of the situation will be presented here. If necessary techniques of work study, organization and methods, together with methematical queueing theory, could be applied.) If all orders arrive by post at 9 a.m. or 2.30 p.m. then continuous picking note production is largely irrelevant as the data is naturally batched. Similarly, if the warehouse staff have dinner between 12 a.m. and 1 p.m. then the arrival of a batch of picking-notes on each hour will mean that two batches of work need to be done at 1 p.m. Assume that, from the documentation, the systems analyst or the users, it is known that 40 per cent of the orders arrive by post before 11 a.m., and that the rest of the orders are received over the telephone throughout the day. The sales staff currently work from 9 a.m. to

5 p.m. with flexible breaks. There are approximately 400 orders per day, with an average value of £50 and an average of 1.8 order lines per order. The warehouse staff work from 8.15 a.m. until 5 p.m. and get two fifteen-minute breaks at 10.15 a.m. and 3 p.m., with half an hour for dinner at 12.30. It follows that the warehouse must currently clear 52 orders per hour, and Figure 70 diagram depicts the situation.

The effect of this distribution of work is that warehouse staff will be working against the backlog of the morning's postal orders for the bulk of the day, and will not be waiting for the next picking-note. It is also important that there are orders to be filled between 8.15 a.m. and 9 a.m., which suggests that the orders received between 3.30 p.m. and 5 p.m. be sent to the warehouse for the following morning.

If the workload and capacity were more evenly spread throughout the day, a real-time system might have been justifiable; however, at present the near-time production of picking notes will be as effective. Data flows can be sent to the

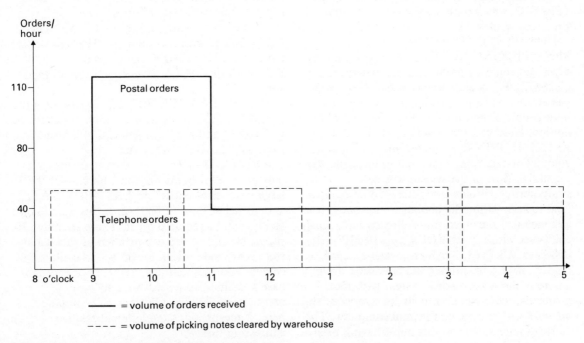

Figure 70  *Near-time processing: picking note production*

warehouse at 9.15 a.m., 9.45 a.m., and then every $1\frac{1}{4}$ hours until 3.30 p.m., with a final end-of-day flow at 5 p.m. This scheduling would be acceptable to stock control giving them information up to eight times daily on products which have gone out of stock. Thus near-time processing is acceptable.

The implication of these output timings is that the RECEIVE-ORDER process must be performed very soon after the ORDER enters the system, especially for the production of the 9.15 a.m. picking notes. This process involves the conversion of the possibly textual order into a standard format. Unless a fifth-generation system with natural language I/O is to be used, a person needs to be involved with this process in order to receive the order. If the CUST-NO is missing, the full name and possibly delivery address would need to be given to a machine so that it could obtain the CUST-NO. Similarly with the ITEM-NO and ITEM-DESCRIP. In this first-sketch design, it is suggested that the standardization is done by people who will be able to handle the variable input with the use of their own memory and the data flows CUST-ID and ITEM-ID, which could be from printed stores produced weekly.

How will STD-ORDER be sent to SEND-PICKING-NOTE? So far the system as described could be performed manually; the STD-ORDER could be written on a form and passed to a typist for picking note production, both people using card files for reference when needed. However, the processes after RECEIVE-ORDER are algorithmic, with large volumes of data being processed in the same way regularly. Most of the system will be computerized. Which computer? To be realistic (and to keep within the bounds of this book) it is assumed that the organization already has a small computer with say six VDUs, two 10 MB disk drives (5 MB fixed, 5 MB removeable), card reader, 600 l.p.m. printer and a cassette drive. There is also a key-to-disk system with four terminals; these will eventually be scrapped, and all work will be done on the mini computer. The existing system runs on this mini, having been converted when the old hardware was phased out.

If the STD-ORDER is composed by a person sitting at a VDU it can be entered at the same time. Data flow can then be achieved with a transaction file of STD-ORDERs. This file can subsequently be processed to produce picking notes intermittently, and a new transaction file created. At the end of the day the eight transaction files so created could be merged together and invoice production performed.

The next area of concern is the stored data, what accesses need to be made and how much time is available to make them. Shortly after the recept of a file of STD-ORDERs, picking notes need to be flowing. The average transaction file will contain 50 orders with 90 order lines. This means 50 flows of CUST-DAT and 90 flows of ITEM-DAT, with CUST-NO and ITEM-NO as the search arguments. If there were only 60 customers and 100 products, any file organization would be acceptable. If the organization is taken to have 1500 customer accounts and 6000 product lines, sequential processing will be quite slow: on average 4 per cent of the customer records and 1.5 per cent of the product records will be accessed for each file of STD-ORDERS. These hit rates suggest that some type of direct access facility would be worth while, using the ITEM-NO and CUST-NO as search arguments. The data structures CUSTOMER-DATA and ITEM-BASIC-DATA have these fields as their keys.

The SEND-STOCKOUT process also uses the ITEM-BASIC-DATA with a search argument of ITEM-NO, followed by retrievals of information from LAST-BUY-DATA and SUPPLIER-DATA. These data structures are only accessed infrequently but, because of the large number of entries on LAST-BUY-DATA, anticipated at over 12 000, some direct access facility will be required for it. There are only 220 suppliers, and so the organization of this data store is not too critical. Direct access could mean content addressable file systems, back-end data base machines, or a software data base management system. On the small computer here, it means index random and relative addressing files.

As a result of the warehouse manager's interest

in a magnetic version of the picking note flow, and a company policy of encouraging departments to perform their own data processing (according to organization-wide standards), the transfer will take place by means of a wired link between the small computer and the new warehouse micro. Once in the warehouse the data will be stored on flexidisk and printed, and then processing from the flexidisk can take place. The STOCKOUT data flow will be on ordinary computer paper.

The data flow PICK-STK will be via a common area of the operating system used for interprogram communication, with SEND-STOCKOUT running as long as there is data for it to process. This process and SEND-PICKING-NOTE should not be merged together because they originate from two different classes of objectives and may need to be run independently. If for some reason processing power is reduced, SEND-STOCKOUT does not have to be run; this gives the system a fall-back position which would be lost if the processes were merged.

The invoicing system is now relatively simple in that the STD-ORDERs will arrive in a file at the

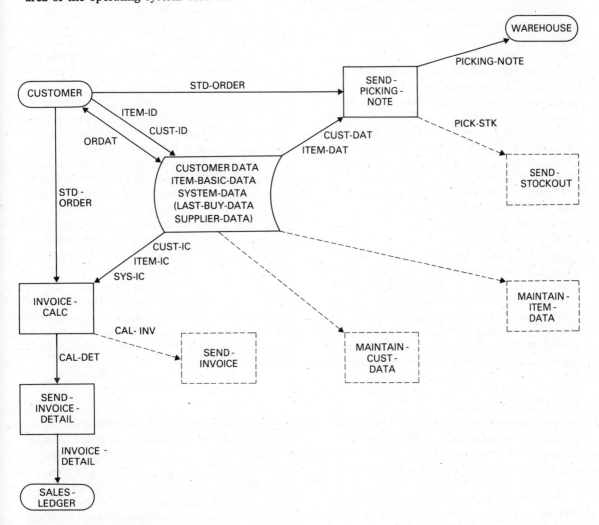

Figure 71   *Fall-back position*

end of the day. The functions of INVOICE-CALC may be performed and the data for storage on the sales ledger prepared. After the completion of the INVOICE-CALC process the merged file of the day's STD-ORDERs is no longer needed for processing. The essential process SEND-INVOICE-DETAIL and INVOICE-CALC, upon which it depends, may be merged together because of this dependency, which means that INVOICE-CALC must also be classed as essential. The full invoice production may again be a background job which is communicated with via the interprogram communication part of the operating system. The output to the sales ledger is a file of invoice details, and the invoice data flow is produced on preprinted stationery.

We now turn our attention to the systems reliability. The necessary tasks have been kept separate from the essential ones, and so in the event of reduced resources, a fall-back position can be operated (Figure 71). In this situation the two data flows PICK-STK and CAL-INV would need to be stored until the processes which use them could be reinstated. Eventually detailed operating instructions on how to switch these flows from interprogram communication to a storage unit, and then to retrieve them, will need to be specified.

In the event of a complete systems failure, it is important to know precisely what data has been processed and the state of the data stores. The general principle is to return to a known point and restart from there. This organization operates a crude but reasonably effective and very common method of data security. At the end of each day, after all users are logged off the system, a physical copy is made of all the stored data. In the event of a failure during the day all jobs need to be restarted from the beginning of that day. In the example system this would be feasible for the postal orders but not for the telephone orders, of which there is no hard copy. Partly to overcome this problem, all orders entered on to the system are immediately written to a transaction log on cassette at the terminal. After system recovery, this transaction log can be used as input instead of the keyboard. This has the further advantage that data entry on to cassette could take place while the rest of the system was down, assuming that an intelligent terminal was being used and that batch exception processing was designed into the cassette reading program.

This system does not fully solve the problems of system failure in that there would then be two copies of each data flow out of the system. A complication here is that although a complete day's transactions may be known, it is not known how far through the system the transactions had passed at the point of failure. If it is taken that the file of INVOICE-DETAILs was lost with the system or can be deleted, then all the cassette transactions can contribute to that data flow. The data flows to the printer, STOCKOUT and INVOICE, will be spooled prior to printing, and the operators will need to start printing off the new STOCKOUT or INVOICE at the point where the old one stopped so as to ensure that only one copy of each document is sent. The picking note can only be inspected once printed in the warehouse, and so procedures will need to be established to inform the warehouse that duplicate flows may be transmitted and to check for and remove them.

## Checking the design

Checking of anything must involve the comparison of two things which are measured in the same units but derived from different sources.

The first check which must be made is for completeness. Are all the data flows, stores and processes, as described in the logical model, defined in the first sketch? If an omission is found then the designer needs to reconsider the first sketch in the light of the omission. The most likely situation will not involve a change to the sketch, but rather the explicit statement of an assumption. The second major area of checking refers to performance.

**Example: order processing**
The following lists define the physical characteristics of the data processes, stores and flows of the order processing system, derived from the first-sketch description.

*Processes*

| | |
|---|---|
| INVOICE-CALC | , batch<br>trigger = end-of-day routine |
| RECEIVE-ORDER | , real time, VDU<br>trigger = receipt of ORDER/fall-back to reading transaction log |
| SEND-INVOICE | , batch<br>, trigger = INVOICE-CALC |
| SEND-INVOICE-DETAIL | , merge with INVOICE-CALC |
| SEND-PICKING-NOTE | , near time<br>trigger = time of day (eight times daily) |
| SEND-STOCKOUT, | near time<br>trigger = SEND-PICKING-NOTE |
| and | |
| STORE-ORDER | , fall-back only, to store orders on the transaction log only trigger = receipt of order while minicomputer is down |

*Stores*

| | |
|---|---|
| CUSTOMER-DATA | , DA/key = CUST-NO |
| ITEM-BASIC-DATA | , DA/key = ITEM-NO |
| LAST-BUY-DATA | , DA/key = ITEM-NO, SUPL-NAME |
| SUPPLIER-DATA | , any |

*Flows*

| | |
|---|---|
| CAL-INV | , global memory for interprogram communication/fallback to file |
| CUST-DAT | , read from disk |
| CUST-ID | , printed report |
| INVOICE | , preprinted stationery |
| INVOICE-DETAIL | , file of transactions |
| ITEM-DAT | , read from disk |
| ITEM-ID | , printed report |
| PICKING-NOTE | , communication line |
| PICK-STK | , global memory for interprogram communication/fallback to file |
| STD-ORDER | , one to eight files of transactions |
| STOCKOUT | , printed on standard listing |

There are in fact seven processes defined here, and eight in the logical model. This is because of the STORE-ORDER process, which is an alternative route for orders entering the system. In addition there are the two processes for the maintenance of the stored data which can be performed on demand by an operator at a VDU. If there are several changes to be made these can be done together, or a single change can be input if it is urgent. These nine processes could all be defined in a data dictionary, and the entry include the fact that they all contribute to the outline design. If the dictionary were searched to retrieve the logical model, only the eight processes which contribute to it would need to be identified.

The method of storing SYSTEM-DATA is not specified. The system data is best held in a global area of memory after having been read in from a small parameter file on disk. All the other stores as defined in the logical data model are included in the first sketch, although no information is given for SUPPLIER-DATA. The supplier data may be put on the most convenient device – in this case it must be on disk and can be sequentially organized.

There are twenty-seven data flows in the logical model, compared with eleven in the sketch (counting the two occurrences of STD-ORDER as one flow). Some of the unspecified flows move data to processes from a store, and may be described simply as disk reads; any other characteristics are defined either by the data store or by the flow itself, e.g. is there a key or a search argument? A consistency check is possible here; if the stored data does not contain the data specified as a search argument for a flow then there is a problem because the store cannot return the data requested. When this situation is identified a review of the meaning of the flow and store needs to be undertaken, looking at the logical process and data modelling. The other unspecified flows are involved with maintenance of the files. All the flows to these A/I/D processes should be in writing, and the flows IMODS and CMODS will be disk updates.

If the sketch is complete, the design can now be compared with other design criteria. The criterion which is most likely to cause change, and which should therefore be considered first, is the system timing. The comparison here is between the times within which the system must operate, possibly defined by the organization, and the estimated timings of the new system. The intention here is not to describe the detailed calculation of disk, tape, printer etc. timing (which will vary with the configuration chosen), but rather to consider how the timings will vary depending upon the overall system design.

The information needed for system timing, apart from hardware performance figures, is the volume of transactions and the number of occurrences of each stored entity. For the order processing system, this includes:

|  |  |
|---|---|
| 400 | orders per day, with |
| 1.8 | order lines on each, and approximately 10 per cent having a purchase order number, 1 per cent having a special delivery address, 50 per cent not including the CUST-NO, and 20 per cent not including the ITEM-NO |
| 1500 | customers |
| 6000 | product lines |
| 12000 | records of previous purchases, and |
| 220 | suppliers. |

The process RECEIVE-ORDER will need to standardize the information. If done manually with printed lists in CUST-NAME + DELIV-ADRS and ITEM-DESCRIP sequence, and an average look-up time of 15 seconds (allowing for people remembering common codes), then:

$$\text{customer look-ups} = 400 \times \frac{50}{100} \times 15$$

$$= 50 \text{ minutes}$$

$$\text{item look-ups} = 400 \times \frac{20}{100} \times 15$$

$$= 20 \text{ minutes}$$

If this were to be done by the computer following entry of the data, and if there were approximately sixty characters more in each name and address than in the CUST-NO, and twenty extra in each description, then the data input would be

$$\text{customer input} = 400 \times \frac{50}{100} \times 60$$

$$= 1 \text{ hour (at 12 000 keys/hour)}$$

$$\text{item input} = 400 \times \frac{20}{100} \times 20$$

$$= 8 \text{ minutes (at 12 000 keys/hour)}$$

There would also be some computer time itself to be included. The situation is not clear cut, particularly as the number of customers providing full details can vary with pressure from salesmen. The computer option will be taken at present. This will keep the operators' jobs relatively simple and can be subsequently reviewed in the light of statistics gathered on the live system. In order to keep the computer time to a minimum, secondary indexes will be needed on CUSTOMER-DATA and ITEM-BASIC-DATA.

The RECEIVE-ORDER process then has the entry of 400 standardized orders with 1.8 lines on each. Data entry is:

| CUST-NO | , | 5 characters, | 400 times |
|---------|---|---------------|-----------|
| DELIV-ADRS | , | 45 characters, | 4 times |
| PURCH-NO | , | 8 characters, | 40 times |
| ITEM-NO | , | 6 characters, | 720 times |
| QTY | , | 3 characters, | 720 times |

The daily total of 8980 characters is equivalent to approximately 45 minutes data entry at 12 000 keys/hour. Add to this the time to enter the characters to identify customers and products, giving a daily total of approximately two hours keying in.

The data flow ORDAT, with LAST-ORDNO-USED and TODAYS-DATE, is from global memory and therefore virtually timeless. Writing each STD-ORDER to disk will take a matter of milliseconds, and again is not significant. For 400 customers, 720 items and 400 standard orders, with an access to an index for each customer or item, then the total daily disk accesses for RECEIVE-ORDER will be 2640. At approximately 100 ms each this is equivalent to 4.5 minutes. The reader should note that in this example no validation involving file look-up, no error processing and no complex file update/insertion is taking place. These operations can take a significant amount of time in live systems if large data volumes are being processed.

RECEIVE-ORDER will employ one VDU and operator for around two hours per day, although the continuous receipt of ORDERs by the organization will mean that the amount and type of contemporary work which can be done by this person is very limited.

SEND-PICKING-NOTE will operate eight times a day, reading the STD-ORDERs on disk and sending data down a wire to the warehouse. A delay here will be the time taken to set up the job, i.e. notify the warehouse that they need to be ready to receive data; this will probably be a minute or so. The PICKING-NOTE will consist of approximately 142 characters of data (70 characters for PICK-NO, name and address, and $1.8 \times 40$ characters for the PICK-LINE). If the link to the micro is rated at 300 baud (and therefore 30 characters per second) at each of the 8 data flows contains 50 picking notes, then each flow will take about 4 minutes. The flow

PICK-STK is to be held in global memory and will take 9 characters per PICK-LINE (6 for ITEM-NO, and 3 for QTY). This will occupy 810 bytes of memory. There will also be 50 flows of CUST-DAT and 90 flows of ITEM-DAT, taking about half a minute. SEND-PICKING-NOTE will therefore take approximately 5 minutes, 8 times a day.

The SEND-STOCKOUT process will read from ITEM-BASIC-DATA with the key of ITEM-NO for each PICK-STK in memory, at 100 ms per read with one read for an index and a read/write for data; this is 27 seconds for each batch of picking notes processed. If 1 per cent of order lines are for out-of-stock items, then there will be roughly one STOCKOUT for each batch of picking notes. To obtain the flow PURCH-INF involves a search of LAST-BUY-DATA using ITEM-NO as the search argument. This will not identify a unique record – rather a set of records, probably two. If LAST-BUY-DATA is organized index sequentially on the composite key ITEM-NO, SUPPLIER-NAME, then this data can be obtained in about three reads (one for the index, one for the first record, and sequential reads until the ITEM-NO changes). This would take approximately 300 ms. A sequential read of the SUPPLIER-DATA would involve reading 110 records on average, which would probably take about one second. The time to start the printer and print the headings and data could be calculated. Suffice it to say that SEND-STOCKOUT would take about a minute to run.

These calculations to estimate the time taken for each process can be performed for the INVOICE subsystem and the file maintenance processes.

The checking really begins when the results are compared with some standard of acceptability. Frequently the only standard used is a subjective assessment of what is reasonable, with no reference to alternative designs or standards. On some occasions the timings are considered by a data processing manager to ensure that present resources are sufficient, or to estimate possible charges which will be made on the user. The user may be asked to agree that the timings are acceptable as a basis for further design work. It is difficult to define what will be considered acceptable, and it is only the exceptional designer who has such hard figures as 'one hour's machine time and 30 minutes printer time, per day' as guidelines.

Consider the possibility that the performance estimates of this system were not acceptable. The existing system is designed to be very flexible and easy to maintain. As mentioned earlier, this does conflict with performance, which means that there is room for improved performance. The system could consist of one program which:

1   Accepted orders
2   Transmitted a picking note
3   Reported on stockouts
4   Wrote to an invoice detail file
5   Printed an invoice
6   Allowed insertion of stored data when it was not found to exist already
7   Allowed amendment of stored data if inconsistency was identified
8   Allowed deletion of customers and items.

The data store could consist of just two structures, one for CUSTOMER-DATA and one for ITEM-DATA.

The time taken to enter an order through the keyboard would be approximately the same as in the first sketch, possibly slightly longer as more options and messages would be encountered by the operator. Time would be saved by only reading from the data store twice, once for customer and once for product data. This could be followed by a maximum of two rewrites. The disk access time would be severely reduced and there would be no need for interface files, saving both time and space. The disk space saving will however be more than offset by the extra space occupied by ITEM-DATA, with the repetition of supplier data for each last buy. The transmission time to the warehouse would remain constant.

The overall effect of this way of implementing the logical design is to reduce the disk access time and to have all tasks performed in real time. The implications of this are that many resources will be tied up throughout the day waiting for orders

to arrive, in the same way that the VDU and operator are busy in the first sketch. For example the line to the warehouse micro may have data transmitted at any time, and this calls into question the feasibility of this link. The explicit interfaces of the system between the tasks would all exist within one program, which may or may not simplify the design depending upon the program design. There would be an increase in data redundancy and storage requirements which follow this implementation of the data model. Over and above all these considerations is the reduced flexibility. If the LAST-COST-PRICE field is expanded by one digit, the one giant program will need modification rather than just the SEND-STOCKOUT program. The complexity of the change and the risks to the system are obviously much greater in the single-program system. A similar problem exists with changes to logic, e.g. a different way of calculating discounts would not be confined to INVOICE-CALC.

Between the two extremes of outline design there is room for compromise. Orders could be entered in real time and then every other job done in batch mode at regular points in the day. The designer could combine the SEND-PICKING-NOTE and SEND-STOCKOUT processes. However, the reader is reminded that this would involve the merger of processes from two different classes of objectives, E and N, and so undermine a fall-back position. The ITEM-BASIC-DATA and LAST-BUY-DATA could be merged. The logical design as developed here represents a very flexible system, and wherever possible the physical implementation should follow it. Moves away from the logical design can lead to increased performance, but will also lead to increased maintenance costs.

Where performance is not acceptable, then the first step is to look at improving performance by combining the logical processes together. Much has been written on module sizing and its benefits and pitfalls (see Gane and Sarson, 1979, Chapter 9 and Gilbert, 1983, Chapter 5). In general, processing units should exhibit (1) high cohesion, in that a module performs a single task and contains all that it needs to do this, and (2) low coupling, such that the interfaces between processing units are as simple as possible.

If the data model is not to be implemented as in the logical design, performance can be improved by joining stores together. In the extreme, a process would perform with the minimum execution time if all the data it required was input in a single step, and likewise output was just one step. To achieve this, all input flows could be joined together as could the output. Although this minimizes execution time, the price in terms of storage and flexibility will usually be too high to justify this extreme. A usage factor UF could be calculated for each field in the system, subsystem, process or (more likely) part of the data model, such that data items which had similar types of usage were grouped together:

$$UF \propto \frac{F}{SA}$$

The usage factor *UF* therefore varies directly with the frequency *F*; the more often an element is required, the higher its usage. Size *S* is inversely related to usage because the overheads involved in providing for small items of data are less than those for very large fields, and as such their increased efficiency can be taken into account. *A* is the time within which the item must be accessed. If an item must be accessed very quickly then the usage factor should be increased accordingly; similarly, a large access time would allow an item to be grouped with low-usage fields on a slower physical medium. Once all data items have a computed usage factor assigned to them, storage of data can be designed to take account of this usage. The intention here is not to say that the designer must build physical storage entirely around access patterns; however, to ignore them entirely is unwise. Usage factors are just one technique which can be used to decide upon the physical implementation of the logical data model, if performance constraints necessitated it.

Performance requirements cannot always be achieved for the logical design. This may be because of a lack of processing power, or possibly a fast system could be designed but the estimated maintenance costs are prohibitive. For whatever reason, the designer must then return to the logical design and the classes of objectives.

Prior to looking at the classes of objectives, it is worth noting that the system performance and ease of maintenance are only two of the criteria by which an outline design may be judged. In the section 'Design objectives and constraints' in Chapter 1, such factors as storage requirements, project life and funding, system integration and security are described, together with some of their implications for design. The ideal project will have its goals in terms of these factors clearly specified. The designer will then be able to appraise the outline design in such terms and refine the system towards the optimum mix of goals. Where such goals are not explicit, the designer needs to check that the outline design is 'acceptable' on each count. The criteria described here all come under the heading 'technical'. There are also the financial aspects in terms of capital and revenue costs and benefits, as well as the more difficult to define (and yet more real) social factors. This whole range of criteria should be employed in checking the outline design; in effect the feasibility of the design is checked.

The order processing example began in Chapter 6 with eight objectives. In the situation where resources are limited it may well be that some of these objectives will not appear in the final system. At the beginning of outline design, a choice was made as to which of the logical designs should be chosen as the basis for the first sketch. This cannot just be the essential system, because without the necessary objectives being met the essential system would gradually fail. The first sketch will be E + N plus as many desirable objectives as the designer anticipates will be supported by the resources. Upon completion of the first sketch it is checked against the constraints, and here there are three possible outcomes: >, < and =.

If the sketch and the resources match up exactly and there is no slack capacity, then it can be taken that the choice of objectives to physically implement was correct. The designer will still need to review the sketch to make sure that

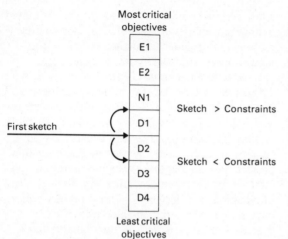

Figure 72   *Constraints on first sketch*

improvements cannot be made; but, on the assumption that the sketch is correct, the outline design has been completed.

Where the sketch fits within the constraints such that there are resources available to meet desirable objectives, the sketch needs to be expanded. The expanded sketch will include less critical objectives, which are incorporated by first referring back to the logical design to see what will need to be done to achieve an objective. From this logical design the sketch can be developed and then checked.

If the checking process reveals that the sketch will not fit within the constraints then something will need to be lost from the sketch. If the sketch includes desirable objectives then it is possible to redraw the sketch without a desirable objective in order to better fit the constraints. This is in effect the reverse process to that described in the preceding paragraph (see Figure 72).

A problem arises where the first sketch was based upon just the E + N objectives. In order to make the system fit the constraints a drastic revision of objectives is needed, because although an objective may be classed as necessary and less critical than others, it must still be achieved at sometime. The objectives are reviewed to assess the need for each objective. This process will not usually reveal any objective(s) which can be

wholly abandoned. However, before proceeding this needs to be confirmed. The next step is to check that the boundaries of the system being designed are broad enough; for example, whether the system has been designed to be wholly mechanized when some parts could be done better manually, or vice versa. The designer needs to break out of any mental ruts and see the system afresh, to do some lateral thinking. A common pitfall of design is concentration upon detail with consequent loss of objectivity, and a middle way between these extremes is probably the hallmark of the good designer.

If all the objectives are critical and the design cannot be improved upon, then the next possibility of change lies with the constraints themselves. Must the system run on the mainframe? Must the system be live in three months' time even if the hardware desired will not be available for four months? The constraints all need to be investigated for their validity. Many constraints are established on the basis of estimates made early in a project, and may be revised following the more detailed information available at this point in the project. The review of constraints needs to be done in conjunction with the systems manager, computer steering committee, or whoever is responsible for the overall planning and setting of the constraints in the first place.

The final possibility which must be considered is the abandonment of the project. If the system is the best which can be designed and yet does not fit within valid constraints, then there is no alternative but to stop work on the project. The stage of detail design is probably the most expensive part of the systems design activity; it is better to stop work before incurring these costs if the system will not meet the requirements, even though such a decision will be unpleasant in the short term (especially for the staff who have worked on the project so far, and those who initially approved the project). Again it is a case of balancing long-term benefits against short-term costs.

The variables and decisions described here are very similar to those of the feasibility study. This is not to suggest that only at these two points are

questions of the validity of objectives and
constraints considered. During the feasibility
study and after the outline design it is important
to stop and explicitly review the project. At all
other times the designer should try to adopt a
questioning and evaluative approach to the
project: as stated in Golden Rule 13 (page 27).

# 10 Hardware provision

Hardware (and software) provision is a specialist area requiring a breadth of knowledge ranging from organization policy to computer architecture, and calling for specialist skills in, for example, capital appraisal or demand forecasting. The intention here is to consider selection from the point of view of the systems designer providing input to a separate decision-making process. This limited view is further restricted by the emphasis upon input and output media. The justification for this limited view is that these are the areas with which the designer is most likely to be involved, and that further specialist texts may be consulted if required.

## Selection overview

Any purchases need to be made as part of an overall plan for the organization, in the same way that the individual project must contribute to the long-term plan. This is emphasized because much hardware and software is not purchased purely for one application system but is a shared resource. The long-term or strategic plan should advise on migration policies, for example to mainframes or micros, towards centralized software development tools or distributed programming. The plan needs to specify what standards (if any) the organization will attempt to achieve, and who will be responsible for co-ordinating effort. Many organizations do not have such a plan, and many organizations have a variety of incompatible and underused equipment contributing to the suboptimization of the total system. All individual purchases need to be consistent with such a plan. Following on from this primary objective, others may be specified. These objectives may be of a general nature such as to purchase:

1  From an established supplier with good support services;
2  A product with many satisfied customers who can be contacted;
3  A product for which ongoing maintenance is available.

More specific objectives will be in relation to the current system being designed and an estimate of future demands which will be made upon the facility. For example, backing store might need to provide:

1  Capacity of 48 Mb

2  Minimum of 12 Mb removable
3  Average seek time of 60 ms
4  Total time to back up 48 Mb of less than 15 minutes
5  Initial cost less than £10 000
6  Recurring cost to be less than £500 p.a.
7  Quiet operation on standard power supply.

In general, selection procedures start by establishing a list of objectives. These must then be specified in enough detail for there to be no doubt as to what is required. This usually means quantifying the objective. Once such a list is established, each of the objectives needs to be classified as either essential or desirable. Essential objectives must be met; desirable ones have a weighting attached to them according to their importance. The weights might be either numbers used for subsequent calculation of a points total, or be a money value placed upon the objective. Thus the need to have terminals which can withstand damp might be worth £1000, because otherwise special cubicles would need to be built to house the terminals, and the anticipated cost of this is £1000. Either a points basis or pound equivalent basis is generally used. Both are arbitrary and to a large extent artificial. However, their value lies in providing a common unit in which several different factors can be expressed.

The table of objectives and the weightings needs to be very carefully drawn up to reflect the needs of the system and plans for the future. Even with such preparation the results may surprise the selector, and the validity of the table needs to be

| | Objectives | Weighting | Pompadour 69 | Consumer plexus | Poser's prince | Waster wonder | Notes |
|---|---|---|---|---|---|---|---|
| 1 | Cost ≤ £200 | E | ✓ | ✓ | ✓ | ✓ | |
| 2 | Can act as a videotext terminal | E | ✓ | X | ✓ | ✓ | Information from vendor only |
| 3 | Colour graphics | E | ✓ | ✓ | ✓ | ✓ | |
| 4 | Supplier within 15 miles | 2 | 4 | | 0 | 10 | Y = 10, −1 point for each extra mile |
| 5 | Games software available | 4 | 9 | | 0 | 9 | |
| 6 | Education software available | 5 | 0 | | 8 | 0 | |
| 7 | Prolog available | 8 | 0 | | 10 | 0 | |
| 8 | Recommended by consumer groups | 8 | 6 | | 8 | 0 | |
| 9 | Can attach flexi disks | 6 | 0 | | 7 | 10 | 7 points or 3 points given if only suspect information is available |
| 10 | Can attach printer | 6 | 10 | | 7 | 10 | |
| | Total products | max 390 | 152 | | 268 | 176 | |

Figure 73  *Points table*

reviewed continually. The totals should be taken as guidelines which can give direction. Where two or more alternative proposals receive similar and acceptable scores, a different means of selecting between them should be employed. Usually more subjective and personal factors are employed in contrast to the formal, literal factors of the table. It has been stated that relatively small purchases (e.g. microcomputers or printers) are selected by means of objective assessment of their costs and benefits, whereas for larger purchases (e.g. a mainframe with networking equipment) the facts and factors are so numerous as to lead to a reliance upon subjective assessments, attitudes and opinions. Such a situation is not difficult to envisage, nor is it difficult to see some of the problems which could follow from such non-rigorous selection. It is worth noting that hardware and software purchase is not significantly different from any other purchase. If one is buying a bicycle there may be ample sources of advice, but these will be biased or deliberately designed to obscure the facts, and few people would make a decision purely objectively.

An example of the use of a points table in the selection of a home computer is shown in Figure 73.

Finally, it is necessary to emphasize the role of the users in the selection of any equipment of software with which they will be directly involved. Users may be involved in identifying the objectives to be met, assigning weightings, and in some cases evaluating products. Once a shortlist of acceptable products is established, the final decision should be that of the users who will have to live with the decision, and make a success of it.

## Input media

Input design represents an interface between man and machine, and is distinct from the design of purely human or purely machine interfaces. Traditionally batch data processing systems contain the following 'input stages':

1  *Data recording*  Some process takes place to record an event in the world, e.g. writing down the arrival of goods.
2  *Data transcription*  This is an optional stage and allows the recorded data to be rewritten for input purposes.
3  *Data batching*  Data is collected into groups for control purposes.
4  *Data conversion*  The media on which the data is recorded is changed to become machine readable; traditionally this means card punching.
5  *Data verification*  This is the process whereby data is reconverted to machine readable form, such that the machine compares the original and second versions, reports on inconsistency and allows amendments to be made (usually after an investigation into which version is correct).
6  *Data control*  This is a process which records all data passing through it to check that all necessary data for a system to run is entered once and once only.
7  *Data movement*  To physically move the data to the computer and into some input device.
8  *Data validation*  This is the process whereby a program of some description reads the input data and checks it to a varying extent to ensure that it is valid.

There are a great many possible variations to this basic pattern of events, depending upon the system being designed and the hardware chosen.

As well as the general factors relating to the supplier (delivery dates, level of support, number of installations and the like), the designer must consider the technical aspects (i.e. will the equipment meet the requirements of the system), the social aspects and finally the financial factors.

Technical aspects of input design derive chiefly from the volume of data to be input and the time available for that input. The lower the volume of data the easier input will be, and so data compression (e.g. with codes) is often useful. If a field appears several times then consideration needs to be given to automatic repetition of the field by the machine. For example, the transaction date could be presumed to be the last one entered unless explicitly changed. The effectiveness of such data saving techniques depends upon the balance between the additional complexity of the processing and the volume of data not input.

The volume of data should be expressed in terms of characters of information which need to be input. This provides a subsequent basis for comparison and ignores for the moment any extra key depressions associated with entering fields or error rates. These factors vary with the input device and contribute to estimation of medium capacity. The timing requirements are frequently more difficult to estimate because any one of several factors may prove critical. Can the week's data be input in a week or will a backlog continually build up? This is a question simply of volumes and capacities. More subtle problems can arise when there is a delay such that data is not continually available for input and will arrive in batches after certain times. The capacity needs to be such that these peaks can be processed within an acceptable period. Conversely there may be hardware, software or human bottlenecks, which mean that deadlines exist by which point all data must be entered. The reader is referred to the first-sketch order entry for an example of uneven work flows. The designer needs to express these timing requirements in terms of throughput, which is the number of characters of information to be input in a given period. The period could be an hour, a day or a week, depending upon the system. Several throughputs could be specified, corresponding to peak, average and minimum, together with details of the requirements for each level of throughput. For example, a college library might wish to record issues of books at 4000 characters per hour normally, but rising to 10 000 characters per hour at the start of term and possibly needing no more than 500 characters per day during college holidays. Resources could be scheduled to meet peak requirements and allocated to other systems when possible.

The capacity of the equipment needs to be estimated and manufacturer's performance figures need to be adjusted to allow for:

1  The time taken to set up a job, e.g. loading cards into a card reader or changing programs on a VDU;
2  Down time of the equipment for maintenance or faults (back-up input procedures having been designed into the system as part of outline design if needed);
3  Operator capacity, allowing for breaks, sickness, training and holidays;
4  Data which is entered to control the input machine;
5  Anticipated repetition of input due to errors.

For example, in a library a VDU might be used for data entry. An experienced operator could achieve 17 000 key depressions per hour. Assuming the time to set the job up is ignored because the terminal is dedicated to the task for the whole day, then the next question is availability. As there are likely to be several compatible VDUs, and assuming this task has highest priority, then average down time may be considered negligible. The operator may be paid from 9 a.m. to 5 p.m., but because breaks and interruptions while working lead to less than

optimum performance, a figure of five useful hours per day is probably a better estimate of the capacity which will be achieved. Assume staff turnover is very low and several staff are capable of doing the job and covering for each other. This reduces the hourly rate by three-eighths to give an average capacity of 10 625 keys/hour. If the average field is five characters long and the return key needs to be pressed for 90 per cent of the entries which are less than the maximum field length, then there will be a reduction in capacity given by

$$\text{reduction} = \text{frequency} \left( \frac{\text{new length}}{\text{old length}} - 1 \right)$$
$$= 90 \left( \frac{5 + 1}{5} - 1 \right) = 18\%$$

giving an average of 8712 keys/hour. If on average 0.5 per cent of characters are incorrect, and when an error is identified by a validation program it needs to display a message which causes a delay equivalent to entering 30 characters, and the whole field needs re-entering, then there is a reduction in capacity of

$$0.5 \left( \frac{30}{5} - 1 \right) = 2.5\%$$

reducing the average to 8494 key depressions per hour.

Only when both the throughput and the capacity are known can a decision be taken upon the suitability of a particular input medium, in a particular configuration of machinery and manpower. The designer may need to consider several alternative versions of resource allocation in order to arrive at a potential solution.

The social factors to be considered concern the impact of the equipment upon the operators. Equipment may not be suitable for use in a particular environment, e.g. voice input in a machine shop or standard keyboards in a cowshed. Such equipment will place unnecessary requirements upon the operators. The medium may affect the environment, e.g. noise from card punches and readers or the heat generated by many VDUs in a room. Furthermore there is the degree to which the operators will find the equipment logical and consistent to use. For example, a point-of-sale terminal may simplify entering sales of common items by having special keys for them, or alternatively may infuriate a harassed operator with a complex routine for cancelling a transaction if a customer finds he has no money with him.

The need for close co-operation between the designer and operator is obvious. Where specialist data preparation staff exist, they may well be more knowledgeable regarding input media than the designer. End users may be very well informed of office equipment or workshop aids that are available.

Consideration of the financial aspect, with which the designer may be concerned, increases the number of variables which need to be taken into account. Financial appraisal will consider costs and benefits in terms of both the initial value and recurring value to the organization. Where equipment is already owned by an organization and has some spare capacity, it may well appear a very cheap input medium and will tend to be selected. This apparently obvious choice is not always valid if a broader view of costs and benefits is taken. Variables which need to be considered include:

1  Space used by the equipment and its requirements for power, sound-proofing or other environmental controls;
2  Overheads incurred on the main computer to control or interpret the input;
3  Initial costs for staff training and recurring staffing costs, together with any savings in either the user department or the computer section;
4  The cost of maintenance of the equipment and technical support;
5  Provision of consumables.

A picture of the costs and benefits of each input medium can be built up for both the short and the long term. The results can then be expressed as costs per 1000 characters of input capacity. This can be useful if the equipment will be shared between two or more applications in the future, and provides a basis for apportioning costs. However, costs per 1000 characters may be misleading if the equipment has a large capacity which will only be partly utilized, and should therefore not be used without an appraisal of how the machinery will be used overall. The input methods which will meet both technical and human requirements can therefore be compared in terms of cost. The cost must be such that the new system can afford it; moreover, cost may be used to select between alternatives if more than one is acceptable on all counts.

## Output media

The data which will be output from the computer is known from the logical design stage, and will be the data, the whole data and nothing but the data that is *needed* by the destination of the flow. Output may take place from the system being designed to another machine. For example, many financial systems produce magnetic tape output which is later processed by the banks. In such circumstances the output media, and probably format, will be determined by the destination system. Machine interfaces should follow standards and will not be considered here where the man/machine aspects are aired.

The usual output stages described for batch systems contain the following:

1  Data formatting and media conversion, to produce something that is of use to human beings;
2  Operators of the output device check that the quality of the output is acceptable/legible, and possibly that the job has terminated correctly;
3  The output is moved to data control who log its receipt, and check for duplicate output and that the output correctly follows from the input previously recorded;

4 Data preparation staff trim, burst, decollate or otherwise prepare the output;
5 The output is distributed by such means as internal post, or special delivery services;
6 The users should log receipt of the output and check it before using it. This is because the checks made by the data processing system are predominately syntactic. It is only the users who know the world which is being modelled and who are in a position to assess the validity of the output. Finally the output should be used for some purpose, unless the whole use of the output is for checking purposes, e.g. an audit trail.

The medium of output may change this sequence of events, most obviously when the output device is physically located with the user. Distributing the data in electronic form with local media conversion does not reduce the checking which needs to be done, but does mean that it is all done by the users themselves. It does, however, cut back on the numbers of interfaces, and therefore the time delays and chances of error are reduced.

The attitudes of the users to output is very important, and user suggestions or preferences should be given serious consideration even if they do not appear to be the best technical solution. If data is difficult to read or laid out in such a way as to make its interpretation tedious, it will lose some of its value. For operational documents poor output will result in an increased error rate and reduced job satisfaction. Where the data should be used as part of a decision-making process, poor design can lead to its being largely ignored.

This concern with the user's attitude to the output leads to an emphasis on the aesthetic aspects of output design, as well as ensuring that the information content is correct and the medium acceptable. It is well worth considering how an artist would look upon output design, and the composition of the screen or page. Commercial artists are employed to work in the area of information transfer, and where possible their advice and skills should be sought.

The output throughput may be calculated in a similar manner to that for the input, the first step being to calculate the output volumes. This is frequently expressed in lines, because of the need for spacings and blank lines; however, in some cases this does not form a valid basis for comparison, e.g. when output could be in characters to a printer or as a bar chart on a screen. To avoid this problem, output volumes can be expressed in information units such as the whole output, a meaningful section of output, or individual fields. Examples would be a whole report on customers, a single customer account and a data value for a customer, respectively.

The needs of the user are not evenly spread throughout the day and timing restrictions play an important part in output media selection. There are two major types of restriction – reponse times and absolute times. The response time for output is the amount of time which can elapse between input ending and output beginning. With conversational dialogues this is of the order of two seconds, which means that the whole computer system needs to be geared to this restriction. If someone wishes to receive a large report within two hours of requesting it, then the use of microfiche produced at a remote bureau is not likely to be able to meet the necessary response requirements. Absolute timing constraints are in the form of deadlines which need to be met, e.g. the statements are produced by the fifth of the next month or a report is to be on someone's desk at remote site by 9 a.m. each morning. In such a situation the designer may have the choice of electronic or traditional movement of data, and alternative throughput values will need to be calculated to allow for the reduced delay when traditional data movement is not used.

The capacity of various media to meet the throughput needs to be calculated. Again manufacturers' figures need to be tempered with such factors as:

1 Job set-up time, e.g. loading special stationery on to a printer and then aligning it;
2 Equipment down time for maintenance or following failure;
3 Operator capacity in its broadest sense;
4 Repetition of output due to illegibility or other loss.

Conversion may be required from such units as

lines per minute or characters per second to the meaningful units of information in which the throughput is expressed. If both the size of the job to be done and the ability of the equipment are known then a decision on suitability can be made. Although this is the principle, many decisions will have to be taken in arriving at these figures which may now need to be reconsidered; for example, if a report can be printed locally by 4 p.m. perhaps it can be sent by overnight courier to a remote office rather than sent electronically.

Two important human aspects of output design are first the aesthetic aspects already mentioned, and second noise. A very large amount of output is printed and printers are predominately electromechanical. Concern for the noise level of office machines has led to better sound-proofing for some printers. Ergonomic aspects of equipment selection may be treated formally, as for example in the book by Damodaran *et al.* (1980). Frequently ergonomic factors are ignored entirely or decisions made on the basis that the equipment 'seemed easy to use when it was demonstrated'. Occasional users may be able to tolerate much lower standards of design than staff for whom the equipment is part of their daily routines. Here specialist advice, and the staff themselves, need to contribute to the selection process.

Financial factors to be considered are very similar to those for input media, including environmental costs, overheads, staffing, consumables and the like.

The range of output media is constantly expanding to use a greater range of communication channels. The designer needs to be aware of the possibilities, for example by reading the trade press and manufacturers' announcements. When media is being selected more information on these media will be needed, and the design may benefit from a knowledge which cautiously extends beyond the traditional methods.

# 11 Detailed design

Once a system has been designed at a logical level and in outline, the job of specifying the physical detail can begin. In many cases the designer is selecting between alternative methods which have become standard solutions, ready made for implementation. Although this can save time and thought, it is a very dangerous practice. The users may well end up with a system which does not meet their needs because their problem was subtly different from a standard problem and the designer did not see the full implications of this difference. This cautionary note is intended to emphasize that what follows are standard solutions and techniques for standard problems. The fact that there is no such thing as the standard problem means that design needs thought as well as a basic knowledge of the alternatives frequently found useful in the past.

The treatment of this stage of the design starts with the all pervasive code design, prior to moving up in scale to look at data flows, in particular the design of forms, including output definition and dialogue design. The next area of concern is data storage, again starting at the item level and proceeding through record and file design to disk mapping. The next areas for attention are the control of the quality of data entering the system, and access to stored data. Chapter 12 gives guidelines on program specification, with the aim of reducing that 'chief time waster, the system query' referred to earlier.

Many books provide a great deal of information on the various aspects of detailed physical design. The intention here is to describe the basics, concentrating on the most important and the most common while trying to maintain some independence from current technologies. Reference to other texts and manuals should be made to obtain information for specific needs, whether they be magnetic tape storage or communications standards.

## Code design

The general principle for codes is that one should avoid designing them. Most systems will already exist in some form, and any codes used within them should be preserved because they will be familiar to the people using the system. There are, however, situations where no comparable system exists or the codes can no longer serve the current purpose.

Codes, as with other symbols and language, exist to store and communicate information. In many cases they are simple abbreviations, e.g. M/F for male or female. Where conciseness is considered, care should be taken to balance the space saving against the time taken to code and decode the information. Binary coding of months would only use 4 bits, but JUN is more readily understood then 0110. If the correct balance is found then codes can prove much quicker for people and machines when manipulating information.

Frequently codes are used as convenient identifiers for groupings of data. The identification may be unique or of a class of data corresponding to unique or generic keys. In this situation an essential feature of the coding system is that it discriminates between data and forms mutually exclusive sets of data. It is the failure of existing systems to provide this service which gives rise to their obsolescence.

Once implemented, coding systems are rarely completely redesigned. Minor changes are made, such as the addition of a suffix or prefix which give the code a new lease of life. The modified code carries on but is no longer as concise or simple as it could be if a new coding system had been developed specifically for the present circumstances. However, user relearning is avoided. Typically codes grow in this manner, becoming complex and of variable length and format. The design of codes which are flexible enough to cope with change is difficult, particularly in view of the longevity of coding systems. Flexibility can be found in non-significant codes. These codes are not based upon any aspect of the data and do not convey any information, purely acting as identifiers. They may consist of a number taken from a sequential or random number list. If the range of data being described expands then new numbers are allocated, and if the code length has to increase then addition of a prefix of one to all existing codes is relatively untraumatic.

Significant codes contain information, and are therefore based upon the data. It follows from this that they are more susceptible to change than non-significant codes. Provision needs to be made for future expansion, and this often means gaps are left in the coding system where growth is thought likely to occur. The situation is very similar to the problems of overflow handling with sequential files. Errors in using codes can be reduced if the codes have a readily understood structure, e.g. three alphabetic characters, three numerics and an alphabetic character. Here the seven-character code is split into three sections, with some validation being easily applied to each section. Where possible sections should be numeric or alphabetic, not alphanumeric. Separation of long codes (over five characters), or those composed of logically distinct parts, should be achieved with the use of hyphens or other separators. Codes can become self-checking by incorporating a check digit, typically modulus 11 for numeric data. This is a number derived from the code by an algorithm and added to the end of the code. It can detect almost all errors of transposition and transcription. The digit is calculated and added when the code is first generated. Thereafter it may be checked whenever necessary, usually each time it enters a mechanized subsystem.

Codes may be used by people and/or machines. The need for space saving or collating codes for machine use is of decreasing importance with the increased power:price ratio of computers. The needs of people who use codes should therefore receive more attention than the needs of the machines, for which codes are convenient rather

than essential. This leads to codes which are meaningful to the operators – codes which can easily be assigned and understood. In many circumstances it may well prove advisable to get the users to design their own coding system with guidance from the professional designer.

Before we turn to some specific coding systems, some other general points need to be made:

1 Where codes are written, letters and numbers which can be confused should be avoided, e.g. do not use I, O, Z, 2.
2 For spoken codes, phonetic confusion can take place between such letters as B, D, P and T.
3 In order to obtain standard length codes the beginnings may be padded with null values, but the code should start with something noticeable, e.g. 100037 rather than 00037 or 37. This takes space but improves consistency.
4 Once a code value is allocated to some data it is best not to change it (to reduce the chances of confusion). This means that code allocation needs to be carefully designed and controlled.

### Non-significant codes

Non-significant codes, as mentioned earlier, are relatively simple. Sequential lists are commonly used for transactions, starting at one and returning to it when all values in the range have been used. Obviously the range needs to be large enough to ensure that no code value is likely to be assigned to two transactions at the same time. In some cases a date is added to the number to eliminate this possibility.

### Block codes

Block codes are given to a group of things which share some property, for example:

| | |
|---|---|
| 00–49 | students |
| 50–59 | staff |
| 60–99 | disciplinarians |

Operating this coding system would involve three separate sequence lists, a person being allocated to a classification and then receiving a non-significant code.

*Mnemonic codes*

Mnemonic codes are derived from the data to which they refer. The usual intention is to reduce the size of the code while retaining meaning. Problems arise because of non-uniqueness. For example, an algorithm to produce four character codes from names may take the first character of the first name and non-vowel letters of the last name until the code is complete, or if less than four characters make up with Xs:

| | |
|---|---|
| Peter James | PJMS |
| Stephen Lee | SLXX |
| Keith Shaw | KSHW |
| Konrad Showman | KSHW |

Typically if unique codes are required a two-numeric-character suffix would be added to each set of four characters starting at 00 for the first allocation. In such a system the mnenomic would allow a user to narrow down the range of codes which were under consideration.

*Faceted codes*

Faceted codes hold different information at different points in the code. For example, character positions 1 to 4 may be derived from the name as described for mnemonic codes; positions 5 and 6 from the last two numbers in the year of birth; and the last character may be odd or even depending upon whether the person was male or female (making the code somewhat cryptic). Thus:

| | |
|---|---|
| Peter James born 1948 | PJMS/48/1 |
| Doreen Grenaway born 1956 | DGRN/56/6 |

Such codes may be more complex if the value of one field alters the meaning of another field. In the above example the last digit might not refer to sex but might rather denote that the preceding numbers were the year of birth or age at 1/9/80 (even and odd, respectively). Thus Pedro Jomaz, born in 1948, could be;

PJMZ/48/4   *or*
PJMZ/32/3

Codes are commonly used in many walks of life and it is possible to find examples quite readily by looking for them, e.g. library classifications, personal identifiers, product identifiers etc.

**Example: order processing**

In the order processing system, for all objectives, the customer number could be derived from the customer's name but combined with a non-significant code which gives flexibility. When a new customer is established the field CUST-NO is given 'according to set rules', and the data flow I/CUST is sent from SALES-MGMT to the process MAINTAIN-CUST-DATA. These set rules could say

1   Extract the first three consonants from the main word(s) in the name;
2   Set the last two digits to zero.

The insert procedure could be written so that it checked to see if the code was in use, and if it was it added one to the non-significant part and tried again. This would allow 100 customers to share each set of three letters, which would be ample, following the assumption in outline design that there are 1500 customers. Obviously the program would need to cater for the possibility of exceeding this number, but this would most likely be an error rather than a real overflow.

The product code information and the product group information could in theory be held as a single physical field by using a faceted coding system. The first character could be in the range 0 to 9 to indicate product group, followed by three numerics to uniquely identify the item within the group. This would cater for the assumed 6000 product lines as long as no single product group contained more than 1000 items. If this situation did arise, either an unused first digit would have to be taken by the product group, or the numeric fields would have to be changed to alphanumeric, or worst of all the length of code would have to be extended. Similarly, if product analysis were required on more than ten groupings the code would have to change, possibly affecting programs which only wished to identify an item irrespective of its group. All these problems stem from the 'space saving' decision to combine two types of information in one field, and to limit the amount of flexibility. The disadvantages of storing the identifier for 6000 products and the product group information in four characters are quite likely to outweigh any benefits.

## Form design

Most organizations have hundreds if not thousands of different forms in use. As electronic media become commonplace for moving information, more forms become electronic rather than on paper. The major difference between VDU screens and paper forms is that the screen may be changed to suit the user, whereas a printed form is fixed for some time. The principles of design are, however, the same. The reader who thinks that good form design is a matter of common sense, such that everyone can do it, is asked to address the question of why so many forms are badly designed.

Forms are used as a medium of data flow and storage. The information to be entered on the form may therefore be taken from the outline design. The concern here is with the medium of transfer. A form may contain several individual transactions, or groupings of data, such that subsequent page turning of the form is reduced. Such a structured form may only be justified if the data will always be handled together as long as it is bonded on to that form. In practice this means until it is entered on to a computer. The design of structured forms is an extension from the normal design described here.

A form needs to have a title by which it will be known. This should be short and meaningful so that it will be used and easily understood. A reference number will usually be included on the form to aid reordering of stationery. These identifiers should be placed somewhere inconspicuous on the form so as not to interfere with the processes of completing or reading the form, which is its true purpose. The identifier which needs to be conspicuous is the filing reference or transaction number which identifies the information on the form. Although a title can be placed in a margin, to be lost when the form is filed, the information identifier must remain prominent.

If a form contains data which will be used for validation purposes, e.g. a sequence number, or a field for batch or hash totalling, then it should stand out from the rest of the data on the form. The reason for this is that these data items will be used by a 'controller' who is only interested in this data, not in that which logically precedes or follows it. Therefore, these items have two separate users to serve with conflicting interests. Typically such fields are grouped close to an edge of the form or have a shaded background.

Headings are one type of instruction on how to use the form. They need to be related to the anticipated user so that they give extensive direction to those unfamiliar with filling in the form. For frequent users headings can be much shorter. All instructions and headings should be in the language used by the user population, including colloquialisms and industry-specific terms as appropriate. Having separate formal and natural languages only leads to confusion. If more detail is needed than can conveniently be put in the heading, further instructions should be near by, e.g. the left-hand side of a form may have instructions corresponding to the data to be entered on the right half of the form. If instructions are on a separate sheet, or in a manual, the user must be able to refer from one to the other very easily, e.g. the form might say 'for help refer to' followed by a reference number in an operator's manual which can be open alongside the form during its completion. Headings should be close to the space where data is to be entered. If boxes are used for data entry then the heading should be either outside the box or in the top left corner of the data entry box. Unless complex groupings of headings are needed, the headings should not be boxed in. If typewriters or frames to hold the form are used, then any headings or instructions should not be obscured by the equipment.

The layout should aim to get the physical sequence of the form to match the logical sequence of how the form is used. There is also the general desire to make the layout of all forms used by an organization conform to a standard, e.g. left to right and then top to bottom rather than vice versa; this row-by-row completion is appropriate if typed completion is possible. The user who completes a form may do so in a different sequence to another user who reads the form. Such inconsistencies may be reduced by the design of forms, screens and job tasks, but is unlikely to be eliminated. In arriving at a compromise layout the designer should emphasize the needs of the person completing the form over those of the reader. This helps to reduce errors which could pass into the system. Reading errors are comparatively local and can be corrected by referring back to the form. It may occasionally be valid to have two forms for one group of data which originates from two sources. In this situation the data may be entered on to a machine by operators for whom it has no logical significance anyway, and output, (if necessary) in a single format.

The layout should use limited choice answers where possible, in order to reduce errors. These choices may cover the most frequent situations, other data being entered in full. Where such choices are used, organization-wide standards on whether to circle correct replies, cross out wrong replies, tick correct replies or whatever should be established. All questions should be phrased in a positive form so as to eliminate the possibility of double negatives. If many similar questions are being asked they should be blocked together, i.e. four blocks of five questions are easier to become familiar with than twenty questions.

The space required by data entries is generally agreed to be $\frac{1}{3}$ inch vertical by $\frac{1}{4}$ inch horizontal for handwriting, although this may be less for office staff, and 1/6 inch vertical by either 1/10 inch or 1/12 inch horizontal for typewriters, depending upon the type size. The $\frac{1}{3}$ inch vertical spacing allows double-line spacing if completed by a typewriter. The space is proportional to the entry, not the heading. It may be necessary to have fixed-length fields on a form in which case boxes, corresponding to character separators, should be included. Similarly decimal points, or slashes for date separators, can be built into the form. Margins need to be included for filing forms so as not to lose information. Similarly, if a particular filing system always means that the right top corner becomes very dog-eared, then information should not be put in that corner.

Physically, forms may be on different qualities of paper, depending upon how frequently and by whom they will be used. The range of papers, print sizes and styles is such that many designers will need advice when this stage is reached. The designer should know how many parts each form

SRI CLIO Y FLEXI

ORDER FORM

Name

SRI number if known

Address for delivery (see note 1 below)

Purchase order no.

Description of goods required

Quantity

Code number if known

*Note*

1 If you do not know your SRI number you must enter your usual delivery address, otherwise delivery address need only be entered when it is not your usual delivery point.

2 Use the back of this for special instructions.

ORP/P3

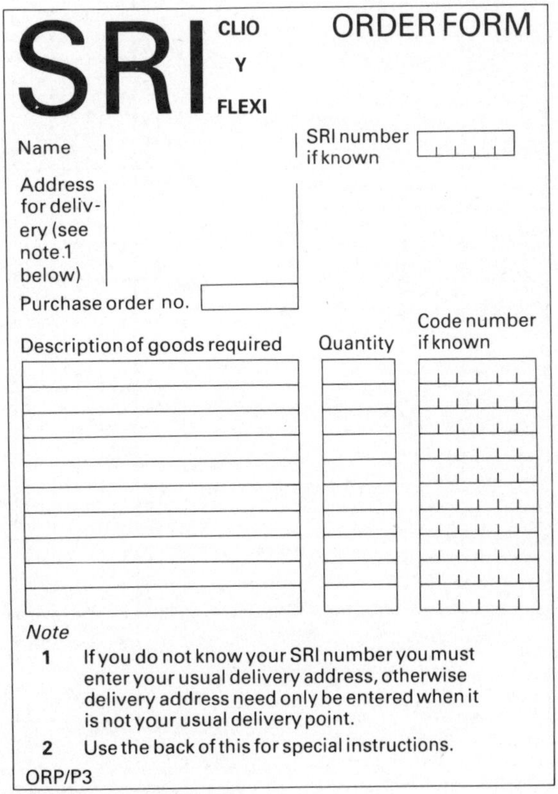

Figure 74 *Order form*

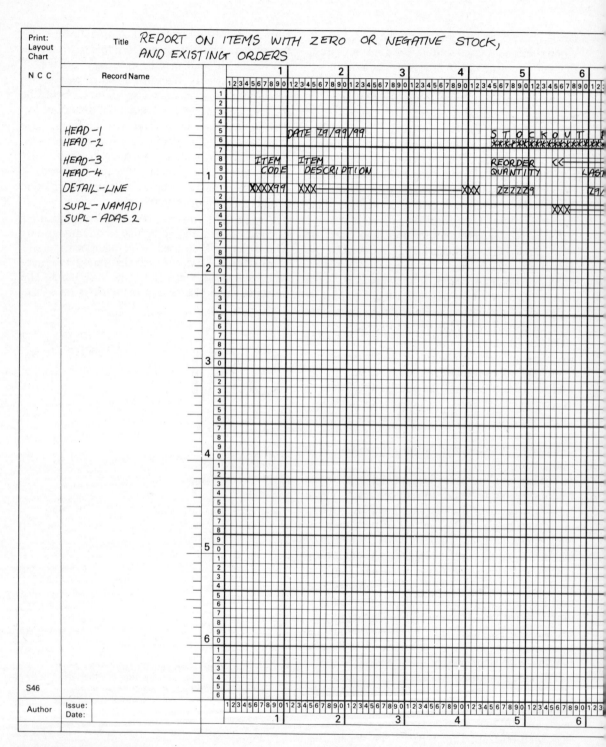

Figure 75   *Report layout*

| | System | Document | Name | Sheet |
|---|---|---|---|---|
| | ORP | 4·3 | STOCKOUT | 1 of 1 |

| 8 | 9 | 10 | 11 | 12 | 13 | 14 | 15 | 16 |
|---|---|---|---|---|---|---|---|---|

R T
XXX

PAGE NO Z99

————SUPPLIER DETAILS————————————————>>
LAST COST     CONTACT PERSON

££££9·99   XXX————————————————XXX

XXX    XXX                    XXX

will have, and then has to choose between carbon copies and chemical copies. The chemical coatings remain sensitive to pressure whereas the carbon can be removed. Forms need not be black and white. Green printing on red paper is still only a one-colour print process, and may aid the emphasis upon the data rather than the form. The use of several colours can help to separate a form into sections, but will only be cost effective if large numbers of the forms are to be used. Many of the physical decisions will depend upon the printing and ancillary services which are available to the designer, and the cost of the products.

The emphasis here is upon how forms are used and the impact of this on form design. It seems most appropriate, therefore, that the potential users of the forms should be involved in their design. Again, the reader is directed to their daily environment for examples of forms which have been designed and implemented.

### Example: order processing

Figure 74 is a form which could be used as part of the order processing system being designed. Note that the top right-hand corner is left blank so that it can be stamped with the date of receipt. The notes are placed at the bottom of the form, which is an area used to clip the forms together after they have been received. This means that no information to be read from the forms will be put here, although the notes are easily read by the person filling in the form. The form's reference number is in the lower left corner, and its title is prominent at the top alongside the company's logo.

The data which will be entered can vary from pure text on the back of the form, to a limited number of characters for customer and item identifiers. The name and address entries are not forced into a box, thereby allowing the use of a rubber stamp.

Reading the data as part of the RECEIVE-ORDER process is simple if the CUST-NO and ITEM-NO fields are present, as all the data for most orders will be on the right half of the form. The left half provides a means of validation, the entry of optional fields or alternatively a means of identifying the customer and item.

## Output definition

Output definition may be regarded as a special type of form design. The data which is to be conveyed is known from the outline and logical design stages, and the definition can concentrate upon how this data will be used. This contrasts with form design proper because there need be relatively less concern with how the output will be written, this being done by a machine.

The use of VDUs for output is considered part of dialogue design and is included in the next section. Other means for output may include microfiche, microfilm, videodisk or the more mundane printers, be they laser, line or letter quality. Where a choice exists, media selection needs to take account of:

1 The physical environment, e.g. sheets of printout are not very practical in a machine shop;
2 The task(s) which will use this data, e.g. output needs to be printed and durable if it is to be written on and used as a turnaround document;
3 The frequency of access and volumes of data, e.g. microfiche used to archive transaction data.

The organization of the data items on the chosen medium should be in such a way as to minimize the work of the user. Thus the physical layout is prescribed by the tasks to be performed and their organization. Examples include the presentation of information in graphic form if an overview of it is required, or the printing of a key data item at both ends of a long line of printout. A printout could mix characters and graphics and colour may be used to benefit.

As well as the data items themselves, it is wise to include control information on most outputs. At its simplest this is a name for the output and the date on which it was produced. This is useful to distinguish different occurrences of output, as well as providing a means of backtracking if problems are encountered.

## Example: order processing

Within the order processing system, the data flow STOCKOUT is sent by the process SEND-STOCKOUT to STOCK CONTROL whenever the difference between the quantity on hand the quanitity ordered is less than or equal to nothing ($QOH-QTY \leq 0$). STOCKOUT has the following structure:

(ITEM-NO, ITEM-DESCRIP, RE-ORD-QTY, SUPLS* (SUPL-NAME, SUPL-ADRS, SUPL-CONTACT, LAST-PURCH-DATE, LAST-COST) )

Figure 75 describes a possible report layout for a printed version of this data flow, as envisaged in the outline design.

## Dialogue design

Machines operate with very tightly structured information, and even the highest-level programming languages currently available have nowhere near the flexibility of natural languages. The man/machine interaction which takes place at a VDU needs to overcome this large difference in language. An example could be the machine's need for a date in the form of numerics DD/MM/YY, whereas the same date may be known as MM/DD/YY by some users, DD/MMM/YY with the month in characters for other users, or even DD/MM/YYYY by others.

The type of VDU operator will be significant, because a member of the general public without experience of computers will be accustomed to natural language whereas the person using the program every day will be used to the program's limited language. Between these two extremes users may be trainees, staff experienced with other dialogues but not the current one, or staff familiar with paper rather than electronic forms. Other factors, such as the amount of harassment or interruptions, will tend to move the type of user along the scale from experienced to inexperienced. This leads to the designer needing to know about the user population for a particular dialogue, which will then be designed for that type of user, possibly by the users themselves with some guidance. The complex situation of a mixed user population means that the dialogue must itself be flexible, for example:

1 A concise dialogue for experienced users can have 'help' facilities built into it for use by unfamiliar operators; in this case the 'help' messages could refer the user to a manual for full explanations.
2 Conversely, a dialogue which uses full words of input can be speeded up for experienced users by allowing abbreviations.
3 Alternatively, a dialogue could exist at several levels and the user could switch to a chosen level.

There is the further possibility of machines using natural language. There is much research into this area and some prototypes do exist where the person is no longer required to translate into the machine's language: the machine must try to do that translation. In general the more flexible the input/output the greater the machine processing required to support it.

In designing a specific dialogue the information flows should already be known. The flows may need to be restructured so as to form blocks of information meaningful to the user. This should include linking the dialogue into any other activities the user performs, and the sequence of user activities. The response time required at each point in the dialogue may be estimated because it is unlikely to be the uniform 2 or 4 seconds often quoted. Such activities as page turning, filing or stamping documents may create natural pauses which can be used by the program, e.g. to rewrite previously read records. The terminology on the screen should be the same as used by the user, and not the official language.

The designer must be familiar with the organization's standards for dialogue design, and keep within them. Where such standards do not exist the designer must inspect any other dialogues which the users encounter and develop the new dialogue to be consistent with these implicit standards. On some occasions existing dialogues may appear so bad as to be best ignored. Against this tendency must be weighed the problems caused to the user in repeatedly switching from one type of dialogue to another.

As well as the 'user' variables described so far, the designer needs to know what facilities are available on the VDU, e.g. reverse video, flashing or underscoring. However, care needs to be taken to ensure that only standard and widely occurring features are used so that a dialogue does not become dependent upon particular hardware and therefore a limitation to future flexibility. Ergonomic aspects of VDUs and the workplace, e.g. document holders or available work surface, are described by Damodaran *et al.* (1980).

One of the most common types of dialogue is the menu, in which the user is asked to select from several alternatives described on the screen. This is particularly good for inexperienced users. Experienced staff can input the selection prior to the alternatives being displayed if an appropriate prompt is given. The null answer of the inexperienced user or invalid answers leads to the full display.

Form-filling is widely used as a means for data input. Here the form is presented on the screen, usually omitting the boxes and lines. Headings and instructions exist as necessary. After entering one data item the cursor will jump to the next position at which data is to be entered. Users generally need some instructions and experience of forms to be able to use this type of dialogue well. Panel modification is an extension of this where the form appears on the screen full of data, some or all of which may be amended. This type of interface is best limited to experienced users.

Instruction and response may approach the normal idea of a dialogue, and may be initiated either by the computer (e.g. ENTER USER-ID) or by the person (RUN PROGRAM). This can be used by a variety of types of user, and its suitability is determined by the fullness of the prompts and the variation of input which is acceptable.

The reader is urged to find examples of these and other dialogue types in their environment. For example, Prestel uses menus, text editors may use panel modification, some cash dispensers can hold instruction and response dialogues. The JCL for many operating systems is based upon abbreviated keywords in either free or fixed format, which is yet another 'class' of dialogue.

Irrespective of the type of dialogue, the user may wish to go back to something on the screen and amend it. This creates an extra task to be performed. Frequently dialogues end with a question 'Screen OK?' which if answered negatively leads the user into an amendment routine. If the cursor control keys are used to go back to change a displayed field, the cursor movement must be known by a processor, possibly the VDU if the data is still buffered, or the computer itself. At the very simplest the whole of any input data may be re-entered if it is not acceptable, although this is only an efficient technique where such an occurrence is rare and the amount of data involved is small.

Errors of various types can be identified during the dialogue. It is important that users have good error messages which assist in the correction of the problem. This does not necessarily mean that extensive text should be displayed by the machine. In most cases the most efficient method of describing the error is a short message on the screen giving a reference to a hard copy manual for further details. This gives two levels of message, which are suitable for the experienced and inexperienced operator respectively. The design of screens needs to take into account the possible display of operating system error messages. If these are normally confined to the bottom two lines of the screen then these lines should not be used by the application system. Program error messages could then use the next two lines up the screen. When errors are frequently encountered, frustration and hostility may build up, and this needs to be avoided if possible. The program needs to be reasonably flexible in the syntax of input which it can accept. The messages need to be informative so as to detect the present cause of the problem and help avoid its reoccurrence.

### Example: order processing

In the order processing system there will be a great variety in the form and content of orders received by the company. Some will be written,

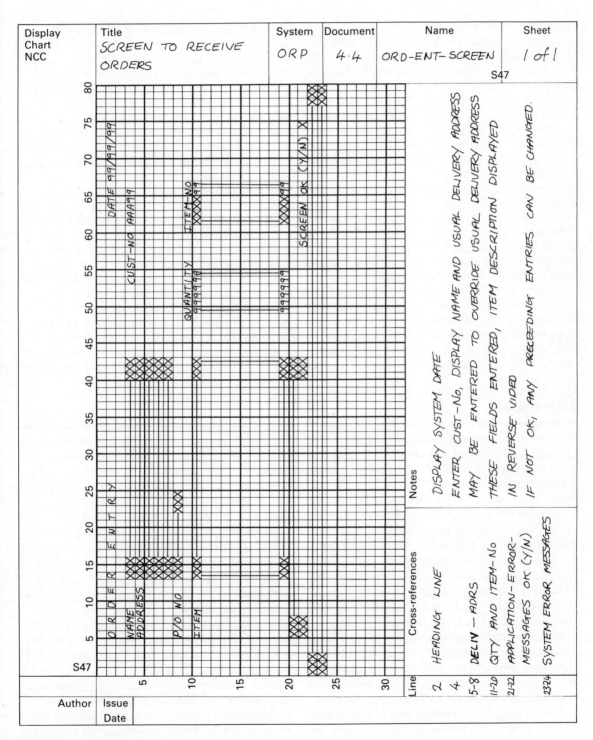

Figure 76 *Screen layout*

others accepted over the telephone. The person entering the data at the VDU will also have to standardize it. As described in outline design, this could involve the use of printed reports to determine the customer and product identifiers.

Figure 76 describes a possible screen layout which closely follows the form design of Figure 74. Most of the data will be entered on the right half of the screen, the left being for validation, e.g. customer name and occasional entries such as purchase order number.

The envisaged sequence of events would be the entry of a customer number. If END, QUIT or STOP were entered here the dialogue would end. The cursor then moves to the displayed address, which may be changed line by line until the entry of purchase order number is prompted. If there were no changes to the delivery address's first line the cursor would move directly to the P/O NO. Next entry of quantity and then item code would be prompted by the cursor moving to the appropriate position. The item description is displayed on the left for validation purposes. When a null value of quantity is entered, or ten

lines have been completed, the screen OK question is displayed. A negative answer allows any entry to be changed, using the cursor control keys; eventually, upon receipt of a new line character, the dialogue again asks SCREEN OK (Y/N). When this is Y the STD-ORDER is written, and then the screen cleared for the next order. Application and system error messages are displayed at the bottom of the screen, and include references to further explanations of the errors as well as allowing corrections.

The dialogue has been designed in this way because the operators will mainly be experienced staff working under pressure, particularly in the mornings. It is therefore possible to sacrifice explanations for the sake of speed and use form-filling techniques. In this situation it is probably best to highlight any errors, not only on the screen but also with a noise because the operator will probably not be looking at the screen. The work station would need to have room for the written orders on the right of the screen with, say, the customer and item printouts CUST-ID and ITEM-ID to the left of the screen.

## Data storage

The physical storage of data underlies the processing system and will frequently determine what is considered worth while or feasible. Ideally a storage system would act like a magical bin into which individual items of data could be inserted very easily but from which any related collection of data items could be retrieved equally easily. There is a conflict between insertion and retrieval, because in general the easier one is made, the more difficult the other becomes. The easiest way to insert data items into a bin is just to drop them in; however, this would make retrieval of specific data items a lengthy if not impossible task. If retrieval of data from the bin is to be easy, it needs to be organized in some way. This leads on to two questions: how will the data items be organized, and when will this organization take place?

Which data items are to be grouped together will have been determined as part of logical and outline design, and will be the descriptors of an entity and/or a collection of items which will be

processed together. This leads to a consideration of how the items will be physically grouped together. The simplest way is to physically place the data items together and separate them from other items; this is a typical physical record. In such a record data exhibits positional dependency, in that a value of say '6 feet' only has meaning because it occurs as the height data item in a record for a person called Robert, as distinct from having the meaning 'locomotive method' associated with it. The position of the data needs to be known in order to be able to interpret it. This is the common situation, but alternatives are possible; for example, the data items in the bin may be held in separate places but linked together for easy retrieval. Data linked in this way is said to exhibit path dependency because it is interpreted according to the path by which it was reached rather than its position. Path dependency is found in some data base systems which hold a record as several linked segments.

The time at which this organization will take place will vary depending upon the time available at either insertion or retrieval. If the system needs fast retrieval of data but there is not time pressure at insertion, then it is sensible for the organizing to be done when data items are placed in store. In systems which require both fast insertion and retrieval of data, a compromise in performance of these two operations may need to be found. Alternatively, an intermediate process can be introduced, to allow optimization of insertion and retrieval separately of each other. An example of this is the on-line bibliographic information retrieval systems, which allow very complex and fast retrieval of data but have the data inserted on to serial files in batch mode so that large volumes of data can be quickly added to the system. Once the serial data is loaded a separate process organizes it to support the retrieval requirements.

Frequently the systems designer is faced with a limited range of options which are available from the hardware and software with which she is working. The designer needs to be able to understand the common methods of organizing stored data so as to be able to choose between alternatives offered by the software, to optimize performance for a particular data organization, to assess the impact on the system, and possibly design enhancements to the standard solutions so as to meet the system requirements.

## Data items

Data items usually hold values which describe something, the attributes of an entity. In the previous example '6 feet' is an attribute of Robert, and describes his height. Consider the 'person' record for Robert (Figure 77), which contains six data items. The first name 'Robert', the last name 'Wolly', the height '6 feet' and the name of his sibling 'Caroline' are all attributes of a person. Much more information could be held about this person and stored elsewhere but linked to this record. Such links are made by pointers which are able to identify other groups of data relevant to Robert and held elsewhere. There are three basic types of pointer (Figure 78):

1  Absolute pointers, which hold the physical

| ROBERT / WOLLY / 10213E / 431 / 6FEET / CAROLINE / |

Figure 77  *Person record*

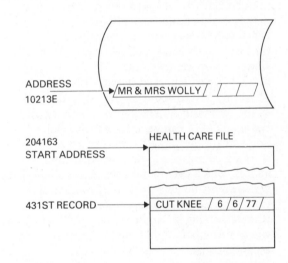

Figure 78  *Pointers*

address of the associated data, e.g. 10213E could mean that on disk 1, cylinder 02, track 13 and block E the data will exist which describes Robert's parents or guardians.

2  Relative pointers, which hold the position of the data by reference to a known point. For example, details of Robert's health could be in the 431st record on a health care file. As long as the location of the beginning of the file and the length of each record is known, the system can calculate the absolute address of Robert's health record.

**3** Symbolic pointers, which allow access to other data by containing meaning rather than an address. 'Caroline' gives information as a data item that Robert has a sibling called Caroline, but further information may be obtained by finding Caroline's own record. In this way the data item has the dual purpose of being both an attribute and a pointer.

Absolute pointers are the fastest. If the pointer is known the physical address is known. Problems arise when the data needs to be moved and all the pointers must be changed, even if the whole parent/guardian file was only moved one block. Relative pointers are usually only used to point to files with fixed-length records, and are slightly slower than absolute pointers. However, they are much more widely used because files may be physically moved about on the disks, and as long as the operating system knows where the file begins the data can be accessed. Symbolic pointers are the slowest means of access because the data item needs to be processed into an address which may be a complex operation. They are the most flexible method of linking data together because they rely upon a logical link. Robert's sibling is Caroline, irrespective of how or where the data is stored, and information can be accessed using 'Caroline' as the key.

Key fields are of two types, unique and generic. Unique keys are able to identify a single group of data items, one record. Generic keys identify several groups of data which have something in common. In the above example the last name can be used as a key, and for any given value will return records of all people who share that name. If there are no duplicate first names then 'Robert' and 'Caroline' will be unique keys. If unique keys are used then duplicate values for that field must not occur, but any field can be used as a generic key field.

Some data items do not describe the entity but exist to control the processing itself. Such data could be:

**1** Contention flags to signify that the record has been read by another program which may amend it;

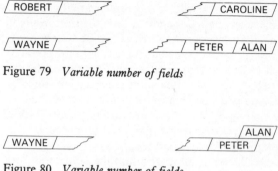

Figure 79    *Variable number of fields*

Figure 80    *Variable number of fields*

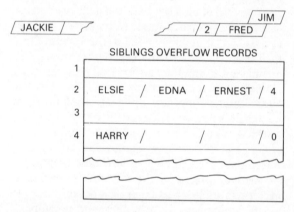

Figure 81    *Overflow record*

**2** An activity stamp to show when and by whom the record was last used;
**3** A poison flag to show whether or not the data is trustworthy; this is particularly useful for large files while discrepancies on a specific record are being investigated;
**4** Statistical; or
**5** Security status.

If such fields are to be held at a record and/or file level, then the whole system will need to use them, possibly with a shared subroutine.

**Records**
There are several standard types of record, depending upon the data items which compose them.

The most common and easy to understand records are the simple 'flat' records. These are composed of a fixed number of fields, which are all of fixed length and always occur in the same position within the record. The preceding person record for Robert is an example of such a flat record, as are all the data stores described by the logical design process. The simplicity of such flat records means easier maintenance and a more flexible data store; these attributes are often seen as outweighing the compactness of the more complex record structures.

If the number of fields in the record is variable, the record becomes variable in length (e.g. Figure 79). If Wayne has two siblings the second name could also be part of the record, adding an extra fixed length field. This is sometimes depicted as in Figure 80, to show the repetition of the sibling field and gives rise to the notion of 'non-flat' records. A problem with such records is deciding the maximum numbers of occurrences of the sibling field, so that the software can allow for this. If a large number is chosen, space can be wasted, but a small or average number will exclude some cases. One possible solution is to allow for the usual case within the main record and have a special record type for those occurrences which have many siblings. For example, if two siblings are allowed within the person record then the names of the third and subsequent siblings could be held in an overflow siblings record, associated by a pointer (Figure 81). In this example there is a pointer to the overflow siblings record, which holds the relative address of the associated data. If it was zero then there would be no additional sibling data. In a similar way the pointer in the sibling overflow record allows a chain of sibling names of indefinite length to be built up. This chain ends when a value of zero is encountered. In the above example it might well be worth making the person record fixed length with space for two siblings, so that the person file could have relative pointers addressing it. This would also save the software overheads of processing variable-length records.

A more complex situation occurs where the fields themselves are of variable length. In this situation the beginning and end of the field need to be explicitly notified to the software which cannot assume that fields start in fixed positions. There are several techniques for doing this; the simplest is the idea of the field separator, a special bit pattern used to denote the end of one field and the beginning of the next. If the space used by the name in the siblings overflow record is to be the same as the numbers of letters in the name, and therefore variable, then the arrangement is as in Figure 82, where $^F_S$ is the field separator and $^R_T$ signifies end of field and record. In order to read such a record the software continues reading each character until it encounters either $^F_S$ or $^R_T$. One alternative system holds the length of the next

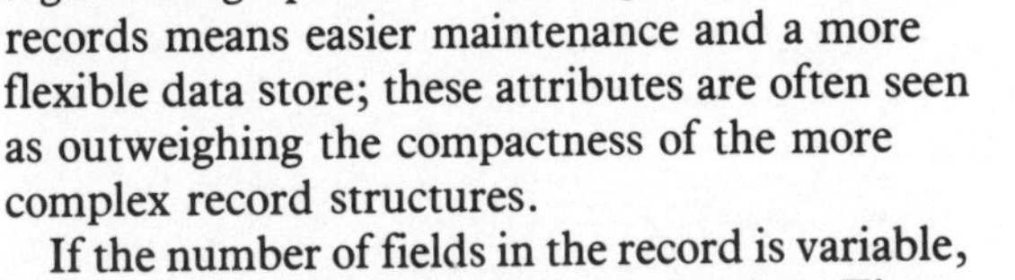

/ ELSIE / $^F_S$ / EDNA / $^F_S$ / ERNEST / $^F_S$ / 4 / $^R_T$ /

/ HARRY / $^R_T$ /

Figure 82  *Field separator*

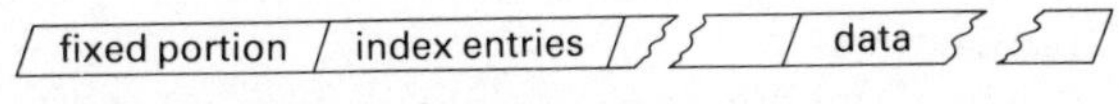

/ fixed portion / index entries / / / data / /

Figure 83  *Record indexing*

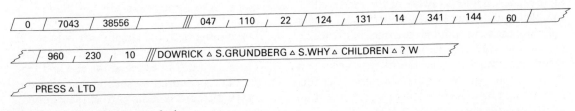

Figure 84  *Identification numbering*

field with the $^F_S$ to avoid this character comparison. Variable-length fields are used where saving storage space, at the cost of extra processing, is considered worth while, and examples can be found in some large data base management systems which offer data compression facilities, and in point-of-sale terminals which record transactions on cassettes.

The combination of a variable number of variable-length fields is fortunately not frequently needed. The major exception is bibliographic systems, which must allow for one, two or twenty-two authors, zero, one, two etc. editors, title, possible subtitle, translated title and so on: each field is of variable length. One system allows a record to consist of approximately twenty short mandatory entries followed by a selection from 950 possible fields. Many of these possible fields are capable of further subdivision by the use of field separators. To cope with this situation, the information which identifies and separates the fields is all held at the beginning of the record as an index to that record (Figure 83). The index entries contain a number to identify the type of field held, its start position and length (Figure 84).

## Files

Records are usually collected together into files, also known as data sets, which may contain one or more types of record. Where several types of record are held in a single file a field is usually added to each record to identify which type of record it is. Usually other restrictions are necessary, such as that any key or sort fields must be in the same position in each record type. Files composed of a single type of flat records, i.e. flat files, are the simplest to design and process and are easy to maintain. Wherever two or more record types are joined together in a single file, the designer should be aware of the increased complexity and reduced flexibility which is being built into the system. It becomes more difficult to process one type of record independently of the other, and changes to one record type mean that the other type will be affected. In some cases the performance benefits of storing two different but related records alongside each other will be

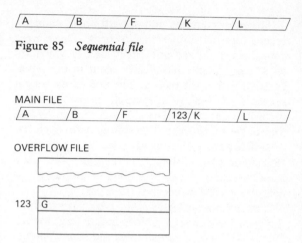

Figure 85   *Sequential file*

Figure 86   *Overflow file*

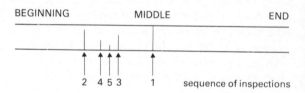

Figure 87   *Binary chop*

deemed to justify these disadvantages.

The simplest file organization is the serial file, where records are added at the end of the file. This usually means a chronological sequence for the file, which is used by logging files for recovery of a failed system with correctly ordered transactions.

Sequential files maintain the records in some sequence according to the value of a key field. When new records are added the sequence must be maintained (Figure 85). If a record with a key value of G is to be added to this file, then:

1  There must be space already left between F and K into which to insert the record G; or
2  The record can be added at the end and then the file reorganized by sorting it so that the inserted record is in its correct place; or
3  A new file may be created by writing the

existing records to it, and pausing to add G when appropriate.

These are the three most common techniques.

It may be possible to maintain the logical sequence of the records, but not the physical one, by using pointers and an overflow area. Records then overflow in a manner similar to the overflow of sibling fields described earlier (Figure 86). When the software reaches the pointer, also known as a tag, which it must distinguish from a normal record, it can then retrieve G before proceeding with K. In this way a logical sequence is maintained.

Serial and sequential files require a lot of records to be accessed prior to finding a single desired record. If there are $N$ records in the file, serial files will average somewhere between $N/2$ and $N$ accesses depending upon the ratio between finds and not-founds. Sequential files average $N/2$ access for both situations. These file organizations are not well suited if single records are to be processed, and are therefore said not to support direct access. However, if a sequential file consists of fixed-length records, then a binary chop search technique can be employed. This looks at the middle record and compares it with the desired key. The software then knows that half the file can be ignored. This process continues until the record is either found or not found (Figure 87). On average the number of accesses to find one record will be slightly less than $\log_2 N$, depending upon the number of 'lucky' hits. The software needs to know where the file begins and ends, the sequence of the records and the length of each record, so as to calculate where to search next.

Direct access is usually by means of indexes or hashing algorithms. The purpose is to convert a logical value of the key into a physical address. Indexes do this by storing an array of addresses and key values.

A basic index has an entry for every record on the file, and these are usually kept in sequence (Figure 88). The address may be either the relative address of the record, if they are fixed-length records, or the relative address of the block which contains the record. The software searches the index, sequentially or using a binary

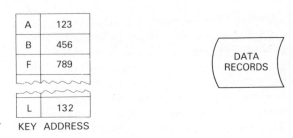

| KEY | ADDRESS |
|-----|---------|
| A | 123 |
| B | 456 |
| F | 789 |
| L | 132 |

Figure 88   *Basic index*

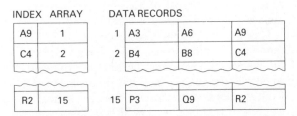

Figure 89   *Limit index*

chop, to find the address of the data. It will then read a block from disk into memory and proceed to search it for the required record. This searching is assisted if the record offset is known. Note that the address for record L is between those for A and B. The records need not be in sequence if a basic index is used, and all sequential access occurs through the index, i.e. a basic index supports an index random file. Overflow is not a problem with index random files because new records are simply put in the first available free space and the address recorded in the index.

A limit index only holds entries for selected records on the file, and so reduces the space requirements and search times of the index. This is achieved by having the data records in sequence and in groups. The highest, or in some systems the lowest, key value in the group is held in the index with the address for that group of records. The index allows direct access to the group and sequential access within the group. A group frequently corresponds to a physical block (Figure 89). In searching for C2 the software looks at A9, and can ignore it because A9 < C2 and there is an ascending key sequence. Next C4 ⩾ C2, and so the records at address 2 are searched sequentially and it is found that C2 does not exist. To maintain the sequence of the records the techniques described for sequential files may be employed, i.e. reserving space for insertions, reorganizing, rewriting the file or using pointers from the data area to an overflow area. Alternatively, the overflow area itself may have an index held alongside the main index. If a file is very large a hierarchy of indexes may be employed to reduce the number of accesses required to convert the logical key value into an address.

Hashing algorithms, also known as randomizers, are routines which have as their input a possibly meaningful logical key value, and as output a number which has no meaning apart from the fact that it is derived from the logical key value. For example, assume it is desired to store records for 100 people, using their names as unique keys, and assuming there are no duplicate names. An algorithm may take the bit pattern for the first 15 characters of the name, i.e. 120 bits, and add the first 60 bits to the last 60 bits. This is termed folding. The 61-bit result may then be treated as a number and squared. The middle 10 bits of this operation could be extracted, giving a value in the range 0 to 1023. If the records are to be placed in an area which allows one record at each address and there are 200 addresses, then the final step could be to divide the number by 200 which would leave a remainder in the range of 0 to 199. This could be used as the address. Such an algorithm could be used to convert the key to an address when a record is being inserted or retrieved.

It is possible that two or more keys may be given the same address and the records are then termed synonyms. The number of records which may be stored at an address is termed the bucket capacity. Inserting records will only result in overflow if the number of synonyms for an address is greater than the bucket capacity. The National Computing Centre has suggested that a bucket capacity ⩾ 10 will significantly reduce overflow problems. If the ratio between number of records held and the available space, i.e. the packing density, is low then overflow will not be

FIRST NAME INDEX

| ALAN | 3 | | |
|---|---|---|---|
| CAROLINE | 4 | | |
| JOHN | 6 | | |
| MAUREEN | 7 | | |
| PETER | 5 | | |
| ROBERT | 1 | | |
| WAYNE | 2 | | |

LAST NAME INDEX

| ALLENBY | 2 | | |
|---|---|---|---|
| OLARED | 3 | 6 | 7 |
| PIDGEON | 5 | | |
| WOLLY | 1 | 4 | |

HEIGHT INDEX

| 2 FEET | 6 | | |
|---|---|---|---|
| 4.5 FEET | 4 | 5 | |
| 5 FEET | 2 | 3 | 7 |
| 6 FEET | 1 | | |

PERSONS' FILE

| | | | | | |
|---|---|---|---|---|---|
| 1 | ROBERT | WOLLY | | 6 FEET | |
| 2 | WAYNE | ALLENBY | | 5 FEET | |
| 3 | ALAN | OLARED | | 5 FEET | |
| 4 | CAROLINE | WOLLY | | 4.5 FEET | |
| 5 | PETER | PIDGEON | | 4.5 FEET | |
| 6 | JOHN | OLARED | | 2 FEET | |
| 7 | MAUREEN | OLARED | | 5 FEET | |

Figure 90　*Indexing: secondary*

LAST NAME INDEX

| ALLENBY | 2 |
|---|---|
| OLARED | 3 |
| PIDGEON | 5 |
| WOLLY | 1 |

HEIGHT INDEX

| 2 FEET | 6 |
|---|---|
| 4.5 FEET | 4 |
| 5 FEET | 2 |
| 6 FEET | 1 |

PERSONS' FILE

| | | | | | C1 | C2 |
|---|---|---|---|---|---|---|
| 1 | ROBERT | WOLLY | | 6 FEET | 4 | * |
| 2 | WAYNE | ALLENBY | | 5 FEET | * | 3 |
| 3 | ALAN | OLARED | | 5 FEET | 6 | 7 |
| 4 | CAROLINE | WOLLY | | 4.5 FEET | * | 5 |
| 5 | PETER | PIDGEON | | 4.5 FEET | * | * |
| 6 | JOHN | OLARED | | 2 FEET | 7 | * |
| 7 | MAUREEN | OLARED | | 5 FEET | * | * |

Figure 91　*Chaining*

signficant. Apart from the techniques described for sequential files, hashed files can use consecutive spill for overflowed record. This technique, also known as linear probing or linear open addressing, simply places the record to be inserted in the next free space in the file. When the record is to be retrieved the software must look at the expected location of the record, the home bucket. If the record is not present it will read forward until either it is found or a free space is encountered. The reasoning is that if the record had been inserted it would have been placed between the home bucket and the free space. This means that, when a record is deleted, either all records following it need to be checked to see if they are overflows and moved back one stage, or (more usually) the record is flagged as being an available free space if the software is trying to insert a record, but not a real free space if a retrieval operation is being undertaken. Where overflow is allowed to occur in the prime data area, it can result in build-up of records in one area of the file, and a separate overflow area may be needed.

Files which require direct access by several keys can be constructed by employing the techniques used for single-key files. If extra indexes are constructed, the file may be said to be partly inverted, or to employ secondary indexes. Consider the persons' file, which may be indexed by first name, last name and height (Figure 90).

First name is a unique key, and there are as many entries as records on the file because a basic index is used in this example and the key is unique. Each index entry consists of a key value and a single relative address. Last name and height are generic keys and have an entry for each key value. This is followed by a variable number of addresses depending upon the number of records which have that key value. The techniques described earlier for handling a variable number of fields can be employed here to simplify index processing. One possible method involves only holding a single address in the index and then spreading the remaining addresses throughout the data (Figure 91). C1 and C2 are the data items which hold the address of the next record in the chain which has the same last name

or height; an asterisk denotes the end of the chain. Files containing chains such as these are often termed multilist files. It is possible to replace the asterisk with a reference back to the index. This allows a chain to be entered at a midpoint, possibly via first name, and all other records with the same value retrieved.

Returning to the conflicting interests of record insertion and retrieval, we may broaden the approach somewhat to include deletion with insertion under the heading of maintenance. The amount of maintenance work done on a file is sometimes termed its volatility. A volatile file will require many insertions and deletions. In a multilist file this will involve not only inserting the record, and recording this in the primary index, but also:

1  Checking that the data values for the other key fields already exist in the secondary indexes and expanding them if necessary;
2  For each key field changing the index to point to the new record and making the new record hold the address which was formerly in the index. This assumes the sequence on the chain is not important.

A similar sequence of events must take place for deletion. This means that maintenance is a complex operation. Conversely, retrieval is relatively simple and flexible. A similar situation occurs with secondary indexes, where such questions as 'How many people are called Olared?' or 'Are any Wollys under 4 feet tall?' can be answered without even retrieving records by simple logical operations on the index arrays.

No two pieces of data management software will handle all the different operations in the same way. The reader can create a new combination of the techniques which support writing, reading, rewriting and deleting data, according to a specific set of needs. The objectives are simple – to perform these operations in such a way as to minimize the overall time spent processing the file.

This coverage of data storage is of necessity brief, and reference to specialized texts should be made to cover free space management or other techniques for overflow, indexing, hashing, etc.

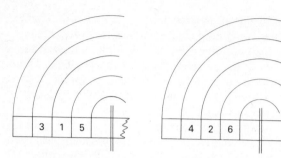

Figure 92   *Disk mapping*

## Disk mapping

The physical location of a file on a disk may affect its performance characteristics markedly. An example of this is the time taken to sequentially read a file and write an updated version of it. If the files are on separate disk drives, it will be possible to read and write independently and virtually eliminate seek times. If the files are on the same drive adjacent to each other, then after each read the head must travel to the new file to write and then return, involving a maximum seek time. If the files must both be on one multiplatter disk drive they would best be placed one above the other on the same cylinders, thereby minimizing seek time.

The situation is rarely as simple as this; instead, several programs usually all require disk access independently of each other. The designer needs to map the files on to the disks to meet either the most frequent set of requirements or, where this is different, the most critical set of requirements. Once the mix of programs is known, the estimated volumes can be applied to them to produce an overall estimate of the number of accesses to each file. If it is possible to select the location of index arrays, the frequency of access to each type of index may also be estimated. The list of files may then be ranked according to access frequency. The most heavily used file is then located at the centre of one disk and then the second file is placed in the centre of the next drive (Figure 92). The third file is placed next to the first, and so on.

This again is a simplified description, assuming that there are two single-platter disk drives and that files can only occupy a single physical area. It does, however, illustrate the principle of disk mapping, which is the minimization of seek time. Consideration needs to be taken of files which are only used together and periodically, such as payroll. A removable disk can contain all the payroll data and be loaded when necessary. If whole disk copying is the back-up method, the frequency of back-up for each file will be a variable to consider. Each situation has its own factors which need to be taken into account; that is, assuming that the operating system is not so user friendly that it automatically manages the space allocation!

## Example: order processing

We turn now to the order processing system. The outline design for E + N objectives has already determined that the data stores ITEM-BASIC-DATA and LAST-BUY-DATA would need to have direct access facilities, whereas the SUPPLIER-DATA could be organized in any manner and still offer acceptable performance.

ITEM-BASIC-DATA (ITEM-NO,
    ITEM-DESCRIP, BIN-NO, ITEM-PRICE,
    ITEM-DISCOUNT%, ITEM-TAX%,
    RE-ORD-QTY, QOH)
LAST-BUY-DATA (ITEM-NO, SUPL-NAME,
    SUPL-CONTACT, LAST-PURCH-DATE,
    LAST-COST)
SUPPLIER-DATA (SUPL-NAM,
    SUPL-ADRS)

These three data stores could be physically implemented on the presumed minicomputer's disk using indexed sequential organization for direct access for the first two, and serial for SUPPLIER-DATA. When the process SEND-STOCKOUT identifies an out-of-stock item it could obtain the data flow PURCH-INF by setting SUPL-NAME to a low value. This performs a direct read on the file LAST-BUY-DATA, which would not retrieve a record, followed by sequential reads to obtain the desired records. This technique is sometimes

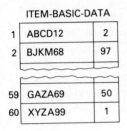

ITEM-BASIC-DATA

| 1 | ABCD12 | 2 |
|---|--------|---|
| 2 | BJKM68 | 97 |
| 59 | GAZA69 | 50 |
| 60 | XYZA99 | 1 |

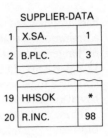

SUPPLIER-DATA

| 1 | X.SA. | 1 |
|---|-------|---|
| 2 | B.PLC. | 3 |
| 19 | HHSOK | * |
| 20 | R.INC. | 98 |

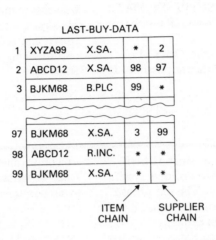

LAST-BUY-DATA

| 1 | XYZA99 | X.SA. | * | 2 |
|---|--------|-------|---|---|
| 2 | ABCD12 | X.SA. | 98 | 97 |
| 3 | BJKM68 | B.PLC | 99 | * |
| 97 | BJKM68 | X.SA. | 3 | 99 |
| 98 | ABCD12 | R.INC. | * | * |
| 99 | BJKM68 | X.SA. | * | * |

ITEM CHAIN    SUPPLIER CHAIN

Figure 93   *Using pointers*

referred to as milestoning. The supplier addresses could then be read from the SUPPLIER-DATA, by reading until the record was found or not.

If at some time in the future information about items supplied by a given supplier was required, this could be obtained by either reading through the whole of LAST-BUY-DATA or by means of a secondary access route. For example, another index could be created using the unique entries (SUPL-NAME, ITEM-NO) to allow milestoning. Alternatively, a relative pointer in the SUPPLIER-DATA could identify the first of a chain of last buy records. Access from the ITEM-DATA could similarly be speeded up using pointer chains.

The use of the pointer system (shown in Figure 93) would speed up retrieval of data, particularly if the elements in the chain were organized to help this, e.g. the supplier chain having entries in ITEM-NO sequence and/or the item chain being in LAST-PURCH-DATE sequence. It is worth noting that the more the physical organization is tuned to meet the data retrieval requirements, the more difficult insertion and deletion become.

If it is necessary to reduce storage requirements, the two fields ITEM-NO and

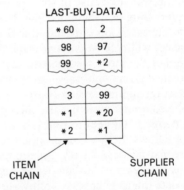

LAST-BUY-DATA

| * 60 | 2 |
|------|---|
| 98 | 97 |
| 99 | * 2 |
| 3 | 99 |
| * 1 | * 20 |
| * 2 | * 1 |

ITEM CHAIN    SUPPLIER CHAIN

Figure 94   *Eliminating data*

SUPL-NAME could be omitted from LAST-BUY-DATA, if and only if the end-of-chain markers were changed to also point back to the 'owner' items and suppliers.

As can be seen in Figure 94 the identifiers have been replaced by pointers, although the other three data items, SUPL-CONTACT, LAST-PURCH-DATE and LAST-COST, would not have changed. This type of file organization could mean lengthy chain searches if one supplier had supplied a great many products. There is also a limitation in that the file LAST-BUY-DATA is no longer very meaningful on its own. The ITEM-BASIC-DATA and SUPPLIER-DATA also need to be accessed to answer all but the most trivial requirements.

These and a great many other ways of physically organizing this data are possible. It is important that the physical organization is determined by the requirements of the system, both short and long term. The designer needs to bear this in mind during the detailed design of the physical storage system, because data cannot be stored and retrieved without costs, and it is the requirements which give guidance on balancing these costs.

## Data control

If a system is to produce data which is both reliable and valid, then all parts of that system need to be working correctly. The old phrase 'garbage in, garbage out' is true; however, it is the system designer's job to ensure that garbage does not get into the system. A phrase such as 'garbage out = design error' would better describe the responsibilities of the designer.

Initially, errors may arise in the capture and manual processing of data. Good job design leading to increased job satisfaction and work performance, will help to prevent errors here. The design of the input mechanisms can again help to reduce errors, and these areas may have error detection and processing features built into them. The computer system must then process the data correctly (system testing is a separate topic and follows the work of program testing). Hardware may fail occasionally (system reliability is considered as part of outline design and includes data integrity checks, archiving and recovery procedures). The purpose here is to describe the control of data quality during the initial stages of getting it into machine readable form.

All control procedures depend upon a decision being made by comparing two values. (In the feedback model described in Chapter 1, comparison was between the plan and the output. Here a similar comparison will be performed, although the control function may be spread physically over several parts of the system.) The designer needs to take great care, first that these two values come from different sources, otherwise they will always agree, and second that the values are comparable. For example, a teacher may be asked how many students are in a particular class by an administrator who is checking that figures for student enrolments held in a central office are correct. If the teacher looks at the front page of a register and replies with that number, then the check is worthless if the register was originally issued by the central office with the number of students entered on it from their records. Alternatively, if the teacher counts the number of students attending classes and replies with this figure, then there will probably appear to be an inconsistency because the number of attendees of a class is not the same thing as the number of enrolments. Mistakes such as these are commonly built into systems.

The types of data error which are most likely to occur during initial processing involve:

1  Loss of data or its duplicate entry, which may apply to items of data, transactions or whole batches of data;
2  Unreasonable data, which is beyond acceptable limits, or inconsistent with either its contemporary input or previously input (stored) data;
3  Data which is reasonable, entered once and once only, but wrong.

A computer can detect and handle errors of types 1 and 2 but not of type 3, which requires an understanding of what is happening in the real world which the computer does not have. For example, if a potential passenger asks for a ticket to Brinscall, a Lancashire village, and Brinscall is a valid destination, then it would be impossible for a computerized ticket printing machine to know that the person did not want to go to Brinscall and in fact meant Brisbane, Australia. An operator of the machine might be able to detect the error. Only when output was generated for the passenger would the error be identified. It is in order to identify this type of error that system users are required to check the output they receive.

### Prevention

It is almost invariably true that what constitutes good design work helps to prevent errors occurring; the exception arises when the decision is made not to prevent errors arising. Data control incurs costs as with anything else, and if the benefits are not sufficiently high then it is good design to accept a certain level of error. It is to be expected that different levels of errors would be tolerable in nuclear defence systems, banking systems and home games systems; with this exception, good design of forms, codes, clerical procedures, dialogues, the production of job instructions and the creation of a positive attitude towards the system and trained staff, all help to prevent errors.

A reduction in the number of errors being generated can be made if the number of manual processes and interfaces is reduced. This is a major reason for the widespread use of terminals by users. Data may be captured and entered on to the machine very close, in time and space, to its source. Where data is captured as a by-product of the activity itself there is a mimimum chance of error, e.g. point-of-sale terminals which store details of sales as they are put into the till by the cashier. Usually there will be at least one person involved to structure the data into an acceptable format, e.g. a VDU operator accepting telephone advertisements for a newspaper. In general, the simpler the input procedure the less chance of error.

### Detection

Accepting that some errors will occur leads to the design of procedures to detect them.

At the level of the individual field, checks can be made for:

1 Missing, illegible or duplicate values occurring where they should not do so;
2 Wrong data types, formats or sizes;
3 Internal consistency, by recalculating a check digit;
4 Reasonable values, by checking with stored data, possibly a system parameter file which defines an acceptable domain of values.

Typical checks made at a record or transaction level ensure that all the data needed for the transaction to be processed is consistent with itself, e.g. a goods received note must contain a header and one or more detail lines before coming to the totals. A transaction may appear valid, but be in error because it has already been processed once. To detect this requires that the system stores information on transactions received, possibly by using numbered transactions in ascending sequence, although this is very restrictive. Transaction numbers assigned manually can be logged, or an identifier generated from the data which is kept for a period; if synonyms are detected full transaction comparison could follow. To assist the single processing of transactions they may have kept with them a log of the processing done to them. For example, a form might have a section where the dates on which certain actions were taken are recorded (see Chapter 12).

Further checks are often incorporated if batches of data are processed. These may include control of hash totals, transaction counts and usually a log of all activities performed on that batch and by whom. To detect errors the totals and counts need to be done whenever the data enters a new subsystem. If a hash total is accumulated by each operator and then by the computer, it should be relatively simple to identify an error and where it was introduced.

Finally, at the highest level, checks can be made to ensure that the correct output is received for the given input. Such checks may be performed by data control staff, or by users themselves. The use of an audit trail to record all transactions entering a system, together with relevant totals, is generally found to be an effective way of monitoring the flow of data into a system and checking for completeness.

## Action

Where an error is identified some action needs to be taken. The first thing to be done as part of the error processing is to identify the severity of the condition. It may be such that processing can continue with a warning printed on the audit trail, or an 'are you sure?' question confirmed by a VDU operator. If processing of the data cannot continue, the extent of the problem is the next significant factor. The individual field may be ignored, if it is an optional entry, or the transaction stopped, or possibly the whole batch of data may be suspect. The general principle is to continue processing as much data as possible.

If the error is not identified immediately upon data entry, processing may have taken place which has caused the spread of false information. Procedures to reverse such effects need to be designed. For example, if stock figures are reduced by an order which is later rejected, orders subsequently received may have been back ordered for lack of stock. To make the system correct such back orders should be tracked down and released, although this may be costly. The later an error is identified the greater the cost of its correction; hence the emphasis upon checking input.

The data which is not to be further processed must then be corrected. To do this, details of the condition need to be given to someone who is in a position to establish what is correct. All relevant information needs to be provided to assist the resolution of the problem. The ideal situation exists when the original source of the information is still available, e.g. a patient is with a doctor's receptionist while an appointment is being made and the system cannot find a record of the patient. It has been claimed that the ability to get errors resolved quickly at the source of information is the biggest benefit of on-line systems. Where such a situation does not exist, the details need to be passed to the most likely source of correction.

Eventually, when the correct data is known, either the whole parcel of rejected data needs to be reinput or the correction must be applied to the stored erroneous data. As stated elsewhere, the latter is the best method in most circumstances. The designer needs to build a procedure to allow the corrected data to be processed, and this may mean that it needs to be merged with that previously entered.

Error identification and processing is a very complex task and takes an inordinate amount of design and testing time compared with mainline processing, but is often a critical factor in the effectiveness of a system. Error processing needs to be controlled itself so as to avoid the loss of the data in which an error was identified or its duplication, e.g. by complete reinput as well as correction. There should be the minimum disruption to work patterns, and any timing or sequence constraints may need to be held to. An error log is frequently used to monitor and control such processing.

### Example: order processing

We return now to the order processing system and the process STORE-DESPATCH-CONFIRM which receives the data flow DESPATCH-CONFIRM (PICK-NO, ITEM-NO, DESPATCH-DATE). This process uses the first two of these fields to identify a specific occurrence of ORDERED-LINE-DATA, into which it writes the date the goods were despatched. The control of the quality of data going into the system starts by trying to prevent the occurrence of any errors. The picking note produced in the warehouse could be used as a turnaround document, but this does not allow for orders which are split into several despatches on different dates.

The warehouse staff could notify the despatch of an order line by writing on a form, which is then used by a VDU operator in conjunction with a program. The form would need to be carefully designed, to be used alongside the picking note, so as to minimize transcription errors. It could contain fields for validation purposes as well as the true data, e.g. ITEM-DESCRIP and QTY.

To detect any errors, the program could verify that the date was valid and that the order line data existed. The operator could enter the quantity despatched, which would be cross-checked against the quantity held in the data store. Once this check was passed the item description could be obtained from ITEM-BASIC-DATA, and displayed on the screen for the operator to visually cross-check with the form. Note that unless the ORDERED-HEAD-DATA held the CUST-NO, no similar check with the customer name would be possible. The value of such a check would need to be assessed, together with the cost of adding the field to the store, prior to deciding on whether or not to go back and change the design. This is an illustration of the iterative nature of design and a characteristic of bottom-up data design.

(What might appear to be an 'obvious' attribute of an entity is not considered unless it is explicitly used in the application modelling or for some other reason is deemed necessary to the design. For example, the field ITEM-NO which allows some of this validation was only added so as to uniquely identify lines on an order, during the normalization process. Top-down data modelling techniques, such as entity relationship, have their own benefits and limitations, but could be used to complement and validate the bottom-up modelling done here.)

Procedures to follow in the event of an error being detected need to be established. The first possibility is miskeying by the VDU operator, and it must be possible to re-enter the data if this is the cause of the problem. If the problem is in the data on the form, then this must be returned to the warehouse for comparison with the original picking note by the staff involved. Here the object is to determine exactly what was despatched to whom and when. Once this is known the correct despatch data can be stored.

Procedures could be set up to control the whole batch of data transmitted to and processed by DESPATCH-CONFIRM. Similarly, procedures need to be established in the warehouse to keep track of partially filled orders and to control the flow of documents through the department. This could potentially involve a periodic report based on the ordered head and line data stores, stating what the computer thought was still outstanding.

In order to reduce the possibility of transcription error, and to speed up the resolution of errors, a VDU could be located in the warehouse. The warehouse staff could then enter the data immediately the goods were despatched.

## Access control

The data which is to be held on computers, and the rights of access to it, are areas of concern for many people. Prior to consideration of the technical aspects of access control, it is worth while looking at some of the broader issues.

Most countries in the world that are heavy users of computers have legislation on data privacy. In the United Kingdom, central and local government tend to look upon themselves as elected bodies looking after information for the overall good of the community. Debate regarding this role has contributed to the delay in United Kingdom privacy legislation. The possibility and increasing reality of transborder data flows casts doubt on many national attempts at control, and is a topic for debate in its own right. Within an organization some data may be considered too sensitive to place on a computer system; a typical example is the directors' payroll. In most cases a consensus regarding what data shall be held, who has access to it and for what purpose, needs to be achieved prior to any technical work being done. This is to say that the objectives need to be defined before looking at the methods. If such a consensus is not reached, attempts to breach security will be more common and the problems of maintaining privacy correspondingly greater. Likewise, where end users are not able to check the output then some types of error are most unlikely to be detected (see previous section, 'data control'). It is relatively easy to cloud the issue in emotional terms when one considers one's own personal data. A more balanced view may well be obtained by including the data personal to tax evaders or embezzlers in such a debate.

It is worth noting that the general image of computers as either 'all powerful genie at the service of mankind' or 'evil, powerful machines dominating mankind' will not decline with popular use of microprocessor-based equipment. The new technologies of fingerprint storage and analysis, already developed, together with voice and picture recognition facilities, will mean a continuing debate on their application.

### Golden Rule 0
Being a good human being is far more important than being a good systems designer.

The two roles need not be incompatible, but the point about this rule is that the designer is human (neither god nor beast) and needs to take responsibility for his or her actions. The day-to-day pressures of living and of systems design can lead to all but the most moral of people ignoring this fundamental principle. Some of the consequential possibilities and dangers are described in accounts of the Milgram (1974) experiment, to which the reader is referred.

Access to information is not a problem which is unique to computer systems. In manual systems data is already in legible language, although it may be difficult to retrieve any volume of data or perform complex matching. In batch computer systems a computer and its data could be physically guarded, and access is relatively slow and obvious because input and output usually need to pass through several groups of staff. Problems are greatest with on-line systems, where the hardware may be widely distributed, and the system is designed to support fast, complex access to data and is controlled by a terminal operator. The data controls which exist in most computer systems, and the machine enforced standards, probably mean a much lower percentage of errors in computer-held data than existed in the manual equivalent.

Under the heading of access control is included not only control of access to data but also unauthorized updating, this usually being part of some type of fraud. People may be authorized to access data for one purpose but not to use it in a different way. An example could be a member of a personnel department who may look at the whole of any individual's personal record, but who is not permitted to ask for a list of pairs of staff who have taken half-day holidays at the same time; such

data is beyond that normally needed for man management!

Attempted breaches of privacy can be classified in three ways. The first is casual attempts by relatively unskilled staff, which for present purposes approximates to those without programming skills. These attempts can usually be stopped by standard security techniques built into application systems. The second is the casual attempts by skilled staff. These may be stopped by using standard techniques, although the number of possible access routes to be protected needs expanding. Finally, there are the determined attempts by skilled staff. These are very difficult to stop, and start with positive vetting of all staff. The cost of such extensive security is considered by many organizations to be greater than can be justified.

The basic components of any access control system are a method of identifying each user, relating the user to permitted functions and data, and finally the monitoring and control of user activity.

Identification may be no more than the computer recognizing one of its own terminals, and by implication a valid user. Keys, badges or cards may be carried by staff and used to gain access to a terminal and identify the operator. Generally data entry is required, which may range from a simple unique password to a series of responses to questions asked by the machine. These questions will vary each day but are based on personal information previously given to the machine. Where passwords are employed, operators may be able to change their own passwords to add security to the system, especially if, as is now usual, the computer uses an encryption routine to store the password. However, if someone forgets their password, it is lost forever. If passwords are centrally controlled, forgotten passwords can be rediscovered, but the main list now requires securing.

Once the user is known the system can then extract from store a profile which depicts what that user is allowed to do. Many systems allow the definition of a matrix for each password, which plots function against data. The functions cover read, write and modify, and the data may be at data base, file, record or field levels of detail. Control is usually exercised over whether or not a user may use some operating system commands, such as compilation, text editing, file deletion or creation. A user may not be allowed to use the printer, or may only be permitted to execute one program which is a master menu and security system. A detailed definition of activities which are permissible for each user, or class of users, needs to be established.

Exercising control of access to data is possible and requires some software to compare the task being attempted by a user with the permitted activities. This is often done within the application programs, although this offers no protection against skilled staff who can write their own programs. If a wide-ranging security system is needed then the software needs to be equally wide ranging, such that a particular file is made non-accessible to either a program or a system utility if the wrong password was given to the access controller. Consideration then needs to be given to ensuring the integrity of the access controller itself.

To allow for human beings making errors, several attempts at the correct password are usually permitted before a user is rejected by a system. Where such a rejection occurs, all known information on the attempt should be recorded on an access control log. By establishing a log of all attempted security breaches, the designer is collecting data which can subsequently be analysed. This may reveal that certain terminals have more access problems than others, which could be investigated, and may be able to assist with the diagnosis of weaknesses if breaches are subsequently discovered. The psychological effect of such a log may alone justify its design.

Access control can be an emotive issue, and frequently such security depends upon the attitudes to the data of all those involved. Basic techniques exist to cover most eventualities, but care needs to be taken to ensure that access control is justifiable in both financial terms and in terms of the extra processing it will necessitate.

### Example: order processing

If a terminal was sited in the warehouse it might be advisable to limit the functions which can be performed by the warehouse operators. For example, they may not be allowed to use the MAINTAIN-CUST-DATA program, produce DESPATCH-STATS or edit and compile programs. In this case there are several operators who are limited to the single process STORE-DESPATCH-CONFIRM.

It is better not to limit the functions of the terminal itself; this reduces the range of options available if a high-priority terminal fails. Rather, identify the group of users by means of a simple user ID code and/or password. Controlling the functions permitted would depend upon the facilities provided by the operating system. Assuming all that is done is to hold the user's identity at a terminal-specific address then each program would need to use a routine which (1) looked at that address, (2) compared its contents with a list of valid users and then (3) either continued executing or generated a security violation message on the screen and audit trail, stopping execution.

If access to system commands and utilities was to be restricted, then they would need to be physically removed from the live version of the operating system. A development version of the system could be loaded when editing, compilation etc. were to be performed. Most operating systems offer more comprehensive access control systems, forcing all users to go through a security process. The warehouse user could be limited to writing to ORDERED-LINE-DATA, reading this file and ITEM-BASIC-DATA, and executing compiled programs. Such restrictions would exercise quite tight control over user activities.

# 12 Program specification

## Introduction

The program specification is a piece of documentation with the purpose of saying exactly what a program does. its original purpose is unambiguous communication between the designer and the programmer. It may then become the key evidence for establishing responsibility for part of the system not working – did the designer design the error, or did the programmer introduce it? In most cases the designer takes responsibility for ensuring good communication with the 'reasonable' programmer, and therefore takes responsibility for most errors in the system. These remarks may appear cynical, but for institutions where programming is farmed out to software houses, contract staff or even another part of the same organization, the program specification is treated as any other binding agreement between two parties. Eventually the program specification becomes part of the overall system documentation, to be used by systems analysts and programmers who are responsible for maintaining the system. Indeed, it may be included in the source code as a comment. Writing program specifications calls for good communication skills, which will ensure a concise and unambiguous statement of the requirements of the program.

Most organizations have either formal standards which apply to the whole organization or local standards which are set by the programming manager, and therefore the designer is given the rules for the communication. If standards are not already established, the designer must select the appropriate method of presenting the information. Whatever standards are followed for the program specification, it is important that they fit into the overall documentation standards used. Thus, if a data dictionary is being used, only references to items, stores, flows etc. may be given in the program specification and the full details can be retrieved from the dictionary as and when required. At the other extreme the designer may be involved in photocopying file and record specifications so that each individual program specification contains all the necessary information. This duplication of information should be avoided where possible as it carried with it the danger of inconsistency. For example, if a field in a record needs to be extended the designer must make sure that every copy of that record layout is changed.

## Specification structure

The following is a possible structure for a program specification. It should be remembered that as with any other standard it cannot be applied to any specific situation without thought. In some circumstances headings will not be appropriate, whereas in other (hopefully rarer) circumstances extra information may be required. Remember Golden Rule 11.

1   Identification
2   Introduction
3   Data
    (a) Inputs and outputs
    (b) Stored
4   Interfaces
5   Processing
    (a) Initialization
    (b) Main
    (c) Termination
6   Programming guidelines.

### Identification
This simply states the short and long names for the program. This is necessary because most programs have a mnemonic name, e.g. SLS002 which could mean sales ledger system program 2, and a full name, e.g. sales ledger invoice posting program. These names correspond to the 'Name'

| | Name | Tel. no. | Planned date | Actual date |
|---|---|---|---|---|
| Written by | | | | |
| User authorization | | | | |
| Systems authorization | | | | |
| Prog. authorization | | | | |
| Programmed by | | | | |
| Program tested | | | | |
| System tested | | | | |

Figure 95   *Program responsibility*

and 'Title' boxes found on all NCC standard documentation sheets.

### Introduction

This consists of two parts. The first gives information which defines responsibility for the program (e.g. Figure 95). The designer who wrote the specification and the programmer who wrote the code are named, as well as the people responsible for program and system testing. The dates act as part of the project control and need to be agreed by all parties concerned as being realistic. Where authorization for the programming is required, this may also be shown here. Telephone numbers are given to assist the speedy resolution of any problems.

The second part of the introduction gives an overview of what the program will do. If a data dictionary is used this can be the functional description or logic summary given there. In some cases it may be necessary to include information describing the role of this program in the overall system; a structure chart with a narrative description may be sufficient. In many cases this information is held in a separate document, the suite introduction and organization which is available to the programmers.

### Data

*Inputs and outputs*

Each data flow to or from the program is defined in turn. The definition can vary from a reference (leading to a full description stored elsewhere in the documentation) to the full description itself. The inputs typically come from files (magnetic or card) or a VDU. Files and their records can be defined on the appropriate NCC sheets S42 and S44; the display chart S47 and a record layout sheet can be used for a VDU.

When the output is to a printer this can be defined with a print layout chart S46, a computer document specification sheet S43, and record layout sheets for each type of line on the printout. It is often very useful to construct a table for each output showing the source of each field. This alone can avoid much ambiguity.

*Stores*

In some situations the designer may need to specify storage structures to be used by the program. This can vary from the use of double precision data items to temporary work files.

### Interfaces

If the program interfaces with any software other than the operating system, details should be given here. Such software could include other programs, modules, utilities, menus, JCL macros etc. which may either call this program or be called by this program. The information given here should be sufficient to ensure that the interface rules are clearly defined. It will be necessary to give a detailed description of the data to be passed backwards and forwards (what to do with the data will be described under 'Processing' to follow).

## Processing

The reader is referred back to the techniques for representing procedural logic, which should be employed here.

### Initialization

The processing which is done once only at the beginning of the program is described here. This may include opening files, obtaining control parameters and setting switches. Here are carried out all possible checks to ensure that once the main processing is started it will be successful.

### Main

The main processing section describes what the program must do in order to meet the requirements of it. There must be enough information to tell the programmer exactly what is needed of the program, and no more. To include information which is not directly relevant is to increase the chance of confusion. Quantity does not mean quality. Similarly the information should be given only once. It is a mistake to think that, by using two or more of the techniques to describe a single section of procedural logic, any ambiguity will be removed. In fact the reverse is often true, as the programmer has two descriptions to assimilate and check for any inconsistencies. It is much better practice to choose the most appropriate method of representing the logic and then to put one's effort into using that technique well and getting the logic correct.

Another common mistake, especially true of designers who have recent programming experience, is to tell the programmer how the program should perform its functions. This is the same dividing line as that between logical (what) and physical (how) design. If the program is going to be written by competent programmers (specifically excluding trainees without much supervision and support, for whom an exception may be made) then the designer should avoid doing the work the programmer is paid to do. Heroic designers who want to do everything themselves and will not delegate work or responsibility, are not likely to be valuable assets to any organization. A frequent justification for

the 'how it is to be done' type of program specification is that the designer cannot think of any clearer way of describing the requirements. The designer should not be thinking about how the program will work at all, but should have the business and system requirements very clearly in his head, and therefore the justification appears somewhat untenable. This does not mean the designer can assume programmers can do anything asked of them; rather the designer needs to be as familiar with the facilities that can be offered by the programming staff as with the facilities of the operating system, hardware or any other potential component of the system. Some institutions have people employed as 'program designers' as distinct from system designers and programmers (who are then mainly coders). The fact that people have found it necessary to formally define and separate these tasks should serve to emphasize the fact that there are different jobs in this area, each with its own skills, knowledge, experience and standards. Where the boundaries are not explicitly defined, the systems designer should keep to systems design.

This emphasis upon defining only the requirements of a program does not mean that the designer can avoid detail. The requirements must be specified fully, and this usually means detail. For example, any program which performs a calculation should have any rounding required explicitly specified. If rounding is not specified, truncation will usually be assumed. It is frequently not too important what rules are followed as long as they are followed consistently. Thus the situation should not arise where program A truncates all calculations, program B rounds at every stage in the calculations, program C only rounds on the last calculation, and program D is run to check that the figures produced by the system agree, stopping the whole system if a discrepancy is found. Rounding problems are, by their nature, intermittent and time consuming to diagnose.

### Termination

There are two ways a program can terminate in a controlled manner. The first is a 'normal' termination following successful completion of processing. The second, 'abnormal' termination, occurs when the program has encountered an error condition which is so severe that processing cannot continue, e.g. a program which reads a file must terminate if it cannot obtain the file. Wherever possible the designer should ensure that the programs cope with error situations without resorting to an 'abnormal' termination, but it is imperative that all possible conditions which must be resolved by termination are identified and fully described in the program specification. For each critical condition the programmer will need to know: what are the symptons of the condition; what processing can be done to achieve a clean termination; what information is to be output to assist in correction of the condition; and is anything else needed which will help recovery from the condition. It is not uncommon for the error processing part of a program specification to be longer than the main processing section.

**Programming guidelines**
Information is given under this heading when the program has special characteristics which are not covered by the institution's normal standards. In particular (1) the maximum run size or response time may be specified, (2) information on optimization and segmentation/overlaying of the program may be necessary, or (3) any library routines to be used can be identified. The objective is to tell the programmer of any constraints which apply to the program or if there are any facilities which the designer knows about and which the programmer should use.

**Example: order processing**
In the order processing system, information on received orders is stored almost as soon as they have entered the system. The process which does this is STORE-ORDER, the flows for which are shown in Figure 64. A program specification for this process could be as follows.

1   *Identification*
      STORE-ORDER (ORPO01)

2   *Introduction*

| | Name | Tel. no. | Planned date | Actual date |
|---|---|---|---|---|
| Written by | Tex Hand | 2321 | 16/8/84 | 16/8/84 |
| User authorization | Reg Owen | 1234 | | 3/10/84 |
| Systems authorization | Gary Ribbons | 1248 | | 13/10/84 |
| Prog. authorization | Audrey Beev | 782 | | 6/11/84 |
| Programmed by | | | | |
| Program tested | | | | |
| System tested | | | | |

Details of all ORDERs which enter the system are stored by this process so that subsequent analysis of them is possible. The logical description is:

For each RO-STO (data flow from RECEIVE-ORDER):
(a)   Obtain C-INFO
(b)   Obtain P-INFO     (from data stores).
(c)   Send STORE-ORDERED (to data store).

The RECEIVE-ORDER process creates eight files of STD-ORDERs during the day, which are merged together for use by the invoicing subsystem. It is this daily STD-ORDER file which is used to provide the data flow RO-STO. The STORE-ORDERED data flow is added on the end of a file ORDERED. This file contains ORDERED-HEAD-DATA and ORDERED-LINE-DATA as record types H and L respectively.

**3** *Data*

An overview; full details are in the data dictionary.

(a) *In*

RO-STO logical data flow is physically:

STD-ORDER
 (ORDER-NO, ORDER-DATE,
 CUST-NO, [DELIV-ADRS],
 [PURCH-NO], ORDER-LINE*
 (ITEM-NO, QTY))

The whole of this sequential disk file is read.

P-INFO logical data flow is physically:

ITEM-BASIC-DATA
 (ITEM-NO, ITEM-DESCRIP,
 BIN-NO, ITEM-PRICE,
 ITEM-DISCOUNT%, ITEM-TAX%,
 RE-ORD-QTY, QOH,
 PROD-GROUP)

Selected records are read from the file, which is indexed sequential.

C-INFO logical data flow is physically:

CUSTOMER-DATA
 (CUST-NO, CUST-NAME,
 DELIV-ADRS, DISCOUNT%,
 INV-ADRS, CUST-GROUP,
 CREDIT-LIM)

Selected records are read from the file, which is indexed sequential.

*Out*

STORE-ORDER logical data flow is physically:

ORDERED
 (ORDER-NO, REC-TYPE,
 ORDER-DATE, DISCOUNT%,
 CUST-GROUP, CREDIT-LIM)

where REC-TYPE = H, and

ORDERED
 (ORDER-NO, REC-TYPE,
 ITEM-NO, DESPATCH-DATE,
 ITEM-PRICE, ITEM-DISCOUNT%,
 ITEM-TAX%, QTY, PROD-GROUP)

where REC-TYPE = L.

Records are inserted into this file, which is indexed sequential.

The source tables for these outputs are:

| Field | Source |
|---|---|
| ORDER-NO | ORDER-NO in STD-ORDER |
| REC-TYPE | always H |
| ORDER-DATE | ORDER-DATE in STD-ORDER |
| DISCOUNT% | DISCOUNT% in CUSTOMER-DATA |
| CUST-GROUP | CUST-GROUP in CUSTOMER-DATA |
| CREDIT-LIM | CREDIT-LIM in CUSTOMER-DATA |

| Field | Source |
|---|---|
| ORDER-NO | ORDER-NO in STD-ORDER |
| REC-TYPE | always L |
| ITEM-NO | ITEM-NO in STD-ORDER |
| DESPATCH-DATE | always ZEROS |
| ITEM-PRICE | ITEM-PRICE in ITEM-BASIC-DATA |
| ITEM-DISCOUNT% | ITEM-DISCOUNT% in ITEM-BASIC-DATA |
| ITEM-TAX% | ITEM-TAX% in ITEM-BASIC-DATA |
| QTY | QTY in STD-ORDER |
| PROD-GROUP | PROD-GROUP in ITEM-BASIC-DATA |

Operation control data is written to an audit trail:

AUDIT-TRAIL
  (MSG-ORIGIN, DATE, TIME,
  STATUS, MESG)

This is a serial disk file.

The source table is:

| Field | Source |
|---|---|
| MSG-ORIGIN | always ORPOO1 |
| DATE | SYSTEM-DATE from operating system |
| TIME | SYSTEM-TIME from operating system |
| STATUS | set by program |
| MESG | set by program |

(b) *Stored*
Not applicable

**4**  *Interfaces*
Not applicable

**5**  *Processing*

(a) *Initialization*
Open all files.

(b) *Main*
For each STD-ORDER:
Add 1 to a tally of STD-ORDERS, TIN
Obtain CUSTOMER-DATA, using
CUST-NO, set up and write ORDERED,
type H
Add 1 to a tally of ORDERED (H),
TOUT

For each ORDER-LINE:
Obtain ITEM-BASIC-DATA using
ITEM-NO, set up and write ORDERED,
type L

If there are no ORDER-LINEs in the
STD-ORDER:
Set STATUS = 'ERROR'
Set MESG = 'NO DETAIL LINES ON
ORDER', STD-ORDER
Write AUDIT-TRAIL

(c) *Termination*
*Normal* is identified as:
TIN = TOUT and TIN > ZERO
Set STATUS = 'OK'
Set MESG = TIN, 'ORDERS STORED'
Write AUDIT-TRAIL
Close all files
*Abnormal*:
If error on opening a file:
Set STATUS = 'RERUN'
Set MESG = file name, 'UNABLE TO
OPEN'
If TIN ≠ TOUT
Set STATUS = 'ERROR'
Set MESG = TIN 'ORDERS IN FROM
STD-ORDER BUT' TOUT 'STORED'

If record not found in
CUSTOMER-DATA:
Set STATUS = 'WARNING'
Set MESG = 'NO CUSTOMER DATA
FOUND FOR CUSTOMER',
CUST-NO, 'ORDER IS', STD-ORDER

If record not found in
ITEM-BASIC-DATA:
Set STATUS = 'WARNING'
Set MESG = 'NO ITEM DATA FOUND
FOR ITEM', ITEM-NO, 'ORDER IS',
STD-ORDER

If any other abnormal file status:
Set STATUS = ' ? ? ? ? '
Set MESG = 'FILE STATUS', file status,
'ON FILE', file name

And then:
Write AUDIT-TRAIL
Close all files

**6**  Programming guidelines
File definitions should be copied from the data dictionary.

Attention is drawn to the fact that this specification incorporates a large number of physical design decisions, such as the use of an audit trail to help monitor and control the operation of the system. This is a file into which any program writes, and which is periodically checked by the operators. The files follow on from the outline and data storage design. If a data base management system had been used, only the fields in the logical data flow would have been known to the program, rather than all those in the physical file. The two 3NF data stores ORDERED-HEAD-DATA and ORDERED-LINE-DATA were physically located in the same file. Similarly STD-ORDER is the physical source for RO-STO. Both of these decisions reduce system flexibility, but may be justifiable in some circumstances. The objective here is to illustrate the difference between physical and logical design. Finally, it is worth noting that the amount of effort dedicated to handling error conditions is far greater than their frequency of occurrence would suggest.

## Exercises for Part Three

**3.1** During outline design many decisions are taken which directly effect the work done by people. List the factors which you believe influence job satisfaction levels, and discuss their relevance for the designer.

**3.2** VDUs are often used for data entry. Describe some of the advantages and disadvantages of this.

**3.3** Briefly describe the circumstances when you would expect software to be provided by purchasing a package. How would it be selected?

Exercises 3.4–3.6: As part of a student record system a program UNPAID is run fortnightly during the first academic term. It serially reads a student file to identify any students whose fees have not been paid. A report is produced which shows the student's name, course, fees due, date of enrolment and fee paying body. This last field is used for sequencing. Subtotals and final totals are produced.

**3.4** What functions could the program UNPAID perform so as to improve the integrity of the stored data in the system?

**3.5** Define a possible report layout which you think would be useful to staff responsible for chasing monies owed.

**3.6** Describe how the data used by this program could be structured into files.

# Postscript

'Finally, as one systems designer to another . . .'

Figure 96

This chapter is intended to draw the reader's attention to some further issues which are associated with systems design.

The storage of data is required in almost all systems, and almost all systems hold data in the form of records. Data base systems often interface programs with stored data using global and local views of data built out of records. Data does not have to be held in records. Data is held to try to describe what is actually taking place in some real world. In the 'real world' a person may be both a student and a teacher. If the data system has student records and staff records, then two records would need to be held to describe one person. These records may be considered as representing roles of an entity. What happens if this person obtains a part-time job as a college cleaner? Is there a limit to the number of roles which can be defined? Alternatively a student record may have space reserved for PERSONAL-TUTOR, but this person may not have one. The field may take a null value. How many more fields will be present but null because

of the fact that each record must have the field present? Conversely, what happens when one student has two personal tutors?

It is possible to store data as items of data and to link these together as required to describe any one entity. This would allow a person to be associated with all and only the fields which were relevant to them. An alternative to this atomistic approach is to store data as text, thus allowing a description to use natural language rather than codes. This would necessitate holding the meaning of the data items in the text together with the data value itself, e.g. 'Grace is 16 months old' rather than just the value '16' being held in a record for Grace, which was interpreted by a process as meaning that Grace was 16 months old. Text processing is becoming increasingly economic and its range of applications is constantly expanding. A further option for storing the data and the meaning together is in a Prolog statement, where the distinction between data, meaning and process breaks down.

Data may be stored in or for graphic form, but a more dramatic type of storage is that of images. These may include the images of faces or fingerprints, the pictures held on videodisk, or even three-dimensional images of airport runways held as holograms. These are all different ways of holding data which require their own types of processing and could form the basis of systems. The record is one way of holding data; it has advantages and disadvantages, many of which have been discussed by Kent (1978).

Throughout this book there has been mention of the problems of defining the requirements of systems which are to be part of human activity systems. Systems which involve people are frequently very complex, and only a small amount of this complexity is used in building an information system to support them. Real problems do not arrive in neat packages, and the situations which give rise to them usually defy understanding by participants. Indeed, a feature of a 'systems approach' is the acceptance of the fact that it is impossible to produce a correct understanding or description of such systems.

The best that can be achieved is a description which is useful for a purpose.

Soft systems methodology is an approach to real world problem solving and described by Checkland (1983) and Wilson (1983). The emphasis is upon finding out what is happening in a situation and then taking action within it. The 'systems approach' lays stress upon a holistic view of the situation and the idea that the whole is greater than the sum of its parts. A systems approach is taken to a situation in which problems are perceived. This contrasts with the 'hard' view, where a systematic approach is applied to a situation which can be modelled and optimized according to knowable objectives.

Many good systems analysts and designers probably embody much of that which is formally defined as soft systems in their daily practice. To produce 'good' systems, the whole of the organization needs to be considered. The information systems need to contribute to the functions of the organization, to be effective and not just efficient. It is possible to purchase one's way out of inefficiency in information systems, but not out of inappropriateness. As hardware and software continue to become more powerful and flexible, the design of 'solutions' will become less important than the identification of contexts within which 'problems' can be tackled.

This book has concentrated on designing record-based solutions for hard systems. This is basic systems design. It involves the use of abstract concepts and of meticulous attention to detail, a thorough and methodical approach combined with the flexibility necessary to adapt to the situation. These characteristics are also necessary for more advanced areas of systems design; as is Golden Rule 10.

# Outline solutions to exercises

## Part One

**1.1** Obviously there is no right or wrong answer to this. The following could be included:

The need for the design was established and the requirements specified. The design balanced the variables to obtain both long- and short-term benefits.
The system met the user's needs, was socially acceptable and not technically too adventurous. The system described the relevant portion of the enterprise's real world in as direct a manner as possible. The system was as simple as possible.

**1.2** The owner of the shop would act as both the project controller (sponsor) and the primary user. The amount of involvement would depend upon the attitude of the owner, which could vary from being only interested in the product to wanting to participate in every stage of the design. The former extreme is unlikely to lead to the design of a very good system, owing to insufficient business knowledge on the part of the designer. This should be explained to the owner. The second extreme could extend the project life and would mean the designer was teaching as well as designing. Again, this should be drawn to the attention of the owner, who may decide that this is what is wanted.

**1.3** The complex interfaces between different parts of systems designed in a bottom-up manner tend to make them less flexible than could have been achieved if a top-down approach had been taken. There is also a good chance of redundancy in the design. An example could be the development of two programs which produced similar reports for different users from one file. If subsequently an extra field was added to the records on this file, both programs would need amendment. A top-down approach would have been more likely to produce either a single program producing both reports or at least a shared file reading and exception handling module. In either case the amount of change needed would be less.

**1.4** First, the criteria used to judge 'success' are often not specified until after system completion. This is not desirable because such a method of evaluation is open to 'political' manipulation and useful information is denied to the designer. Frequent causes of problems are poorly specified system requirements, if any are explicitly defined at all, or requirements which are not integrated with an overall plan. These lead to the most pervasive and expensive problems. Misunderstandings and mistakes during design occur as do program errors (these can be virtually eliminated if code generators are used). Lack of end user involvement in the project increases the chances of problems. This leads to missed opportunities and unrealistic attitudes to the system.

**1.5** Design work is only part of a development effort, and DM/1 does not cover the project management requirements and analysis phases or the implementation and review stages. Many other more specific differences could be identified and explained in terms of the functions of each step in the project.

**1.6** In the system of Figure 97, flows only move structures and stores only hold structures. If it was necessary to describe the elements stored or moved, the entries for the data structures could be redundant, although this would involve much repetition in identifying the elements composing the data stores or flows.

**1.7** IF TYPE = TEMP
  | IF UNIT = F
  |  | CONVERT-TO-CENTIGRADE
  | ELSE (UNIT = C)  NULL
  | END-IF
  | IF VALUE > 40
  |  | IF PROCESS = 1
  |  |   SWITCH-PUMP-OFF
  |  | ELSE (PROCESS = 2)  NULL
  |  | END-IF
  | ELSE (VALUE < 40)
  |  | SWITCH-PUMP-ON
  | END-IF
END-IF

The decision tree for this logic is as in Figure 98. The questions that would need answering are:

What happens if type is not temperature, or unit is neither C nor F, or value equals 40, or process is neither 1 nor 2?

**1.8** The question leaves scope for several answers, which could approximate to Figure 99.

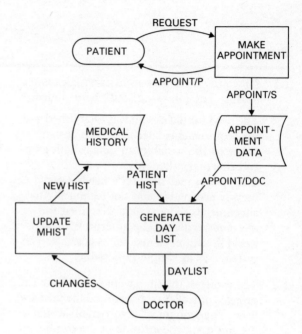

Figure 98   *Decision tree for Exercise 1.7*

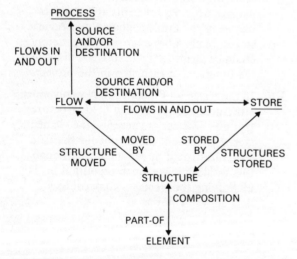

Figure 97   *System for Exercise 1.6*

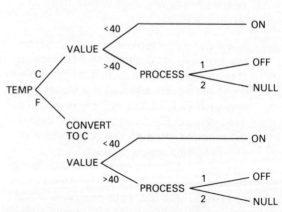

Figure 99   *Flow diagram for Exercise 1.8*

# Part Two

**2.2** Stage 2 defines at an item level the data which is flowing out of the system. For information retrieval systems such as those which provide 'management information' and 'decision support' all the outflows may not be known at the beginning of the project. In this case the primary objectives may define the inflowing data which will be used to support *ad hoc* retrievals. In such a situation stage 2 would need to look at inputs as well as any defined outputs. This would have an impact on stage 3 as well, where the decisions on derived/stored/input would mostly have been made. The design would need to concentrate on supporting a robust data base which would be able to respond to a variety of demands made upon it.

**2.3** Ultimately all data stored in the system must have been input, and it follows from this that the data store is an intermediary between an original input, and a useful output, of data. It would be possible to have no data stores and input all required data each time it was required. The distinction is influenced by such factors as: the chances of data being reused after initial iput; the number of processes which may wish to use the same data; the comparative costs of storage and input; and the chances of the data changing while stored. As is frequently the case, there are no right or wrong answers; each decision depends upon how the data will be used in a particular design. The distinction is important because it will influence the development of the data model. It is also important at a physical level as it may influence what is held in a data

base, as opposed to a work file, or which data is deleted at the end of the day.

**2.4** Maintenance of the stored data is very important to an organization, and the fact that stage 5 checks that all data has maintenance procedures designed for it means that it will never be truly redundant. However, if the primary objectives for the system included the maintenance of data, then there is quite likely to be relatively little change to the application model as a result of stage 5.

**2.5** Assume a person's name is unique.

PERSON
(NAME, ADDRESS, CAR-NO,
CAR-PARK, PAID)
CAR
(CAR-NO, COLOUR, TYPE)

This data model allows a person to use several cars on one car park or the same car at several car parks. The new model is:

PERSON
(NAME, ADDRESS)
CAR
(CAR-NO, COLOUR, TYPE)
PERMIT
(NAME, CAR-NO, CAR-PARK, PAID)

A representation of the new model is as in Figure 100.

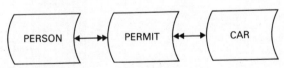

Figure 100   *New model for Exercise 2.5*

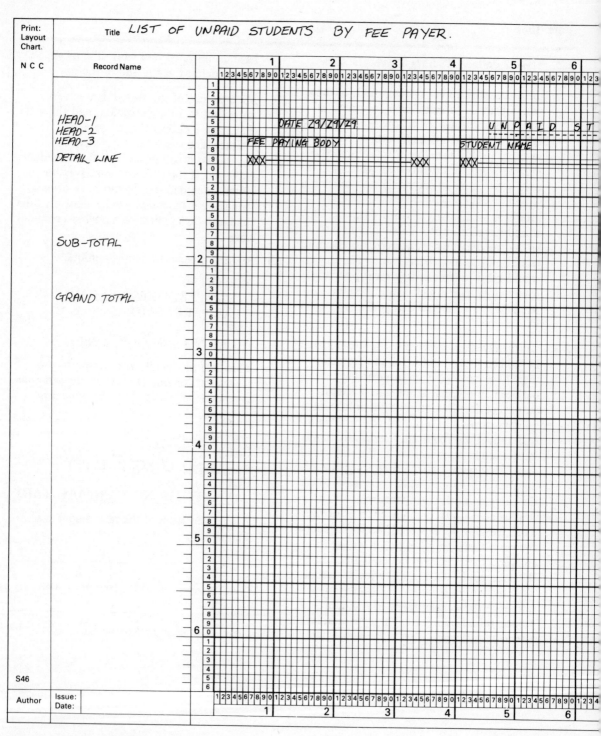

Figure 101   *Layout for Exercise 3.5*

| | System | Document | Name | Sheet |
|---|---|---|---|---|
| | SREC | 4·3 | UNPAID | 1 |

NTS

PAGE NO ZZZ9

COURSE TITLE        ENROLLED ON    FEES

XXX————————XXX    Z9/Z9/Z9    ##99

FEE PAYER SUB TOTAL    ####99

TOTAL OUTSTANDING    #####99

## Part Three

**3.1** Without entering the areas of organization and methods or the personnel aspects of management, then it is impossible to fairly treat the topic.

The following is a list of factors which are frequently said to influence the amount of job satisfaction a person gets. It is by no means an exhaustive list.

The extent to which one is able to identify with the job being done

The amount of contact with jobs which precede or follow one's own job

The amount of involvement with the end users or customers of a product or service

The availability of clear job instructions and performance targets

The presence of feedback on one's own performance, that of the department, or the organization as a whole

The presence of hope for an improvement in one's lot, via one's work

A variety in job content

A reasonably demanding level of work

The constant improving of oneself and one's skill

A reasonable level of responsibility

The ability to control what one does

An effective means of suggesting changes.

These factors are not equally powerful for every person; in fact for some they may be negative, e.g. job responsibility is not always desired. However, in the textbook world, jobs are designed independently of individual personalities in order to achieve a greater degree of long-term system optimization. Whether or not this is desirable, it is rarely done in practice where people are already employed.

**3.2** Advantages include the following:
Errors spotted by a validation program may be corrected immediately while the source is available, possibly aided by on-line 'help' facilities. The reduction in the amount of paperwork may lead to less chance of lost or duplicate data. The relatively direct data entry gives less chance for the introduction of errors, and probably less manual work, than many alternatives.

Disadvantages include the following:
There may be no source document or other hard copy of the data. In the event of a hardware or software failure, data capture will need to be done by some other means, which must also be designed. The design must allow for fluctuations in demand which will be directly experienced by the system.

**3.3** Use a package if:
In-house staff have other work to do which cannot be bought in; or own staff lack expertise; or very short project life; and package meets user requirements, i.e. modifications (to package or requirements) are minor/acceptable, and costs are acceptable.

Selection:
Establish reqirements; identify available packages (NCC, user groups etc.); obtain literature and select possible packages; evaluate facilities, performance, experience of other users, support, documentation; shortlist two or three; visit working installations; select.

**3.4** As the program will be accessing all the student records, the opportunity is available to perform integrity checks on the status of the file. This could be a count of the number of students held, or the production of a hash total. These figures would need to be compared with their equivalents derived from some other source, e.g. whenever students are added to or deleted from file a count in the header record could be updated. More detailed checks might include accessing other data, e.g. to check each student has a member of staff allocated as a personal tutor. If any chains exist which either pass through or start with the student record, their integrity can be checked. The data items themselves could be validated in an attempt to detect corruption. It is important to note that these are all techniques which *could* be incorporated into this program. This does not mean that they should be implemented. This decision must be based upon the system objectives, and built into the whole design.

**3.5** The layout might be as in Figure 101.

**3.6** The data on the report describes three entities: fee payers, students and courses. It is unlikely that all this information would be held in full on one file. A possible structuring of the data could include:

STUDENT
    (STDT-NAME, COURSE-NO,
    FEE-PAY-ID, ENROL-DATE)
COURSE
    (COURSE-NO, TITLE, FEES)
FEE-PAYER
    (FEE-PAY-ID,
    FEE-PAYER-NAME)

Such a structuring would reduce the total amount of space used by avoiding repetition of TITLE and FEE-PAYER-NAME. It would also allow for the files to be processed independently of each other. It is assumed that all fields are fixed length and that only one body pays a student's fees.

# References

Bjørn-Anderson, N. *Information Society, for Richer, for Poorer*, North-Holland, 1982

Checkland, P. 'The application of systems thinking in real-world problems: the emergence of SSM', *First Symposium Internacional de Ingenieria Industrial y de Sistemas*, Mexico City, March 1983.

Damodaran, L., *et al. Designing Systems for People*, NCC, 1980

Farrow, H. F. *Computerisation Guidelines*, NCC, 1979

Gane, C., and Sarson, T. *Structured Systems Analysis*, Prentice-Hall, 1979

Gilbert, P. *Software Design and Development*, SRA, 1983

Grindley, C. B. B. *Systematics*, McGraw-Hill, 1975

Jenkins, A. M. 'Prototyping a methodology for the design and development of application systems', Indiana University Discussion Paper 227, 1983

Kent, W. *Data and Reality*, North-Holland, 1978

Lee, B. S. *Basic Systems Analysis*, Hutchinson, 1984

Lundeberg, M., *et al. Information Systems Development*, Prentice-Hall, 1981

Milgram, S. *Obedience to Authority*, Tavistock, 1974

Munford, E. and Henshall, D. *A Participative Approach to Computer Systems Design* Associated Business Press, 1979

Semprevivo, P. *Systems Analysis*, SRA, 1976

Tsichritzis, D. C., and Lochovsky, F. H. *Data Models*, Prentice-Hall, 1982

Weinberg, V. *Structured Analysis*, Prentice-Hall, 1980

Wilson, B. 'SSM in the creation of MIS', *First Symposium Internacional de Ingenieria Industrial y de Sistemas*, Mexico City, March 1983

Wood-Harper, A. T. and Fitzgerald, G. 'A taxonomy of current approaches to systems analysis'. *Computer Journal*, vol. 25, no. 1, 1982

# Index

## Examples index

*Note*: Entries are followed by the letters E, N or D (essential, necessary, desirable) and refer to the class of objectives with which the entry is concerned. Entries are also followed by stages 1 to 5, normalization, courting, review, or a word describing an activity in detailed physical design. These additions describe the stage of design with which the entry is concerned.